Praise for *The Judas Legacy*

"Like a light-house beacon, *The Judas Legacy* shines a guiding light of consciousness through the stormy waters of collective mind-sets and ideologies adopted as societal norms in American culture. Author Rushing explains the psychological dynamics of C. G. Jung's theory of the projected shadow as she demonstrates how through the ages Christendom has projected the dark shadow component of evil betrayer unjustly onto the character of Judas Iscariot. She gives stark examples of how the collective shadow factor is at work today pointing the dark finger of evil onto "the other," instead of finding it rooted in one's own being. She examines how this is clearly perpetuated by the self-righteous stance in our institutions of government and church. Dr. Jung wrote that the world today hangs by a thin thread and that thread is the consciousness in men and women. *The Judas Legacy* is a strong filament in that thread of consciousness that can awaken humanity to the destructive perils of the unexamined shadow."

>Nancy Qualls-Corbett, Ph.D., Jungian Analyst and author of *The Sacred Prostitute: Eternal Aspect of the Feminine*

"Sandra Rushing probes the Judas story from every perspective, bringing his shadow and the evil of our own prejudices into a new focus. This is a dynamic, fresh and provocative new study."

>Bishop John Shelby Spong (Retired), author of *The Sins of Scriptures*

"In her book *The Judas Legacy*, Sandra M. Rushing offers the reader a far ranging analysis of how the shadow figure of Judas within the individual, politics, the church and popular culture keeps us from adapting to change and overcoming our addictions to anger, sectarianism, and other restricting demons. Chapter 7 alone, "The Christian Church in America: The Link to the Judas Legacy," should furnish enough materials for creative discussion and self-evaluation to keep many a Sunday School class or church session busy for many a meeting."

> Myrl Guy Jones, Ph.D., Professor Emeritus of English, Radford University

"Writing from *inside* the church, Sandra mentions the unmentionable. Whether or not we agree with all of her conclusions, reading this book will stir vigorous thought and discussion."

> Rev. Bernard Bangley, author of numerous books on classic spirituality, including *Nearer to the Heart of God* and *Authentic Devotion*

"A gold mine of religious, literary, psychological, and sociological examples and images keep one turning the pages of *The Judas Legacy*. Rushing has done a remarkable job of linking the biblical past to the stress, strains, and dysfunctions of modern society. As a mediator, I find the discussion of communication, both in terms of content and strategy to be most critical, as well as relevant for our times. The real treasure lies in the last two chapters which offer concrete suggestions for the transformation of self, church, and society."

> Janet Kelly Moen, Ph.D., Professor of Sociology/Peace Studies, University of North Dakota

The Judas Legacy

The Judas Legacy

By Sandra M. Rushing

Brandylane Publishers, Inc.
Richmond, Virginia

Copyright 2008 by Sandra M. Rushing. No portion of this book may be reproduced in any form without the written permission of the publisher.

ISBN: 978-1-883911-77-5
      1-883911-77-X
Library of Congress Control Number: 2008922520

Brandylane Publishers, Inc.
Richmond, Virginia
www.brandylanepublishers.com

Cover Illustration by Sandra M. Rushing

For all those who have been wounded by the institutional church in whatever ways those wounds may have been inflicted.

Contents

	Foreword	xi
	Introduction	xv
1.	The Shadow and the Judas Archetype	1
2.	Who was This Man Judas Iscariot?	21
3.	The Shadow and Our Mind Habits	37
4.	Scapegoat, Ritual, and The Atonement Principle	62
5.	The Cultural Evidence of the Judas Legacy	80
6.	American Shadow Symbols	110
7.	The Christian Church in America: The Link to the Judas Legacy	125
8.	The Money Factor and Judas	153
9.	The Shadow Side of God	178
10.	Transforming the Judas Shadow in Self	201
11.	Transforming the Judas Shadow in Culture and Church	219
	Appendix A	241
	Bibliography	242
	About the Author	253

Foreword
Kim Paffenroth, PhD

There is at the heart of the Gospel story of Jesus a strange character named Judas. The Gospels recount how the authorities enlist his help to find Jesus, a man who routinely appears in public, unaccompanied by bodyguards and never secretive about his whereabouts. In such a scenario, why is Judas' help necessary at all? And from a personal perspective, why would he accept such an offer? The Gospels keep his motives secret, and even offer a confusing picture of his mental state: Judas' outrage against Jesus at the anointing, frequent hints of the disciples' overall dissatisfaction with Jesus' insistence on non-violence, Judas' remorse at Jesus' condemnation, and then his own death, which is told in two completely conflicting accounts—either suicide in Matthew's version, or a fatal accident in Acts. Judas' presence and actions in the narrative have in fact struck critics in the past two hundred years as so implausible that he is now routinely dismissed as utter fiction. Judas is just not logical, from such critics' perspective.

But what is rightly observed in the present book is that, from other—and I would say much more important—perspectives, Judas makes perfect sense. The sense he makes may not be historical—it is quite possible that such a person did not exist in Palestine two thousand years ago, and if many scholars judge the possibility of his nonexistence as probable, they have good reasons for doing so. But he makes perfect sense from the literary and psychological perspectives. The story just wouldn't work as well, or affect us as deeply, were it not for Judas. This has been my main point in my analysis of him, *Judas: Images of the Lost Disciple* (Westminster

John Knox Press, 2001), and Rev. Rushing does a fine job laying out the major points of the discussion in her first two chapters.

The real value and contribution of her analysis are in what follows, however. Drawing on personal anecdotes, Jungian psychology, the social theories of Thorstein Veblen, numerous other examples from science and literature, comparative analysis of ritual and scriptures, and trenchant, well-informed criticism of current events, Rev. Rushing shows how Judas is far from non-existent: he is, in fact, everywhere, in the form of the dark, evil shadow sides of our individual and collective souls. Her analysis of the evils of current American society is a prophetic call to real Christian introspection, commitment, and repentance. We have shielded ourselves for too long by denying our own shadows and scapegoating others we deem evil, thereby cheating ourselves of any real healing and improvement. The psychological and social damage we are daily inflicting on ourselves and the rest of the world is as real, sinful, and deadly as any betrayal inflicted on Jesus by one of his disciples. Indeed, if I could modify any of Rev. Rushing's analysis, it would only be to wonder whether her title does not do yet another disservice to Judas, for her analysis shows clearly and powerfully that it is we who are the betrayers and killers of our God, not the disciple whom we blame and despise in order to avoid our own guilt. And unlike Judas or Peter, we betray and deny over and over, like addicts. We are the negative, destructive shadows, not Judas. Rev. Rushing is to be humbly thanked for shining a sometimes painful but therapeutic light onto our dirty secrets and calling us out of the shadows and into the light of God's love and forgiveness.

Kim Paffenroth, Ph.D.
Associate Professor of Religious Studies
Iona College

Acknowledgements

No book is ever the work of an author, alone, but encompasses the energy and efforts of many others. My grateful thanks to the private foundation which funded a grant for me to return to my home in the mountains of Virginia to write this book. I would never have completed this manuscript without the critical attentions and advice from Mary Lynn Lipscomb, Alex Lipscomb, Dru Tyler, Bernard Bangley, my daughter Jean McCrowell, Kim Paffenroth, Ken White, Mary Jane Mutispaugh, Anna Bangley and Shelley Bourdon. My profound thanks to Linda Baer for sharing her splendid poetry to close two chapters of this book; readers who think it is beautiful should hear her sing these same words. My publisher, R. H. Pruett, and the senior editor, Annie Tobey, have been invaluable in their editorial contributions as I completed this manuscript.

Introduction

This book was completed during a time in the history of the United States when we had made a critical decision to go to war in Iraq for wrong reasons, based on flawed information. Not only was our information flawed, our leadership was equally as flawed. The ineptitude of the George W. Bush administration was not simply that of frail humanity, but it was an indicator of a psychological impetus that few wanted to discuss. After a number of years of war in Iraq, the American people and the news media began to pay attention to factors that should have been noticed long before. With this understanding in place, I intend to discuss one of the underlying factors that has been apparent to me for many years. It was never more evident than during the second war with Iraq.

I intend to explore the shadow in a variety of ways, by first describing the shadow from a Jungian perspective and then emphasizing the negative aspects of the shadow that are so much a part of the American culture.

I have written this book because events in church and state are so potent in the present age, allowing us to look at how unresolved shadow behavior injures others and ourselves. I believe both the church and the state are operating far more out of an unresolved shadow impetus than from cognitive thought. As a theologian I have followed Judas from his role in the Bible to the ways the contemporary world casts him as a favorite scapegoat, far beyond the arms of the church. The better we understand the Judas/scapegoat, and how unresolved shadow affects us individually and collectively, the better we can function.

One of the most potent aspects of the shadow in our culture is a denial of its existence. Its power is equal to the levels of denial that are cast upon it when we look for a scapegoat onto whom we can project our guilt and shame. We look for another to blame far more often than we accept the consequences of our own behavior. Becoming responsible for our choices calls for maturity. Just as children in a multi-sibling family will look for someone to blame when they are caught in something unacceptable, every collective of people will choose a scapegoat subconsciously when looking for a way out of their own guilt.

I had begun the research for this book five years before September 11, 2001, but the events of that day gave the American president, and the people of this nation, a superb target for individual and national shadow projections. Once a target is the focus for the shadow, denial becomes even easier, because those who deny their own internal darkness can do so more easily when there is an enemy to hate.

As the chapters of this book unfold, there may be readers who disagree, perhaps vehemently, with its premise. My intention is to describe, as carefully as possible, the ways the negative characteristics of the shadow feed our cultural reality at this time in our history. Some readers might wonder why a definition is not my first approach. Each time a term is defined, no matter how broad the definition, it creates a tangible obstacle to an enlarged definition. Thus I have found that descriptions and examples provide the best ways to understand the shadow and its power.

There are readers who will not only disagree with the material presented in this book, but will perhaps choose to denounce it for a variety of reasons. One of those reasons may be that clear, logical, linear thinkers are not influenced by the shadow in the ways I have described.

My own life experience provides an ideal example. I don't know about other folks, but I would not want to be married to someone who is unwilling to argue with some vigor when we disagree. My deceased husband, who was an attorney and the dean of a state university law school, never turned away from such arguing. He was a classic linear thinker, so I became quite adept at arguing from the cognitive function. Three-point analogies and articulated rules of engagement were always part of our arguments, and while my husband could not out-argue me in these situations, the two of us always argued from a dual perspective: *We used the cognitive function to give voice to the shadow.* There were times when the argument would wax and wane for hours, but there was always one common denominator: The intellect was always the instrument we employed to sing the song of the shadow.

If you have one leg cut off you cannot walk without aid. In the same way, the cognitive levels of the mind do not function in isolation. Pure, rational or rarified levels of thinking are an illusion. They are always influenced by the deeper subconscious levels of the psyche. Thus, delving into these deeper levels of the psyche can enrich the human experience and enhance the soul journey that is life.

Recent research completed by a professor of psychology at Yale, John A. Bargh, supports the conclusions I have drawn in this book. Dr. Bargh found that the "subconscious brain is far more active, purposeful and independent than previously known." Furthermore, "like neural software programs . . ., the unconscious is perfectly capable of running the program it chooses." The interaction between the cognitive levels of the psyche and the unconscious levels suggest that the rational mind is profoundly influenced by the primordial, or reptilian, brain. Dr. Bargh, as well as Dr. Roy Baumeister, professor of psychology at Florida State University, agree with many other scientists in this field "that the evidence for psychological hot-wiring has become overwhelming." These findings are also supported by Dr. Chris Frith, professor of neuropsychology at University College, London, whose book *Making Up the Mind: How the Brain Creates our Mental World* describes his own work in this area (Benedict Carey, NYT, July 31, 2007)."

It is my hope that those readers who find this material difficult to accept will initiate dialogue with others who resonate with it. No author can respond to the criticism of every reader. Readers who use this information to find new ways to look at the culture or themselves may open new areas of conversation about the ways the shadow influences every facet of our culture.

Chapter 1

The Shadow and the Judas Archetype

Judas has evolved from a relatively flat character in the Bible to a code word for "betrayer." While we may dislike a betrayer, we often search for a scapegoat, someone else to blame for wrongdoing. Judas has become the unspeakable person who betrayed Jesus. Even non-believers will condemn Judas as the sole person responsible for selling out Jesus. Rarely do we recognize our own part in betrayal. Judas became a scapegoat for the shadow denial among the disciples, and remains as a classic example of a scapegoat into the present day. In that way he represents the shadow.

Discussions of the shadow must take us back to places deeply imbedded in the psyche. Delving into the soul is necessary. When one is a child and dreams of flying, it does not seem like a strange thing at all. When one is an adult and dreams of the Holy Spirit in the form of a lavender leopard, which has been capable of changing her own spots, it startles one in a wonderful, but affirming, way. Then for the same dream to introduce the rest of the Holy Trinity as wild animals, as well, brings the wild side of God into sharp focus. Can we understand any part of God as wild? Or do we want a more comfortable God, one more attuned to our own small human perspective? The notion of the wild side of God will be explored in one of the later chapters of this book, and it is my hope that you will read the chapters in-between for a perspective on the wild side of humanity. To encounter God's wildness or the shadow in humanity means looking backward first.

As a toddler, and until I was ten years old, I used to spend many weeks each summer with my grandmother. My grandmother died when I was ten. When I was visiting, she observed a weekly ritual. Every Sunday night, she gathered her skirts around her, and plopped down into the frayed armchair that sat in the corner of her bedroom just past the end of her bed. Turning to the floor model Philco radio beside the chair, she would fiddle with the dials until she found her favorite radio mystery. Then, from its depths a sepulchral voice would utter these words, "Who knows what evil lurks in the hearts of men? The Shadow knows."

I would sit on the floor at her feet, my back pressed tightly against the cold iron of her bed frame. As we listened together to this mystery program, my very bones were inculcated with the cold seeping out of the iron bedstead at my spine. It was a symbolic sort of cold that was magnified by the plot of this radio serial. My knees ached with it, my fingers turned into chunks of ice, and my breath seemed stuck in some nether region of my being. By the end of every program I would feel paralyzed with, and calcified into, pure fright. My grandmother's comforting words and reassuring hugs did little to allay my fear, for I had internalized the haunting laughter of one who was "The Shadow." Nightmares frequently ensued. Nevertheless, I became deeply fascinated with this hidden side of the human being. Now, some sixty years later, *The Judas Legacy* is the culmination of my explorations. The "shadow" is a term applied with a certain level of understanding by those who wrote this radio series, and yet, one that was not fully appreciated for its fulsomeness of character.

The psychological term "shadow" is Jungian. Carl Gustav Jung, a Swiss psychoanalyst, used this word to articulate a powerful facet of the human personality. In this book, I will use Jung's theory and the negative characteristics of the shadow as a sub-structure for an exploration of the dark side of the soul. Then I will go beyond it to consider the socio-psychological and theological dynamics of fractured spirit in our contemporary culture.

For Jung, the human psyche was a multi-layered phenomenon. The uppermost level of the psyche, termed by Jung the "conscious level," is that part of psychic reality most honored and accepted by our culture. It is the place where we hold an awareness of social mores, of the right and wrong thrust upon us by cultural boundaries and limitations. The stipulated rules that govern our lives, everything from federal and state law to church creeds, confessions, and doctrine—all that is legal and legalistic can be found at this level of the human psyche. This conscious level thrives in an information age where the precision of computers delineates the ways we perceive our world and ourselves.

At this rational, intellectual level of the psyche, feelings are pushed aside as invalid; only computer-like understandings of self and world are deemed acceptable. Our educational system, while making strides toward an understanding of self in other ways, still champions this rational aspect of the psyche. From its either/or knowing of the world, we excel in the educational process. Only reasonable data, which can be linked to empirical or scientific proof, is honored at this level of the psyche. British common law—and thus historical, applicable law for the United States—is propounded at this logical, linear site of cognitive function. Exegetical methodology, the translation and interpretation of a biblical text from either Hebrew or Greek, relies upon the rationality of this level of the psyche.

An example of the power held in this psychic layer can be found in the teaching and practice of the law. My deceased husband believed with every fiber of his being in the superiority, and practice, of the law. He also believed it was possible to function solely from the cognitive levels of the psyche, unimpaired and uninfluenced by the deeper, more visceral levels of it. Yet, at the same time he had a powerful shadow. Like most people, he denied his shadow and could engage in profound intellectual arguments about it, as if this deeper level of his psyche could be cast into an abstract and examined like a flea under a microscope. All of his brilliance was used in the denial of his shadow, and in doing so, he was left with a body that threw up symptoms in an attempt to get his attention. His thinking was more familiar with a western medical model that for decades has seen the body in bits and pieces, like individual cogs that could be examined in isolation. He died of a massive heart attack five days after a birthday on which he had declared, "I don't want to be fifty."

In a sometimes dark and lonely place, below the uppermost, conscious level of the psyche, lies the *personal unconscious* element of the human psyche. This is where our personal, individual shadows live. The *shadow* is that *hidden part of self* we have repressed, and buried within, during the years after birth. Its repression is part of our socialization process. For example, when a mother teaches her children not to pick their noses in public, this habit is repressed downward into the contents of the shadow. But if, on a day when this same mother is weary with fatigue, she tells a child who is singing off-key to hush and makes the mistake of actually saying "You're singing off-key," the child may push singing (whether off-key or otherwise) into the shadow, believing that s/he cannot sing. One is an example of repressing unacceptable negative material ("Don't pick your nose!") and the other is an example of repressing positive creative energy (singing, even if off-key). We tuck the contents of the shadow downward inside ourselves in order to survive and to be accepted by the society in which we live.

The shadow can be recognized in two ways. *Its positive characteristics are written upon the faces of our best friends and of our mentors.* These traits mirror the parts of ourselves we find most admirable, but often fail to allow ourselves to claim. They personify the creative energy and vitality of the positive aspect of our own personal shadow. Usually these attributes are most discernable in same-gender friends, although it is possible to find them in opposite-gender interactions.

The negative characteristics of our shadows are most evident to us in others whom we find repulsive. Again, the evidence of shadow is most obvious in encounters with others of the same gender, although opposite gender may apply at times. The person who sets us off, who provokes an emotional kick of angry energy, is usually a personification of our own individual, negative shadow qualities. If, in encounters with a particular person, we are more prepared to hate than to accept, to judge than to affirm, or to shun than to befriend, this person is a mirror of our own negative shadow characteristics.

There are readers who will find this description of the ways one's own shadow can be recognized difficult to accept, for they find child abusers, rapists, murderers and/or bigots repulsive, and thus people to be shunned. These same readers may indicate that they have chosen opposite values as the way they will live their lives, but not because these values represent the shadow they have stifled. Whenever I teach this material, it is always this aspect of the shadow that provokes the most vehement reactions from those in the class. Yet, every human being has a shadow with extreme dark characteristics, as well as glowing positive characteristics. The negative side of the shadow is more often denied. The more it is denied in a culture that believes it represents values opposite those of its criminal element, the more the criminal element becomes the carrier for the collective shadow. For this reason, befriending our own personal, individual shadow is the greatest challenge we ever undertake in the therapeutic process of psychoanalysis.

It is vitally important to understand that the shadow holds both positive and negative qualities. The shadow, like most other aspects of our lives, is multidimensional and diverse. It is not limited to one personality trait or one way of being. It has multiple faces and the guises it wears may seem to be satirically amusing, or on the cutting edge of intellectual discourse. It can both stimulate and stultify. When intense reactions accompany our interactions with another, that other person is the mirror that reflects our own shadow back upon us.

The shadow is capable of enlarging or diminishing who we are, even as it is the impetus for both compliment and criticism of another. It is the encapsulated potential within us; it is the unlived potential held deep inside a psychic room with a closed door. The door is not locked, though, nor is the room inaccessible. We only open this door when we are ready to accept the attributes that represent our most creative (yet unlived) abilities, as well as those unseen shameful traits that we have kept hidden from others, and, quite often, even from ourselves. Each is part of the shadow; one comprises its positive face; the other marks its negative countenance.

A certain amount of tunnel vision and ethnocentric focus comprise the unconscious assumptions of every human collective. This tendency to perceive the perspective from one's own group as superior has been a deciding factor for cultural development throughout the history of the world. Thousands of years ago, the Greek philosopher Plato gave us a splendid example of the dynamics that are "shadow." In *The Republic* he creates a myth about human beings who have been forced to live chained inside a cave throughout their lives. The chains are rigid—they encircle the legs and necks of the people, so that they are forced to face in one direction all the time. They cannot turn their heads to see behind them.

A fire burns behind them, providing the only light by which they can then see. Silhouetted on the opposite wall of the cave, are the marionette-like shadows of those who are moving around behind them. Since the heads of the prisoners are immobilized, they are incapable of seeing the real humans behind them who create the shadows. Their only contact with other beings is through the shadows cast, both their own shadows and those of their captors. Ultimately, they come to believe that beings of any kind are comprised solely of shadow, since the cave produces an echo whenever they hear voices, causing the prisoners to suppose the voice is coming from the passing shadow. Thus, for these immobilized beings, the sum totality of their perception of other beings, and of themselves, is one of shadow.

Plato concluded that, if these poorly treated prisoners were released, and if they tried to turn their heads, they would suffer from shooting pains in their necks. If they were compelled to walk outside into the sunlight, the glare would "distress" them, for the light would hurt their eyes. If these prisoners were confronted with the reality that their previous perceptions had been an illusion, they would still be more inclined to name the shadow as reality. Plato asks, "Will (they) not fancy that the shadows which (they) formerly saw are truer than the objects which are now shown to (them)?" (Paragraph 515, p. 224)

Because the shadow has such powerful energy and an equally powerful energy is used to sublimate it, *shadow denial is a dominant aspect of human interaction.* Despite the shadow's tendency to push one into illusion instead of reality, denial is more common than any other reaction to it. The shadow feeds the aspirations and often unhealthy desires of the ego, especially in a culture where falsely inflated egos are encouraged. When one lives in an egocentric society where extroversion is unconsciously held as a norm, the quietude of introverted self-reflection is rare. The more technology impinges upon every waking hour of our lives, the more the psyche is bombarded with outside stimuli. Thus, silence and introversion suffer, and the benefits of such stillness are lost in the noise of a technology-driven world.

Below the shadow's dwelling place in the personal unconscious an even more fascinating aspect of the human soul is found. At the deepest level of the human psyche lies the *collective unconscious*; Jung also called it the "objective unconscious." It is that primogenial place whose patterns of living were imprinted before birth and carried forward as a soul memory. Here the human psychosocial patterns of belief and behavior that Jung called "archetypes" take form and are revealed in their primitive ways.

When we "adore" a public figure, a military hero, for example, we are responding to the internal "hero" archetype within ourselves and projecting that archetype onto a contemporary person. The heroes of great literature and history form an image in the psyche. That image is archetypal. Military heroes not only carry the projection of the "hero" archetype, but by the nature of their work they also carry the "warrior" archetype. The archetypes of king, queen, princess, father, mother, and child are all carried at the deepest levels of the human psyche and each one is stereotypical in its dimensions and traits.

When political candidates square off to run for the Office of the President, military service is a vital factor in their résumés. In our nation's history George Washington became president by virtue of these two dominant archetypes, setting an archetypal precedent for those who would follow. A nation's population identifies the archetype from a visceral level of the soul and reacts to that feeling, not to some cognitive rationalization, when electing a "hero-warrior" to national office. Dwight Eisenhower also followed this same pathway to prominence, as did John F. Kennedy and George H. W. Bush. Most cultures around the world could identify those who hold the position of "hero" and of "warrior." Military men often become leaders of nations, and aspirations of peace are rare among those who have been trained to go to war.

The primordial aspects of our human understanding of "self" lie within these archetypal characteristics, many of which take on particular imagery familiar to us through films, fairy tales, and dreams. A more obscure, but equally powerful knowing of these archetypal images emerges in bodily symptoms, most particularly symptoms of "dis-ease." Archetypal beings, those well known to us through stories of fantasy, are the inhabitants of this psychic-mystery land within the collective unconscious. In a past age, the archetypes dwelling there also came alive in great mythology and legends. These archetypal beings are the stuff of Star Wars; they are filmdom's monster creatures. The popular Harry Potter series is a dialogue with archetypal imagery. The reason for its popularity is that both children and adults are drawn to the power of the archetypes depicted in its stories. The "wizard" archetype is a classic. He is more than a wise old man—he has magic and knows how to use it. It is natural for the human soul to resonate with these familiar characters. These beings are primitive and have been part of an underlying worldview for literally thousands of years. They are the citizens of our psychic underworld, where we are connected to ancient times and people and places.

Darth Vadar is the walking-talking negative shadow we all carry inside ourselves. His personification of evil is greater than personal shadow. His larger-than-life evilness has touches of "archetypal shadow," for archetypal shadow is more powerful than that of just one individual. During the Second World War, Adolph Hitler was a man who was a living, breathing archetypal shadow. His evil was greater than the capability of one man alone. By the power of the position he held, he managed to trigger the collective shadow of masses of people. Thus, he represented the personification of archetypal shadow.

The apathy of many nations and peoples, including the institutional Christian church, contributed to the strength of this shadow projection. Once that collective shadow was unleashed among so many people, the atrocities that emerged were denied with vehemence, because a concurrent psychic denial had been evoked in vast multitudes of people in Germany as well as the rest of the world. *Denial is the first human reaction to encounters with the negative force of the shadow.* The collective negative shadow acts like a powerful virus, creating a contaminated environment in which such atrocities will be accepted. Acquiescence and abdication of responsibility then followed as German soldiers declared their actions were simply ones of "following orders." Such is the danger of an unleashed collective and archetypal negative shadow; its atrocities are the evidence of its vast and unbridled evil.

Some readers may wonder how such collective or archetypal shadow could so completely squelch the possibility of individual choice. In such cases, the shadow overwhelms the ego and individual choices are made from the shadow. As I explain later in this book, individual choice made from the shadow feels like ego strength. It is never more powerful than when individuals believe their actions are motivated by divine purpose. Without the apathetic complacency of other nations and the institutional church, this contamination would not have been as complete, nor loss of life so great. Our unconscious shadow participation was necessary for Hitler to be so effectively destructive, and that shadow participation cannot be denied, despite a powerful tendency to do so.

The attacks on the World Trade Center and the Pentagon on September 11, 2001 provided an ideal opportunity for the extroversion of individual and collective shadow. These attacks were attributed to one fanatical Muslim leader, Usama bin Laden. Bin Laden now represents archetypal shadow for the United States. Our national, albeit unconscious, need for a collective projection of "enemy" onto some villainous target has meant that Americans project their national shadow onto bin Laden and his al-Qaeda compatriots. Of course, bin Laden has been a willing player in this modern tragedy, since he has actively chosen to carry the projection. The failure to accept any international accountability for American actions that might have triggered bin Laden's hatred infuses a volatile situation with both individual and collective negative shadow energy. From a place of collective psychic inflation and misplaced superiority, many of our leaders and we, as citizens, demonstrate how profoundly we reject appropriate self-reflection. By choosing an infusion of "negative" shadow energy, we exhibit the typical self-righteous failures of those whose unconscious pattern is to extrovert the shadow onto a target. Scapegoats have abounded since September 11, 2001.

President George W. Bush engaged in a massive delusion that became the core element in his decisions. By adding what seemed to be his own personal demon, Saddam Hussein, to the collective target for projections of shadow, he initiated flawed foreign policy. By emphasizing extreme risk and creating collective psychic chaos centered around fear, the executive branch of our government created a constant undertow of negative shadow energy, while refusing to recognize that it was also fulminating collective cognitive dissonance.

Shadow energy is highly effective, even when its denial provokes cognitive dissonance. For example, cognitive dissonance is both the impetus that drives the tobacco industry and the resultant psychological end product. Any smoker who has watched the evening news for the past couple of decades knows there is irrefutable evidence that shows cigarettes cause cancer. The power of the shadow is its ability to support an addiction, despite the fact that, at a cognitive level, smokers know that cancer is linked to smoking. Even without considering the physical addiction, the shadow's energy is great enough to support a powerful addiction, despite the cognitive dissonance created when the intellect knows, understands, and sees graphic evidence of the harm that cigarettes cause. The complexity of a nicotine addiction cannot be discounted. The physical addiction to nicotine is a strong component of this addiction. Research shows that if ten individuals try heroin and tobacco, seven will become addicted to tobacco, but only three will become addicted to heroin. The negative power of the shadow is often greater than the strength of the ego feeding the intellect. The link between the shadow and addictions is one of the reasons that behavior modification rarely works to break an addiction.

Just as tobacco companies denied their product caused cancer, the cabinet members of the Bush administration denied that the nation had been misinformed before going to war in Iraq. Because he projected his own personal shadow onto Saddam Hussein, this president discounted the failure of substantial evidence linking al Qaeda terrorists to Iraq before the United States initiated a preemptive military strike.

When confronted with actual concrete indicators that the administration had misled the American public, its response was one of petulant arrogance and massive shadow denial. Talk show appearances by key cabinet officials, circular propaganda, and repeated messages emphasized that military action was initiated to "liberate" Iraqi citizens from the harsh dictatorship of Saddam Hussein. By reiterating the same message again and again, shadow energy between the administration's supporters and its opponents escalated. The decision to use repetition, instead of truth, fed this shadow escalation. Perhaps each of these vocal leaders was familiar with Vladimir Lenin's opinion that "A lie told often enough becomes the truth." When lies were used to initiate war and to defend it in the succeeding years, perhaps these leaders came to believe the lie was true. The shadow deals in lies and subterfuge, and as collective shadow escalation continues, self-reflection suffers.

When contrasting this nation or its people with either the terrorists who initiated the attacks on the World Trade Center and the Pentagon, or to Saddam Hussein, our leaders fell into an ideological trap of assuming opposite symbols of "good versus evil." President George W. Bush's seeming inability to reflect upon his own shadow is evident in the ways he proclaims his "born-again" Christianity, while claiming not to be prejudiced against Muslims. The original designation of this military action as a "crusade" was quickly changed when politically correct expediency made such a name inadvisable. The United States is now left to repair fractured diplomatic international relationships that have been carefully articulated over many decades.

Vladimir Lenin once wrote, "The purpose of terrorism is to terrorize." A more discerning observer of the shadow side of humans, Friedrich Engels, wrote to Karl Marx in 1870, "Terror is for the most part useless cruelties committed by frightened people to reassure themselves" (Zakaria, B-07).

The preemptive strike against Iraq was a shadow-driven military action that failed to meet accepted standards for initiating war against another nation. In doing so we unconsciously assumed the precarious position of international bully and created our own form of psychic terror. It is one we are neither equipped to maintain financially nor to defend diplomatically. The shadow is very effective when collective fear is triggered. The fear that is an undertow for daily newscasts and legislative actions is an unremitting emotional bludgeon. It has the power to bring our whole nation down without any action from an external terrorist. Fear blocks the doorway to healthy discourse, even as it drives legislation that strips Americans of civil rights guaranteed by the Constitution. The blatant use of fear as an emotional tool can only lead one to wonder, is the federal government impelled by its own fear more than any other impetus? Are the leaders of the Congress and the administration living out Engel's astute observations about human nature? Is the war in Iraq one of "useless cruelties committed by frightened people to reassure themselves" in a global arena? Those who question the political, philosophical, or military stance related to the war in Iraq are deemed both unpatriotic and unchristian. The collective shadow is one of the dominant forces driving such reactions. By labeling those who disagree with national leaders in this way, the negative shadow is denied while creating an environment for its escalation, and cognitive dissonance abounds.

While archetypal shadow may be the most fascinating and dangerous aspect of the collective unconscious, other archetypes also dwell there. These archetypes are most clearly represented by characters in great literature. The gods and goddesses of an ancient time were all archetypal figures whose personality traits were familiar to their worshipers because they were part of a panoply of archetypes available within themselves. Whether a fairy tale king or a mythological warrior, archetypal figures are recognizable for their characteristic personalities.

The man who carries the Western world's energetic projection of archetypal traitor is Judas Iscariot, a biblical figure whose prominence is tied to this one aspect of his being. In such projection Judas can be compared to the internal shadow, in that the negative side of the shadow is the "Judas" dwelling within every human soul. While Judas' positive qualities are largely hidden in the biblical narrative, Judas—like the shadow—embodies positive and negative characteristics worthy of exploration. Whether one is a devout church member of the Christian faith or a casual observer without strong connections to the Christian tradition, the name Judas conjures within the deep reaches of the collective unconscious a distant, yet profound sense of betrayal. The Judas archetype, or the betrayer archetype, is also what Americans conjure when they hear the name Benedict Arnold. If Benedict Arnold is symbolic of national treason, Judas Iscariot is symbolic of much greater human treachery. He is the one who betrayed Jesus.

The Judas archetype continues to flourish because most of us are unaware of the betrayal inherent within our own shadows. The negative side of the shadow reveals itself quite clearly in the ways we are willing to betray. For example, if asked how content they are with the particular job they are doing, many people would respond that they are dissatisfied with their job. A survey taken by Business Week found that worker satisfaction has dropped from 59% to 51% in the years between 1995 and 2000 (Koretz, November 13, 2000). While many of these same workers might insist they have to stay on the job to provide for their families, betrayal of one's own soul is a large factor in "job dissatisfaction." Soul betrayal is that itch you cannot scratch with a linear, logical explanation, but it is the psychic pain you feel at a deep heart level when the job you are doing is not right for you. You feel the same psychic pain when you are in an intimate relationship that is unacceptable to your own soul, for such intimacy is also a betrayal of the soul.

We rarely betray another without also betraying some aspect of ourselves when we function from this negative impetus from the shadow. Such is the nature of betrayal. In betrayal, we reveal our own shadow. When we are betrayed, at some level, whether conscious or otherwise, we have participated in that betrayal. Our lack of awareness of our own shadow material, and its need for acknowledgment, will lead us to participate.

Such shadow betrayal is palpable in the American culture. Fragments of countless multitudes of shadows have been spewed out into the atmosphere in which we all live. There they careen about, contaminating the collective in ways we fail to recognize. If we were to use a biological approach, Rupert Sheldrake's understanding of morphic resonance would apply. Psychic energy from individuals in any particular species forms the invisible environment in which that species develops behavior patterns. This morphic energy is the unseen atmosphere that influences learning patterns, cultural habits, and accepted modes of functioning within that species. As an example, when wild geese form a tight V formation and fly for thousands of miles without bumping into each other, they are tapping into the morphic field for their particular species, and resonating from it.

Every person in a given society unconsciously contributes to the collective energy of that culture, while at the same time tapping into this shared energy through daily interactions. The commonality of this morphic energy becomes a deciding force in the collective psyche of any group or species of individuals. When we encourage or invite fear (as a driving collective emotion) into the national consciousness, then the result will always be a negative energy field surrounding our daily living. The United States, by its actions and the ways it defends those actions, has created a powerful morphic field of negativity, fear, and paranoia. This is the collective spiritual environment that has the most powerful daily impact upon our individual souls. If we were fish, we would be swimming in a vast sea of contamination. While the actuality of world events is part of our daily stimuli, the morphic contamination of fear and negativity that surrounds us daily is less evident because it is both denied and held outside levels of awareness.

Those who would revert to ancient ways and pound plows into swords insist that military battle is the only way to deal with the contemporary international pirates called "terrorists." Saber rattling is a favorite pastime for those who believe in ancient warrior tactics. By emphasizing this exclusive method of combating terrorism, other methods are excluded from consideration. When fear, or any other strong negative emotion, is the dominant impetus for collective national decisions, rational solutions slip into default mode as inoperative.

The psychic underbelly of the nation is the same as the psychic underbelly of the institutional church, for both deny the deeply held negative aspects of their psychic reality. Whenever any social institution believes it represents an ideal, it sets itself up for shadow denial. Two of the most prominent examples of this inflated ideal are the government of the United States and the institutional church. Both deny the negative side of the shadow. This denial itself acts to provide strength to the shadow, since the shadow feeds upon denial. The collective shadow in the United States is fed every time a newscaster uses a term like "the world's greatest superpower" to describe this nation. An overweening national arrogance inculcated by such labeling is the visible attitude we present to other nation states in the world. In both the public political arena and the institutional church there is a powerful tendency to project shadow through ego-inflation, self-righteousness, arrogance, rejection of opposing views and pseudo-piety.

When we agonize over the travesties of the Bush administration and their concomitant damage to this nation, perhaps it would be wise to consider how much the White House with its self-absorbed narcissism is symbolic of today's American culture. The odd juxtaposition of symbols often found in America's public places—the history of warrior gods set side-by-side with supposed Christian belief—reflects a schizophrenic casting of opposites. For example, every church I have ever served has an American flag located on the chancel of its sanctuary, highly visible to those who attend worship services. Given our history of a separation between church and state, such flags are incongruous in the context of worship. We tend to choose symbols and display them, even when they are inappropriate.

During the Iraq War, Saddam Hussein's pistol was seized by the military when he was captured. It was later mounted and presented to the president. This pistol now hangs in the small study off the Oval Office alongside "a photograph of special-forces soldiers in Afghanistan praying after burying a piece of the World Trade Center there as a tribute to those who died in the terrorist attacks on Sept. 11, 2001" (Cooper, *Time* Internet Archives). These warrior trophies are displayed with pride by George W. Bush.

"He was really proud of it," remarked one visitor to the White House after visiting the display, referring to Saddam Hussein's pistol.

There is a difference in authentic warrior courage and the pseudo-warrior ego of this commander-in-chief. Authentic warrior courage is the deep psychic ability to lay down one's life for another or for a vow one has taken. Warrior-leaders do not stand in front of a podium and try to scare their people into a belief or action. Warriors do not use fear as a reprehensible tool for emotional manipulation. Historically, warrior kings were often great leaders because they never sent their armies into war with others to lead them. The king, himself, led them. The disconnect comes in the leading. If the commander-in-chief is not bold enough or courageous enough to stand and lead, then the army lacks psychic potency. At an unconscious level the people of the nation know that. It is one thing to "support our troops." It is a whole other thing to lead them or the entire nation in authentic, psychically healthy ways.

Our national pseudo-piety was evident in our military action in response to the destruction of the World Trade Towers and the attack on the Pentagon. Supposedly, God was on our side when we initiated retaliatory strikes, even when we scoffed at the notion that Usama bin Laden had been answering the call of his God to attack America. Our actions were touted as noble, while the actions of the enemy were termed evil. When the reaction to evil is one with its own undertow of evil, then nobility is stripped from the second action, and one is forced to evaluate what part of it is evil. We cannot pretend to be above evil. Nor can we claim it is absent from our foreign policy decisions, military actions, and reactions to other nation states on this planet regarding the environment. The undertow of shadow evil is highly visible in the corrupt practices of our Congressional representatives, inculcated daily into the programs offered to our youth, and it is the core element in our egocentric and ethnocentric notions of our collective superiority.

Theologian (and Jungian analyst) John A. Sanford wrote, "The deliberate decision to do evil leads to our becoming evil. This is why living out the darkest impulses of the Shadow cannot be a solution to the shadow problem, for we can easily become possessed by or absorbed into evil…; it is one of the qualities of the archetypes that they can possess the ego, which is like being devoured by or made identical with the archetype" (*Evil: The Shadow Side…*, 103).

Pseudo-piety is a mark of the Judas legacy, for pseudo-piety is both an indicator of the degree to which the shadow is denied and a sad demonstration of a lack of connectedness to authentic soul. One of the most troubling aspects of such pseudo-piety is evident in many members of churches and their clergy, for an insistence upon "being good" is a lopsided attempt at covering up shadow contents, while unconsciously revealing them in times of stress or conflict. The scandals that erupted in televangelism were healthy in that they brought high-visibility preachers to an abrupt confrontation with their own shadows and forced them to look into the mirror of imperfect, flawed humanity shared by all humans.

Ultimately, the continuing scandal engulfing the Roman Catholic church may become the means for cleansing its collective soul.

Shadow-denial is evident each time American politicians pontificate before an international audience, decrying human rights violations in nations like China—while denying covert violence against those who do not meet perceived cultural norms in this nation. Not unlike shadow targets of the past, homosexuals now share the pain of those who were historically targeted in history.

Shadow-denial was especially evident when the United States diverted its military attention away from its original "war on terrorism." By targeting a nation whose leader was admittedly a well-known tyrant but whose inexact links to terrorism were never fully confirmed before the military action, our government took the war on terrorism and diffused its focus.

From the beginnings of its history the United States has never been forced to accept its own collective shadow, because it has never been forced to overtly surrender to an enemy force or nation. Few other nations in the world share this experience. Here I am discounting our own internal Civil War, since the entire nation, as a collective, was not forced to surrender. When the collective of a nation's people has never had the experience of surrender, there is no collective understanding of the positive aspects of psychic surrender. When a nation has always "won" or, at the very least, not lost a war in a thoroughly ignominious manner, then the collective ego of the nation feeds upon this notion of its own superiority. The psychic power of the shadow is rarely recognized or accepted without what may be a painful surrender. "Winning is everything" might be our national slogan; aggression is the mode of living we model for our children, and fear is the air we breathe every day.

The shadow feeds such fear, while at the same time, it is denied with remarkable and complete vehemence. Even when political, educational or church leaders want to deny this reality, it still presents itself with consistent and painful clarity.

We are living examples of the cultural texture in Jonathan Swift's declaration: "We have just enough religion to make us hate, but not enough to make us love each other."

Back in 1988 when Jonathan Kozol first wrote of this reality in his book entitled *Rachel and Her Children*, he pointed out the cold and brutal truth of homelessness in this country. He was one of the first to point out the awful reality of mothers and their children living on the streets. Not only has the national government failed to respond with appropriate programs, it has cut programs that would benefit this segment of the population during the last three decades. It is important to note—the leadership of this nation has been both Republican and Democrat, conservative and liberal, during that span of time.

Our perceptions of self, formed within various necessary social institutions—whether family, government, corporation, university, media, or church—are ones which allow us to perceive ourselves without shadow. We can deny our own shadow as long as we can blame evil on external entities, like "an axis of evil," or on individual national leaders like Hitler, Stalin, any Ayatollah, Usama bin Laden, or Saddam Hussein, or…fill in the blank—any one of countless tyrants, nations, or terrorists history can offer as the flavor of the decade. In some ways, our delusion is worse than the people of Plato's fantasy. We have not had our necks chained, even though we refuse to turn our heads and look behind us at our own hidden shadow side. We are busily projecting that hidden side onto some target we have found to blame for everything that is wrong with the world. Any target will do. Through our passive (but willing) participation, the collective shadow projection in our nation has become a powerful presence, an undeniable energetic entity, a powerful morphic field of gloom and pessimistic energy. Because of the potent energy provoked by such shadow projections, we are interacting daily in a morphic fog of fear-induced negative energy.

We deny this shadow at our own peril, for its strength is in direct correlation to its denial. The more we deny it, the stronger it becomes. Like the immobilized prisoners of Plato's imagination, we are very close to living our whole lives in the midst of a delusion, for we fail to recognize the actuality of shadow among us. Such is the nature of shadow; it hides within the illusions we cast for ourselves. Unless each one of us learns how to confront our own hidden side, our own shadow—thus also correcting the ways in which we participate in the collective shadow—we, like Plato's imaginary prisoners, will be incapable of tolerating the sunlight of positive consciousness. This nation gives birth daily to new shadow actions. They are born into a "family" rich in its habits of refusal, the children of denial, whose mother is our collective shadow.

Chapter 2

Who was This Man Judas Iscariot?

We know so little about Judas. We know more about the scapegoat he has become. No name is as strongly linked to betrayal as the name of Judas Iscariot. Nineteen out of twenty-two direct references in the New Testament refer to Judas as the "betrayer." By the time the gospel of John was written, this legend, rumor, or projection of evil had reached its zenith. One commentator declared, "With singular harshness the author of the fourth Gospel consigns Judas to the realm of the demonic" (Klassen, 143). Yet the name "Judas" is a Greek derivative of the Hebrew, meaning "praised" or "celebrated" (Brownrigg, 247).

For a man whose name held hidden connotations of praise and celebration, the being of Judas Iscariot seems wrapped, instead, in death and despair. The betrayer label reflects a poor equivalent in the English translation from the original New Testament Greek word, *paradidomi*, meaning "to hand over," or "to commend to," or "to hand down, or transmit, or teach." The more negative connotations of the English word "betray" were absent from the meaning in the Greek word. Our collective unconscious holds the memory of betrayal as "delivering to an enemy by treachery," or another definition similar to the one found in the Merriam-Webster Collegiate Dictionary. The coloration of this poor translation hangs, like a hangman's noose, over the being of Judas. He carries the archetypal energy of betrayer, without equal.

The designation "Iscariot" has provoked much scholarly debate, for this appellation seems to have diverse meanings, no one of which has been given a consensual elevation. A number of scholars have settled upon "a man from Kerioth" (Kerioth-Hezron is identified as a village about twelve miles south of Hebron in Judea). The Greek word Iscariot, taken from a Hebrew root, "*is Qeriyyot*," would be derived from the Hebrew word *ish*, meaning man, and the place name, Kerioth (Fitzmyer, 620; Metzger, p 26-27; Geldenhuys, 206).

Other meanings for Iscariot depend upon derivations from either Latin or Aramaic. If Iscariot is related to Latin, it could be derived from the root *sicarius*, meaning "assassin" or "dagger-man." The Aramaic root *seqaryâ* applied to this name would give it a meaning of "liar" or "false one" (Marshall, 240). Another Aramaic root, *sêqar*, meaning "to dye red" lends itself to notions that Judas Iscariot was a man with red hair (Albright & Mann, 118) or a man with a ruddy complexion (Metzger, p 26-27). There is also some speculation that this name could have meant a leather apron or girdle, or even the bag in which money was carried, suggesting Judas' greed and overt preoccupation with money. These meanings are suspect, however, since what parent would name a child a "greedy one" or "money-grabber" at birth? These designations suggest later redaction by an imaginative editor.

Judas Iscariot is set apart as the one disciple who is not a Galilean. Whether this is true or not, Judas is the one who becomes most notorious for his role in Jesus' arrest. So, by that action, every other aspect of his being is thrust into the background. No other belief about Judas is as paramount as the accepted belief of him as betrayer, thus an archetypal traitor. No other understanding of his personhood is evident from the canon. Only his role as betrayer is there for readers to speculate about, for his motivations are as unclear as the derivation of his name.

There is some speculation that Judas was a Zealot (Marshall, 240; Albright & Mann, 316) or was associated with a group of Palestinians who most vehemently opposed Roman control (Fitzmyer, 620). If he was a member of such a group, his betrayal of his rabbi might then be tied to a strategic maneuver intended to force

Jesus' hand, so that at the moment of betrayal, Jesus would declare himself a secular messianic leader and thus empower the masses who were his followers to overthrow an oppressive government.

All four gospels depict Judas as a traitor; when he is named among the twelve, he is usually named last, and identified as the one who would betray Jesus. John is the most emphatic in his condemnation of this disciple, labeling Judas also as a "thief." John's gospel (John 6:70) also uses shadow language for Judas, placing these words in Jesus' mouth: "Did I not choose you, the twelve? Yet one of you is a devil." By such language the biblical writer thrusts Judas into the archetypal role of demon and of scapegoat. He is the carrier of historic projections of archetypal traitor because of such labeling. And he seems to be the personification of evil.

Yet one must ask why he was chosen as a disciple; how did this man who would become the betrayer enter the ranks of the chosen twelve? The text is clear: he was chosen by Jesus, like all the others, even though the Johannine writer opines, "For Jesus knew from the first...who was the one that would betray him" (John 6:64b). Here the Johannine author may be imposing his own peculiar need for Jesus to be all-knowing and omniscient, since this text—written so long after the actual events—would be one with the most tendency to present legend rather than actual historic fact. The gospel of John has a polemic coloration that cannot be denied. The reader could also ask, since Jesus healed any number of people who were possessed, even by "the devil," why then, if Judas became possessed by Satan, did Jesus not choose to heal him as well? Why did Jesus fail to exorcise this evil from Judas? When the canonical text was written, most people believed that evil was external to the human psyche. Thus "devil" or "Satan" language became the means by which writers set evil apart from themselves, projecting it onto a target, or an unseen god or spirit, or even upon a race of people who were different from them. For example, evil in the form of the minor Greek goddess Atê, a daughter of Zeus who symbolized blundering, sinful behavior, was typical of the way in which evil was perceived during this time in history (Jordan, 31). It was believed that Atê ranged far and wide upon the earth, known as "the meadow of Atê," provoking humans to sin.

In our modern age, there are still many people with similar unsophisticated ideas, who still believe evil is lodged in some unseen and invisible "devil" persona, albeit one external to themselves. Others unconsciously project devil/evil onto those who are marginalized, whether they be those of a different language and culture, homosexual (a favorite and trendy target for shadow projection in our contemporary time), a different race or color, or the opposite gender. In a long history of collective shadow projections, Judas was among the first targets. The target serves to allow the collective to disown its own evil, so that it can unconsciously abdicate any responsibility for personal shadow.

While many biblical scholars still debate the role of Judas as a disciple and as a participant in the dynamics that led to Jesus' crucifixion, one scholar asks a vital question about Judas. Bishop John Shelby Spong wrote, "There are many elements in this story that cause me to wonder about the historicity of Judas Iscariot. Was his betrayal invented to make the behavior of the other disciples less shocking by comparison?" (*Resurrection: Myth or Reality* 242).

Peter seems to personify the fear and cowardice of the other disciples; he denies his affiliation with Jesus not once, but three times. Yet Peter becomes the one who is exalted as the "head of the Roman Catholic Church" from its earliest days to the present time. During the time of Jesus' arrest, trial, and execution, the other disciples, except for the women, were characterized by their absence from the fray. For Judas to bear the brunt of betrayal would rescue the others, who were not bold enough to claim their discipleship in that time of crisis.

If the life of Judas is historically suspect, his death is no less suspect. The two different and contradictory accounts of the way in which he died are part of the inconsistency of the canon, an inconsistency that does not allow for literal interpretation. Matthew's gospel (Matthew 27:5) declares that Judas flung down the thirty pieces of silver, his blood-money payment for his betrayal of Jesus, departed from the temple, and hanged himself.

Yet the writer of the gospel of Luke and the book of Acts writes that Judas did not throw the blood money away, but used it to invest in real estate. This writer indicates that Judas used this money, "the reward for his wickedness," to purchase a field, where he fell headlong, and his belly burst open and his bowels gushed out. An extra-canonical source, the *Fragments of Papias 3*, may lend credence to the Lukan account in that this source supports the notion that Judas had some sort of disease which caused his body to swell so dramatically that he was unable to pass through a gate where a chariot could ordinarily have passed. If this source is credible, it suggests that Judas was crushed by a chariot, causing his intestines or bowels to burst out (cited by Sanford, *Mystical...*, 239). There can be no reconciling these variant accounts of the death of Judas; they simply are too inconsistent.

This inconsistency in the legends or myths of the death of Judas is not singular in its nature. For example, each of the four gospels describes the story of the anointing at Bethany; but the writers disagree on the actual details of this story. Their stories differ on the location of the anointing. It occurred at the house of Simon, the leper, according to Matthew and Mark. Luke writes of it at the home of a Pharisee. John places it at the home of Lazarus, Martha, and Mary. John's source for locale is apparently secondary and may be inferior (Brown, 453). They have problems with the identity of the woman—whether she was simply the unknown woman of Mark and Matthew's text; or a woman who was a woman of the city, perhaps a prostitute, as Luke has told it; or Lazarus' sister Mary, as John tells it. They disagree on whether she anointed head or feet—Matthew and Mark agree it was his head, but Luke and John agree it was his feet. And the reaction of those who witnessed this anointing is not consistent—Matthew has the disciples, as a collective, reacting; Mark's identity of the responders is ambiguous; Luke has the Pharisee react; and only John shows Judas as the one who has an adverse reaction (Aland, 277). The writer of this gospel seems determined to cast Judas in a negative light, from which there is no redemption.

All these disagreements in the text are a classic example of the reason literal interpretations are problematic. There can be no such thing as a literal understanding of this particular story without addressing the literal aspects of the inconsistencies in the canonical narrative. Each of these writers wrote years after the events they sought to describe. The gospel of Mark was first; it was written sometime around the year 65 C.E. Matthew and Luke followed at least a decade later, with Luke coming as much as "five to ten years after Matthew and fifteen to twenty-five years after Mark" (Spong, *Liberating...*, 263). John's gospel was written still later, sometime between 90 and 100 C.E.

Paul's writings to the churches were written some years earlier than these four gospel accounts, with the letters to the church at Thessalonica (dated around 52 C.E.) as probably his earliest. (Wilson, 65-78). Yet nowhere in Paul's writing is there a reference to Judas Iscariot as the betrayer of Jesus. One reference alone appears in I Corinthians (I Corinthians 11:23), but Judas is not named in this reference to the betrayal of Christ. Paul writes, "For I received from the Lord what I also handed on to you, that the Lord Jesus on the night when he was betrayed took a loaf of bread...."

When Paul refers to betrayal, he does not accuse one individual of that betrayal, nor is a collective named. Surely, if this man, Judas, had been as well known for his betrayal of Jesus, as the implicit and explicit message of the gospels would have us believe, then Paul would have known of him, and condemned him, too. Paul did not hesitate to make accusations. It seems out of character for him to forego an accusation in a matter as important as the betrayal of Jesus. He was vociferous in his proclamations of judgment against those who did not meet his perfectionist expectations. Yet, he does not specifically name Judas as the betrayer of Jesus.

Each of these New Testament authors used sources which obviously did not agree. They each placed within the text their own peculiar bias as to the characters who were part of the scene, and the part those characters played, whether large or small. A careful and critical reading of the text, beginning with Mark, progressing to Matthew and Luke, and ending with John, will show how the Judas legend expands, multiplies, and is most developed by the time it appears in the gospel of John.

Only John's gospel makes Judas the questioner at the anointing. Judas is now the one whose miserly spirit is such that he would question the anointing of Jesus' feet with a costly ointment. John's plot builds on successive references to Judas as that one who symbolizes evil. After John's reference to Judas as devil (in chapter six), the story of the anointing at Bethany takes on this additional color, which is absent in the synoptic gospels.

The author of John adds insult to injury by then explaining that Judas did not feel any particular concern for the poor, for whom his question supposedly applies; but rather John's gospel declares that Judas, himself, is a thief. Judas, who carries the money for the twelve, has been in the habit of dipping into the common treasury for his own purposes, according to this account. Since John's is the only account that has this added detail, the discerning reader might wonder whether this detail has more to do with the writer than with Judas. Biblical scholars have debated the identity of the author of the gospel of John for years, sometimes even speculating that there were multiple authors. Whoever the author may be, perhaps he is simply projecting his own shadow onto Judas.

By writing of Judas as both treasurer and thief, John's gospel more fully sets the stage to condemn a man who will have aberrant behavior related to money. This gospel enlarges the picture we have of Judas, and it becomes one of greed-induced betrayal, of treachery for money. Yet in the actual story of Jesus' betrayal, it is Matthew's gospel that details the betrayal for thirty pieces of silver, money that Judas demands of the chief priests by asking, "What will you give me if I deliver him to you?"

The differing accounts in both Mark and Luke seem to imply that the synagogue leaders were the initiators of this transaction; they proposition Judas, offering him thirty pieces of silver for this treacherous deed. Yet, even the thirty pieces of silver may have a Midrashic coloration, for the counterpart to this New Testament echoing of an older text might be found in the book of the minor prophet Zechariah (Zechariah 11:12-13), when its author writes, "I then said to them, 'If it seems right to you, give me my wages; but if not, keep them.' So they weighed out as my wages thirty shekels of silver."

These Old Testament verses might then give weight to the parallel account in the gospel of Matthew, but only if viewed through the lens of Midrashic technique, not as historical proof, since Matthew is the only gospel that articulates the amount of the bribery sum. The Midrashic technique delves into the hidden aspects of a particular text, looking for what is unspoken or assumed, looking for what has been deliberately omitted. This pitiful amount of money, the worth of a slave in those days, (Spong, *Liberating...*, 261) seems like a lowly price, indeed, for such a powerful betrayal. Does one betray oneself and another, who has been mentor and friend, for such a sum?

Far more critical to the undertow of this betrayal story is the demonic aspect of it. The writers of Luke and John portray Judas as a man into whom Satan entered. These two gospel accounts declare that the devil entered into Judas, thus provoking his action of betrayal. While the writers of Matthew and Mark leave this specificity to implication, the implicit becomes explicit in Luke and John. As the years pass the Judas legend is obviously building, gathering a head of steam. "The devil made me do it" flies out of contemporary vernacular and lodges in the throat of the gospel, where it becomes the overriding impetus for Judas' actions. And yet, this "devil" can also be found in certain works of art, showing Jesus with his disciples.

A remarkable medieval painting of the Last Supper (from The Hours of Catherine of Cleves) depicts Judas receiving the morsel of bread from the hand of Jesus, and in that same moment a tiny demon/devil/Satan leaps into his mouth. This literal depiction of "Satan entering Judas" carries the historic prejudice against Judas as betrayer. Strangely, this painting would have it seem as if Judas' awful destiny comes as food from the hand of Jesus, so that the symbolic bread which later becomes the "bread of life" may have been perceived by this artist as something more akin to a bread of death or even a bread of betrayal. Judas' participation in that destiny would thus be obedience, rather than betrayal (Edinger, 83).

The cosmic battle between evil and good, however, is seen in a dichotomy between a treacherous, greedy Judas whose driving force comes from Satan, and Jesus, whose divine character is affirmed each time he heals, whose divinity has been displayed in his ability to raise other humans from the dead. On the one hand we are shown evil as avaricious betrayal to death—for money; on the other hand we are shown good as resurrection to life—without compensation.

Elaine Pagels wrote, "Satan, like God himself, appears incarnate, first in Judas Iscariot..." (111). Satan, as an identifiable entity, takes on great strength in this characterization of Judas, for Satan is described as living in the heart of this man's personality. Satan is that one who finds his being most appropriately in the man who betrays Jesus. Since Jesus is part of God, as son, then Judas must be part of Satan, and vice versa, part demon, as betrayer.

Here, dynamics that would permeate Christianity down through the centuries become evident, for if Judas is the incarnation of the demonic and Jesus the incarnation of divinity, those who have participated with Judas in the arrest and execution of Jesus must also share in that which is evil. Those who "love the Lord" share, by some sort of default, in that which is good. As the fourth gospel becomes the arbiter for designating both "the Jews" and Judas as responsible for Jesus' death, they become—together—the designated shadow targets for coming generations. This allowed the church, as a thriving social institution clinging to a one-sided view of itself, to disregard the atrocities of the Holocaust and its horrible impact upon those who were Jews.

With a slanted depiction of the events that led to the arrest and subsequent execution of Jesus, the Johannine writer created a negative *habit of the mind* regarding "the Jews." Long before World War II, the projection of demon/Satan upon Jews was fully entrenched. Again, theologian John Shelby Spong has articulated the critical issue about the earliest projection cast by the Christian community.

He asked, "But who was Judas? Was he a person of history who did all of the things attributed to him? ...Or was he purely and simply a legendary figure invented by the Christians as a way to place on the backs of the Jewish people the blame for the death of Jesus?" (259).

Projection will not work unless a target is available. Projection is incomplete without a scapegoat, someone to blame for that which brings shame, humiliation, and degradation. And projection is at its most powerful when it is a projection of denied shadow within oneself (or a collective) onto a target who has been chosen for such projection. The disciples were demoralized by the execution of Jesus. In the face of this cruel Roman fait accompli, they fled to the safety of old occupations, fearful of Roman reprisals against themselves and their families.

When the gospel accounts of Jesus' life were written a number of years after Paul's letters to the early Christian churches, they were polemic instruments, apologetic explanations from a minority who followed Jesus. This minority, while vocal and unyielding in its loyalty to this rabbi, was substantially outnumbered by the Jewish majority. The majority retained an orthodox understanding of God and self, and continued to hold leadership roles in the synagogue. Some even maintained close ties to the Roman leadership.

Pilate, the fifth Roman procurator of Judea, Idumea, and Samaria, became a major player in the final days of Jesus' life. Pilate's family name was Pontius; he had come from an elite Roman family. The name "Pilate" has a Latin meaning that may have been an indicator of the character and personality of this man. In Latin, Pilate comes from "pilatus" meaning a "pikeman," or one who arms himself with a *pilum*, a javelin. One writer noted, "He was a proud, hot-tempered, obstinate and aristocratic young man, capable of childish behavior when his will was crossed and as military minded as his name suggests" (Brownrigg, 366-67).

Pilate was known to be a violent man, who accomplished what he wanted with force whenever he needed to use it. Secular historians of the time reported that Pilate was inflexible and merciless.

The trial of Jesus took place in the third year of his reign. While the canonical text would make it seem as if Pilate might have been the pawn of the more cunning high priest, Caiaphas, it is more likely that Pilate was a proactive participant in the events surrounding Jesus' death. Jesus, as a charismatic leader of the masses, had become so vocal and so well known, Pilate could easily have perceived him as a threat to the order of the day. If the headcount in the canonical text has any veracity and thousands of people were not only seeking out Jesus for healing, but following him in large multitudes, then the power brokers of the day were threatened by his popularity. The large numbers of people who were captivated by Jesus' message and healing would have been seen as a threat by the Roman authorities.

One can only wonder, then, if the impetus to execute Jesus originated with Pilate. Were the Jewish authorities pawns in his effort, in contrast to the canonical accounts? Crucifixion was a Roman form of execution, not one that was typical of the Jewish community. Pilate, however, used this form of execution frequently. If the Jewish community had executed Jesus, he would have been stoned to death.

Yet both groups, the old established orthodox order and the fledgling Christian group, were subservient to the Romans, who had conquered them and controlled their homeland. The Sanhedrin and its leaders sought to maintain their dominant hold on the religious norms for the people, but to suppose they would have held Jesus' trial at the time detailed in the canon does not make sense, for two reasons.

First, the Passover holiday (along with Shavuot and Sukkot) is one of three pilgrimage festivals that are sacred festivals, celebrated with rituals stipulated by law in the Torah. The leaders of the Jewish community would not have desecrated the holiest day of Passover by convening a trial. They simply would have bound Jesus over for trial after the holiday had been appropriately celebrated.

Secondly, the Toraic laws that governed such trials required that the Sanhedrin must render its judgments before sundown, during daylight hours only. Nevertheless, the authors of the gospel accounts in Matthew, Mark, and Luke have written that this trial occurred at night, during Passover. This story does not seem credible, because the orthodox leaders of the Jewish community would never have broken the Passover, or the laws of the Torah, in such a way.

The newly emerging Christian community was struggling to define itself as separate and superior to the old order, while at the same time hoping to appease the Roman government. Even though most of the men and women who followed Jesus were Jewish, when the writers of the gospels told this story, they had a political purpose in mind. Blaming the Jews by using a man whose name was derived from Judah allowed them to abdicate any responsibility for the execution of their leader. When the name alone is scrutinized, a fascinating aspect comes slipping through, since Judas is the Graecized form of the Hebrew word "Judah," from which the word "Jew" is also derived. Was there ever a man named Judas—or is he the pure shadow concoction of a biblical writer?

The conflict between these two groups is part of the historical warp and woof of Christianity and Judaism. The early Christian church, by unconsciously casting its projection of evil onto those who are described in the gospel accounts as "the Jews," created an atmosphere for subsequent historical projection of shadow onto those whom they had labeled "enemy." This projection became the defining norm for the attitudes and educational practices of the Christian community down through the generations of the institutional church.

It created the underlying *habits of the mind* at work when large segments of the Christian church worldwide watched in silence as the Nazi regime exterminated millions of Jews. German Christians, notably Dietrich Bonhoeffer and his cohorts, revolted against the Nazi regime. The Theological Declaration of Barmen is their bold statement against the terrorizing practices of the Nazis. It clearly articulates the difference between authentic Christianity and extreme nationalistic patriotism. Bonhoeffer was imprisoned and executed shortly before the Allies marched in to end the war. However, the Vatican stepped back from efforts to rescue the Jews during the war and became an international player when war criminals sought asylum after World War II (Aarons & Loftus).

In late winter of 2006 the world was finally told what many canonical scholars already knew. A thirty-one-page tractate entitled *The Gospel of Judas* would be revealed to the world of Christianity just in time for Easter celebrations around the globe. This Coptic Egyptian translation of a second century tractate had floated about in the scholarly arena for more than twenty years. When this translation was released, Judas was not portrayed as the treacherous character found in the biblical text, nor as a callous betrayer of the God/man Jesus, but as his obedient and intimate confidant (Kasser, Meyer & Wurst, 22). One striking aspect in this extra-canonical text is that Judas is the one who recognizes Jesus as divine (Kasser, Meyer & Wurst, 22-23). In the biblical accounts, Peter is the one who is given credit for recognizing this.

James Robinson, retired professor of Coptic studies at Claremont Graduate University and founding director of the Institute for Antiquity and Christianity, indicated he had tried to purchase *The Gospel of Judas* as early as 1983. Robinson, the general editor of *The Nag Hammadi Library*, an English translation of the Gnostic scriptures (regarded as definitive by biblical scholars), also vouched for the authenticity of the Gospel of Judas. In his book on it, James Robinson opens with two statements that might startle many readers. Here is what he wrote:

"*The Gospel of Judas*, a long-lost second-century fictional account that elevates Judas to hero status in the story, has been rediscovered! But it has been kept under wraps until now, *to maximize its financial gain for its Swiss owners.*" (Robinson, vii, italics mine)

Robinson may vouch for the authenticity of this tractate, but he also claims this account is fiction. Furthermore, he charges the owners with a crass motive in the timing of their release of this translation.

At the same time, the spokesman for the Roman Catholic

Church quickly asserted his scorn for this material. Monsignor Walter Brandmuller, president of the Vatican Committee for Historical Science, declared it to be a "product of religious fantasy" (Van Biema, 51; Meichtry, www.beliefnet.com). By standing in a place of rigidity, this spokesman for the church, founded upon the quavering rock of St. Peter, seems bent upon keeping Judas in his place as a scapegoat.

However, an Italian lay leader, Vittorio Messori, who has co-authored books with both Pope John Paul II and Pope Benedict, holds a different view. When asked about this new piece of biblical information he answered, "Judas wasn't guilty. He was necessary. Somebody had to betray Jesus. Judas was the victim of a design bigger than himself."

These words lead us to the remarkable fact that after more than two thousand years, the church may have to forgive even Judas. The church does not forgive easily, most especially not those who have carried projections of its collective shadow for so many eons. Jesus did not create the church; the apostle Paul did. Despite the words that claim that Peter is "the rock" upon whom Christ's church will be founded, Jesus did not establish any form of an institutionalized church. He was a vagabond itinerant preacher, whose revolutionary ideas were as foreign to the orthodox rule of the day as they are still in this contemporary age. He did not choose to initiate any formal organization that could be regarded as "the church" during his lifetime, nor did he indicate that such a formal organization was necessary or even helpful for espousing his beliefs.

Another extra-canonical book in which Judas holds a principal role is *The Dialogue of the Savior*. Here the identity of Judas cannot be easily clarified—it is not clear whether this is the man who is Judas Thomas or Judas Iscariot, since this text only identifies him as Judas. In this text the disciple identified simply as "Judas," along with Mary and Matthew, participates in a long conversation with Jesus.

Filled with apocalyptic overtones, this conversation is one that focuses upon matters of the spirit. If this Judas is the man of later betrayal and devil-driven evil, his questions and concern for things of the spirit stand in stark contrast to the picture painted of him in the canon. In one particularly poignant passage, the text reads, "When Judas heard these things he bowed down and [worshi]ped and praised the Lord" (Miller, 349).

The author of John's gospel (John 14:22) does offer a quick glimpse of this unknown Judas, in a verse which says, "Judas (not Iscariot) said to him, 'Lord, how is it that you will reveal yourself to us, and not to the world?'"

In a remarkable parallel from the Gnostic text (in *The Dialogue of the Savior*), Judas asks, "How is the spirit apparent?"

Jesus answers this question with a typical rabbinical reply, a question for a question, responding, "How is the sword apparent?"

Then Judas asks the question in another way, "How is the light apparent?" The response from Jesus has been lost, so that only a three-word phrase ("...in it forever") remains (Emmel, 254-255).

This unknown Judas slips through the tightly bound weave of the biblical text and asks us, as readers, the hard questions. Are we willing to suspend all reasonable inquiry into the gospel texts, elevating them to a place where we are worshiping words instead of God? Or are we willing to read the canonical text with the same critical eye as we read other great historical literature, knowing full well that polemic purposes were served by the Bible just as surely as they have been served by other great literature?

Those readers who find themselves fascinated by the canonical figure who was Judas may find my thumbnail sketch of him too succinct, but to portray Judas as an archetype, this account is sufficient. It is important to reiterate, this book is not about Judas as a protagonist in the betrayal of Christ; *it is about the symbol of Judas as archetypal traitor, who represents collective shadow.* Readers who want to learn more about the person of Judas can turn to a fine book written by a contemporary theologian: *Judas: Images of the Lost Disciple*, by Kim Paffenroth. This book is a comprehensive portrayal of the canonical Judas and a splendid examination of the legendary aspects of his history. Few theologians delve so carefully into the worrisome aspects of projections, onto Judas as betrayer and by Judas as the one who casts the projection. Paffenroth articulated the psychic escalation of the shadow with singular clarity when he wrote:

> Like Othello, once the ideal has been corrupted by suspicion, there is no turning back: everything contributes to increasing Judas's suspicion and destroying his idea of the beloved, until there is nothing left but hate for the one he thinks has destroyed his ideal and resentment for the pain and humiliation this (supposed) betrayal has caused him. The object of his love is pure, but the love itself is completely self-centered. Othello's love for Desdemona or Judas's love for Jesus are ways to ratify and increase their own self-worth: when the love threatens their self-worth, when it threatens to humiliate rather than uplift them, then it is turned into hate, destroying both the beloved and the lover (Paffenroth, 101).

The characterization of Judas Iscariot as betrayer is made more complex when one considers one's own shadow projection as well. Simplistic characterizations of treacherous behavior, and/or accusations of such behavior, are always called into question when the powerful impetus to find a target for shadow projection is considered. All the disciples were passive participant observers as Jesus was arrested, tried, and executed. Whether blaming the betrayal of Jesus upon Judas Iscariot, a man who may or may not have been an outsider, a man who may or may not have been a Galilean like all the other disciples, or whether "the Jews" are blamed, the scapegoated target serves the purpose intended.

This allowed the early Christian Church to distance itself from those who cling to orthodox Judaism while still standing inside the protection of the Roman Empire. In such either/or dualism, the church had its beginnings; Western civilization began its march into a dualistic future; and individuals, social institutions, and nations were educated to deny shadow, while searching, like a heat-seeking missile, for a target onto whom it could be projected.

Chapter 3

The Shadow and Our Mind Habits

In 1996 the Presbyterian Church, USA added an amendment to the sixth chapter of its governing document, the *Book of Order*. That amendment requires those who hold office in this denomination "to live either in fidelity within the covenant of marriage *between a man and a woman*..., or *chastity in singleness*" (italics added). This amendment also contains a cross-citation to emphasize the opposite gender aspect of its articulation. This amendment to the *Book of Order* is directly aimed at homosexuals even though it carefully refrains from using that specific word to identify its blatant bigotry. The underlying shadow impetus for such legislation is obvious. By covertly denying homosexuals any office in the church, this amendment stands in stark inconsistency with previous statements in the fourth chapter of this same book, one of which declares, "Our unity in Christ enables and requires the church to be *open to all persons* and to the varieties of talents and gifts of God's people..." (italics added). The amendment in the sixth chapter strips "all persons" of their choices by covertly revoking the statement in the fourth chapter.

This is a powerful example of the power of the shadow, and of its primary ability to sabotage social change through the psychic energy of refusal. The energy poured into a refusal to accept anyone who seems to be different from ancient understandings of a norm is fed by the shadow. The shadow's energy or force of refusal takes any issue, no matter how simple, and makes it seem complicated by stripping its soul away and gnawing at the bones of its simplicity. This is most often accomplished through complex legislative actions, either in the church or in the government. This shadow energy is a force that drives much of the fearful refusal in a culture as bound by fundamentalist thinking as those in Iran, Iraq, or North Korea, who have been declared "evil" by the leadership of our nation and targeted as "enemy." Each culture looks inward at its own belief patterns, sees them as superior, and denigrates any other culture's knowing of itself or its gods as inferior. This is not a matter of healthy choice. It is an egregious example of collective bigotry, fed by the negative energy of the shadow.

There is a marked difference between healthy choice and shadow-refusal. The cognitive dissonance that feeds the negative energy of the shadow's refusal in hot-button issues such as abortion, rape, or same-gender marriage is an energy that always looks backward over its shoulder at the way things were in the "good ole days." This same energy would claim its freedom of choice as the only choice, while vehemently denying the same freedom of choice to those who do not meet its so-called moral standards. The healthy ability to make life choices through a freedom of the will is not the same as a sinking into negative energy that refuses to focus upon the reality of one's own life in ways that would be growth producing. The shadow feeds refusal in ways that can stop creative energies from emerging in one's life through evolving and necessary change. Such evolving spiritual change and soul growth is held at bay as long as the shadow is denied.

The healthy ability to refuse to participate in matters where one's integrity or honor is compromised is not the same as the shadow's force of refusal that aligns itself with a stasis quo perception of reality, thus preventing positive movement into the future. The world of technology has radically changed so many of the dynamics and paradigms that had been assumed as determining norms. This radical change is not easily accepted by the deepest levels of the psyche. The first reaction is resistance. Yet, rapid paradigmatic shifts drive a technological culture.

The shift from clocks and watches driven by a winding mechanism to quartz-driven ones is a classic example of just one paradigm shift. When the person who invented the quartz-driven movement had perfected his invention, he offered it to the finest watchmakers in the world, the Swiss. Their reaction? They scoffed at the notion that quartz watches would ever be accepted and refused to work with him. He simply got on a plane and flew to Japan, where he offered his technology there, and the rest is history.

At a collective level this resistant dynamic becomes a force, with an individual and collective energy of its own. It has greater strength than individual resistance. The collective shadow force of refusal is very potent. The shadow, lying in the personal unconscious, is a reflection of the archetypal patterns that lie in the collective unconscious; and it participates in a dialogue with them. The human psychic self is charged with the responsibility of using this dialogue for positive growth and healthy choices, rather than following an ancient archetypal pattern as the only possibility. This is a soul-spirit creation, not a mental or cognitive process, although one's cognitive abilities are not eliminated, rejected, or suspended during this process.

The rational mind is much better at recording than at creation. The rational mind functions more like an accountant, but the positive creative energy of the shadow is an artist. Positive creative shadow energy is more like a finely choreographed ballet. While the human self creates itself moment by moment, the healthy aspects of this new process bring the heart and the head together in a melded understanding of soul energy. Yet, in our culture, the opposite dynamic is more evident.

There is something beyond sad in a nation that with unremitting vigor declares itself a Christian nation, but with unconscionable regularity and intentionality cuts programs for poor children and homeless people. Our national leadership, whether Democrat or Republican, spends for war, while cutting programs that would help families and children. Instead, as a nation, we focus upon trivialities.

Our failure to acknowledge, or come to appropriate understandings of, the shadow's energy provokes strange reactions to paradigmatic changes in a technological world. Reality television blurs the line between authentic reality and gross invasions of private places and interactions. Even the nomenclature for such programming is inauthentic, since there is nothing real about the staged situations used to create these shows. These "reality" participants seem unable to recognize that it is much less costly for the networks to cast amateurs rather than professional actors in these roles. When people clamor to appear on such television programs, not only do they open themselves to the indignities devised by clever television producers striving to win ratings wars, they also create a morphic field of acceptance for the complete loss of privacy. In this morphic field anything goes, as long as there is a cash prize in the end. The fairy-tale fallacy that money can be equated with happiness drives these shadow endeavors, but the unconscious cultural acceptance of a loss of privacy drives their popularity.

Numerous young women believe it is not only acceptable but fun to live in the strange fish-bowl existence of a twenty-four-hour web-cam. As they reveal their most intimate private moments to strangers on the Internet, these same people create an environment to allow the culture to more easily accept the intrusion of the government into the privacy of all citizens. This lack of physical or psychic boundaries contributes to the blurring of boundaries for the collective, creating an unconscious acceptance of breached boundaries as a norm, rather than an aberration. The voyeurism encouraged by this aberrant behavior provokes an escalation of dangerous shadow pathology.

When children who have not yet reached adolescence flaunt their active sexual lives on talk-show television and their mothers appear along with them, wringing their hands and declaring their inability to do anything about such a child, the culture is buying into some strange notion that these children have a right to bully adults and behave badly in public. The profound lack of boundaries implied by these self-absorbed-but-needy children, Web-cam exhibitionists, and reality-show participants sets the stage for a relaxation of appropriate privacy for all Americans, because the more these personal boundaries are blurred and assaulted, the more the government will believe it has the right to invade the private home or life of any individual. These sociological dynamics cannot be absorbed into a changing culture without understanding the dangerous impact they potentially represent. They may symbolize a future in which Orwellian predictions pale by comparison. Each time the privacy of one person is breached, the shadow energy surrounding that fractured boundary creates negative energy that opens the collective psyche to an acceptance of an aberration as a norm.

When reality shows tap into the "fear factor" alive in the American culture of the moment, they do so with a firm conviction that capitalizing on any particular weakness is an acceptable mode of achieving success. When the political leadership of this nation uses these same tactics, it grossly abuses its public office and subjects American citizens to forms of despotic strategies that parallel its point of entry into preemptive war against another nation. To use fear-producing strategies of any kind, whether tangible or subtle, is not a way of informing the nation, but rather, uses fear to accomplish a political end unto itself. As such fear is appropriated for political purposes, the incessant drumming to return to old traditional gender roles is a shadow counterpoint, always beating in the background.

As parents became more and more alarmed about adult predators who use the Internet to lure young teens into sexual traps, one network set up a sting operation. In cooperation with local police forces, the network filmed adult men who came to homes where adolescents were supposedly available for sex. The lure seemed to be virginity. When these men were arrested, they seemed completely puzzled by their own behavior. They were out of touch with the shadow that had driven them into a situation where they were ultimately arrested. Entitled "To Catch a Predator," this program aired for many weeks, but even the men who had seen previous programs could not withstand the powerful impetus of their own personal shadow. It was a classic example of the shadow overwhelming the ego.

In a nation where rapidly emerging technological changes

deeply impact the culture, the social institutions of marriage and family are also changing. In a post-industrial age, the paradigm that created marriage is no longer necessary to hold the culture in place. Women no longer need to psychically or physically sublimate their own soul's journey in order to achieve a modicum of financial security. Two-parent households are more ideal for children, but they are only ideal when the parents model healthy, egalitarian behavior patterns, with appropriate boundaries for these children. Former models of dominant-subordinate roles were not healthy, either for parenting children or marriage partnerships. Old rigid forms of belief or behavior will no longer fill the void of spirit in this nation, and poorly allocated federal funding will not change that. Even Jesus understood that old orthodox means did not achieve ideal ends.

He taught his disciples to move beyond old archetypal patterns of non-free-will living to the Christ archetype of free-will experience. This free-will form of living fully incorporated the creative energy of the divine held within each human, but it was the diametrical opposite of the old laws of the orthodox tradition. Christ lived and taught that the human spirit was greater and more complex than any law propounded by the legalistic thinkers who initially set the parameters for the Hebrew faith. While this was the underlying dynamic that led the orthodox leaders to find Jesus guilty of sedition, the later alteration of Christ's teachings into an antithesis of his concepts defined the shadow of the institutional church.

When the followers of Christ became the church, and determined that this institution must protect itself, the rigidity of its governing laws, doctrine, creeds, and rules for living reflected a soulless antithesis to Christ-consciousness. The more rigid the law, the more it stripped the spirit from the teachings of Christ. These laws, doctrines, and rules all have one undertow in common: they carry the denied shadow of the church in their actual articulation. Shadow motives are one of the underlying factors that help to sustain the rigidity and bureaucracy of every formal social institution, including the federal, state and local governments, universities, schools, corporations and the institutional church. They hold old patterns as the only norm, and in doing so protect both the norm and the power derived from it.

This shadow refusal is an energetic force unto itself. It has a penetrating energy with its own qualities, traits, and characteristics. That energy is summoned when we respond to new and different concepts with an emphatic, and decidedly emotional "No!" Or it may go underground and emerge, instead, in deliberate acts of sabotage. When confronted with a paradigmatic shift, the listener who functions from this shadow energy will often do so from a place of cognitive paralysis. A certain psychic paralysis causes the listener to retreat from hearing alternative suggestions. Listening shuts down and the result is adamantly holding to one's position, despite cognitive dissonance, sound reason, hope, or actual necessity. The shadow drives the coercive powers of the institutional church—provoking teachings of guilt, innate sin, and threats of hell. Authentic discernment is cast aside, regardless of any conditions that might indicate otherwise. The stance taken is hard, stark refusal, a refusal shaped and given energy by the negative aspects of individual shadow. It is then compounded by the acceptance of the collective shadow of a group, which gives it further power and greater intensity by their collective agreement with or apathetic acquiescence to it.

One of the most potent and hurtful articulations of shadow refusal is: "You're lying! You're crazy if you believe something as patently stupid as that!" By summoning through the physicality of one's self the shadow's energy of refusal, any flow of positive energy is abruptly halted. Instead, through vehemence and demeaning verbiage, the shadow's negative energy and power is magnified. By accusing an opposing person or group of being crazy, the shadow slips a manipulative dynamic into the equation. By suggesting that falsehood linked to insanity characterizes the opposite view, speakers suggest that they, themselves, are the only ones who are sane enough to offer any truth, and thus the only ones who can be trusted. No matter what political or philosophical belief might be held, this response is a shadow response.

When Ron Suskind's book, *The Price of Loyalty: President George W. Bush, the White House, and the Education of Paul O'Neill*, was released, one of the first reports from the White House referred to Paul O'Neill as "crazy." A CBS news reporter stood just outside the White House, microphone in hand, and declared that sources inside the White House had categorized O'Neill in this way. His manner seemed to imply there was nothing extreme or unacceptable in such a designation.

Political tactics employed by both major parties in the United States have become textbook examples of extroverted shadow energy. Their public statements are suspect because honesty seems to be an orphan child when political handlers design campaigns around derogatory five-second sound bites aimed at the opposition. Simplistic self-congratulatory political ads prevail.

As modern technology changes the world in innumerable and unforeseen ways, the political process in this nation has been damaged by those who "handle" politicians. When consultants determine every word that comes out of the mouth of a political candidate, the candidate becomes a pitiful puppet. Manipulated daily by their handlers, politicians step on public stages as mere performers in a play contrived by these same handlers. Karl Rove was an archetypal manipulator who was extraordinarily clever at scapegoating anyone who threatened the plans or actions of the White House. Bush's refusal to terminate him after the scandals that swarmed around the Valerie Plame outing is an indicator of their intimate codependence. A president who used lies and innuendo to manipulate the entire populace was manipulated daily by his handler. Using lies and innuendo is classic shadow-driven behavior.

When President Clinton stated emphatically that he "did not have sexual relations with that woman," he was functioning from shadow denial, fed by the energy of negative shadow refusal. His ability to believe his own original lie was fed by his own shadow. Such pathology is filled with classic levels of cognitive dissonance. Despite the obvious brilliance of his intellect, President Clinton's shadow is equal to (or greater than) his intellect in its dimensions. When he stepped over the line with a White House intern, he was driven by his shadow. When she participated in or initiated this relationship, she acted from her shadow. When the dust settled and Clinton decided to talk with clergymen, rather than address this obvious psychological problem in a therapeutic arena, he again functioned from the shadow, making this choice from the shadow. This meant that his shadow chose a pseudo-clinical response to its own extroversion.

When we elevate any president in the United States to a suprahuman place, our need to project a form of the "king" archetype onto them is evidence of our collective shadow. Because these men are not suprahuman, their shadow is triggered by the adulation and isolation inherent in the Office of the Presidency. When any president buys into this ego-inflating projection from the collective, as both Presidents Bill Clinton and George W. Bush have done, he unconsciously plays into his own shadow's desire for inflation and self-aggrandizement. Then arrogance becomes the means whereby the shadow's inflation is exhibited.

When the Bush administration refused to acknowledge that the rationale provided to the public for war in Iraq was not true, and was used despite advice from its own intelligence agencies, it acted from the powerful energy of its collective shadow forces of refusal. Just as Clinton had been captured by his own personal negative shadow, the Bush administration tapped into the potent collective negative energy of the shadow, until the collective ego believed the lie it had told to itself. This "belief" then fed more energy into the collective ego, allowing the shadow to convince and delude the collective. From such delusion, this same collective can then scoff at those who would question their motives.

The dynamics surrounding the motives and decision-making process used for declaring war on Iraq are prime examples of *groupthink*. Groupthink is provoked by the shadow and driven by its negative energy. Propounded by Yale social psychologist Irving Janis, groupthink is a dynamic of group cohesion characterized by any group that suspends critical thinking and rational analysis in order to maintain group consensus. This particular dynamic includes the *illusion of invulnerability* (Vander Zanden, 379). When Bush boasted that the United States would go into Iraq alone, even if no other nation agreed with his position, he was verbalizing the underlying shadow assumptions of the White House team. The sheer vanity of their collective shadow drove their sense of America's superior power and, thus, invulnerability.

Morality is also a trait of groupthink. The obvious need to prove the higher moral stance of his actions as compared to those of the former president (or Saddam Hussein or Usama bin Laden) led Bush to continue building upon the first lies that were motivating factors in his rationale for war. His own sense of his personal morality was tied to, and derived from, the rigid dogma of fundamentalist Christianity. His shadow had convinced his ego of his moral superiority, and from that stance of false inflation he stridently defended his position in every speech he made. Moral inflation allows the ego to distort perception. By "preaching" the superiority of our position as "Christian democratic" Americans who value "freedom," the collective consciousness of the nation is led into the illusion that we are morally superior to others. The perception is held up as a substitute for reality, and by sheer repetition is declared to be the reality. Over time it becomes the delusion a large majority of the collective will embrace with fervor.

This trait of morality feeds into another typical pattern in groupthink, that of *rationalization* (380). The administration, by declaring this military action one of "liberation," rationalized its own reasons for initiating combat. Those reasons are more secret than most of us will ever know, because secrecy is a dynamic in the formation of groupthink. To label this an act of liberation is somewhat akin to declaring that our importation of Africans in order to enslave them was, instead, to offer them the fine advantages and "liberties" of American citizenship.

Two other aspects of groupthink are quite evident in the dynamics surrounding the war on Iraq. One is *self-censorship* (381). By pushing for high levels of cohesion among the members of the decision-making group, individual members are pressured to sublimate and subvert their own integrity, honesty and social consciousness. This was chillingly apparent by the time Secretary of State Colin Powell made his historic speech in favor of this war to the United Nations. Until that time, this old warrior—who knew far more about the barbaric realities of the battlefield than his commander-in-chief—had been opposed to a military action in Iraq. By the pressure applied behind the scenes, this man took on the majority opinion, despite his own opposite views that were informed by years of war experience.

Powell's change in attitude was, in all likelihood, provoked by the classic *emergence of a mind-guard*. As this cabinet assumed its cohesive perspective through the defining shadow of its presidential leader, any one individual with a differing view was pushed by peer pressure to conform to the opinions, attitudes and stances of the group. Usually one or more highly vocal individuals emerge as the spokesperson, or mind-guard, who will vocally strive for unanimity. Vice-President Richard Cheney and Donald Rumsfeld, (then) Secretary of Defense, may have played a dual role to achieve this purpose. Perhaps Condoleezza Rice was also a verbal participant, but ultimately *an illusion of unanimity* is the result of groupthink dynamics. After divergent opinions are stifled and then halted, the cohesion of the group is fed by their misperception that a majority of both their leadership team and the public approves their actions.

One of the more profoundly lamentable aspects of Powell's apparent acquiescence to his persuasive peers was encapsulated in his own words. Powell, whose memories of Vietnam were keen and painful, had written in his memoirs, "When our turn came to call the shots, we would not quietly acquiesce in half-hearted warfare for half-baked reasons."

For groupthink to hold, *maintaining the illusion of unanimity* was critical to the process. When both Republicans and Democrats in the Congress acted in agreement with this stance and voted for the war resolution, the illusion of unanimity was given further strength and intensity. Then all the shadow dynamics of groupthink were cemented into place.

In *The Price of Loyalty*, Ron Suskind wrote this about the organizational practices employed by the Bush White House:

> The President was caught in an echo chamber of his own making, cut off from everyone other than a circle around him that's tiny and getting smaller and in concert on everything—a circle that conceals him from public view and keeps him away from the one thing he needs most: honest, disinterested perspectives about what's real and what the hell he might do about it... "*because this is the way Dick likes it*" (293; italics are Suskind's).

Vice-President Dick Cheney was the silent partner to a vocal President George W. Bush. Suskind continued, "...O'Neill had stopped trying to discern where Cheney ended and the President began." Former Secretary of the Treasury Paul O'Neill learned that the Bush White House operated on political ideology, not on sound analytical process. Those who surround President George W. Bush lead by fundamental conservative ideology, not by cognitive or linear strategy. O'Neill concluded, "I realized that it's very hard for an organization or an institution to achieve more than the leader can imagine."

A lack of imagination is characteristic of ideological or fundamentalist thinking, whether one is conservative or liberal. When challenged, those who are ideologues continue to emphasize their basic beliefs, without a rationale for such deeply held beliefs. When a highly skilled weapons inspector, David Kay, returned from Iraq and testified before the Senate, he indicated the assumptions that predicated the preemptive strike on Iraq were simply wrong. President Bush denied the reality of this truth and continued to defend the war on Iraq as one against a man who was a brutal tyrant. No one denies the fact that Saddam Hussein was just that, but Bush's refusal to admit a mistake is a classic characteristic of an inflated ego, one that reflects its own pathology. Descriptions of Saddam Hussein's responses to questioning by military officials seem to mirror similar pathological misperceptions of reality.

At this same time, National Security Advisor Condoleezza Rice attempted damage control by opining that the only logical conclusion that could have been drawn was that Iraq possessed weapons of mass destruction. In making such a statement she implied that the very same man whom the president had labeled a "mad man" was going to function in a logical, rational manner.

If this administration had been wise enough to invite dialogue with those who were not part of their highly cohesive groupthink process, their options might have been explored in a more balanced and analytical way. The shadow stands in the doorway to valuable dialogue with others who hold a different or opposing stance, and the rigidity of the ideological stance is usually maintained by shadow refusal or cessation of dialogue. Quite often shadow refusal is employed in acts or words of aggression, revenge, force of all kinds, authoritarian power mechanisms, tyrannical decisions and motivations to harm others. The shadow, in these times, chooses some form of war, the exact opposite of surrendering to the energy of divine consciousness. The shadow's need to control or to manage its perception of control will not allow it to release the aggression stored there through surrendering to divine energy. By the very act of calling in the shadow forces of refusal, we stop the flow of benevolent energy from a divine source that would provoke positive growth and development.

The shadow forces of refusal feed on every polarized negative emotion. Among these are fear, anger, rejection, jealousy, spite, grief, rage, cruelty, sarcasm, resentment and revenge. Fear is the most primordial and potent energy in the human psyche; it is encapsulated in the shadow's forces of refusal. It builds a duality of negative intensity that, by its negative polarization, provokes paralysis and creates an inability to consider the positive aspects of any given situation. Fear, through this psychic impetus of negativity, calls in the shadow forces of refusal, which then feed and escalate the fear. While criminals or terrorists or tyrants may provoke valid informed concern, fear cripples the intellect, paralyzes the spirit and warps the soul's ability to maintain psychic balance. If predicated upon such fear, national security organizations, whether military or otherwise, can use it in all the wrong ways.

We can look at the reaction of the Roosevelt administration, which urged that "We have nothing to fear, except fear itself," and compare it to the ways the Bush Administration used fear as a manipulative emotional device. The different attitudes reflected by these two presidents show us the difference between healthy informed concern and fear used as a political ploy. Fear used in the latter example creates a spiral of more fear. This spiraling pattern of fear-negativity is given strength and purpose by the closed ranks of leaders who have succumbed to groupthink. The most insidious aspect of this process is that, quite often, "God" is believed to be the driving force for actions that are, instead, motivated by pure fear fed by negative shadow energy.

Individual and collective human apathy, cultural stagnation, and theological rigidity are all driven by the same unconscious impetus, or "habits of the mind." A Norwegian sociologist better known for his economic theories, Thorstein Veblen, propounded this social theory many decades ago, but it is applicable in this contemporary age. This theory can help to explain the power of the negative energies of the shadow, because these habits of the mind are as invisible as the shadow and are often driven by its adverse energy.

Veblen's theory had three basic concepts (Ashleigh & Orenstein, 373-374). First, *habits of the mind are not driven by the rational, linear mind. They are based on cultural assumptions and societal norms, not upon a cognitive consideration of a particular pattern of behavior. Since they are assumed, they are not questioned. To do so is to call into question ordinary cultural dynamics and their accepted norms.* By extension, cultural norms and societal assumptions rest upon the bedrock of archetypal patterns held in the collective unconscious. They are fed by the collective unconscious and strengthened by ancient archetypal models, rather than by intellectual or cognitive perceptions.

As an example, one of the reasons a formal recognition of homosexual unions, or marriage partnerships, is resisted is the habit of the mind that assumes all "marriages" must be between opposite genders. The fidelity of contemporary long-term, same-gender partners is completely discounted in such thinking, and offered as further evidence of unrepentant "sin." The power of this cultural norm feeds upon the intensity of fundamentalist biblical traditions supposedly linked to God's commands for the mythological first couple created to dwell in the Garden of Eden.

The first creation myth in the first chapter of Genesis declares that the male and female were created by God and told, "Be fruitful and multiply." Written by a different author, the second creation myth, from the second chapter of Genesis, says that God made the woman from the rib of the man. Then the man declared her to be "bone of my bone, flesh of my flesh," thus declaring the second human creation to be some sort of clone. A literalistic interpretation of the biblical text does have its pitfalls.

Despite the "morality" implied by proponents of marriage as a cultural norm, nowhere in these two chapters does the biblical writer indicate that God actually conducted some sort of formal marriage ceremony. The canon simply says, in both accounts, that God created these two human beings and presented them to each other for purposes of reproduction. No wedding seemed necessary to the writers of Genesis, and no deep, intellectual debates were initiated on the morality of the apparent cloning process employed by God. Furthermore, God blessed the two of them and labeled all of creation, including this unwed man and woman, "Good."

The *second characteristic* of habits of the mind is that these mind-habits *seem to be suitable and appropriate to the culture in which they are formed, and by their congruity with that particular culture they gain strength*. When the family values argument comes into play, it supports the notion that one can hate the sin but love the sinner by declaring that homosexuality is a sin because the Bible says so. Going for a one-two punch, marriage is declared to be "ordained" between a man and a woman only, and if women knew their proper place in the divine order of things, the family would not be at risk in America today. By this distorted, non-cognitive process, women can be blamed for the chaos in our culture, while also blaming the sin of homosexuality as evidence of that chaos. Actually the canonical text does not call homosexuality a sin but an abomination. The word abomination refers to "unclean" and is specific to the stipulations of the holiness codes related to purity in the Torah.

The beliefs espoused by literal translationists lack grounding in the history of ancient cultural assumptions and practices. Theologian James B. Nelson noted, "A common Middle East practice in that day (was) the submission of captured male foes to anal rape. It was an expression of domination and contempt, a powerful symbol of scorn in societies where the dignity of the male was held in such high esteem" (185).

Nelson continued, "The moral climate of Hellenistic Rome was marred by various forms of sexual commerce and exploitation" (186). Nelson explains that the apostle Paul was speaking against the common practice of heterosexual males engaging in homosexual practices. The culture of that day did not understand or accept homosexual partnerships as ones representing the expressed love between two individuals of the same gender. Paul was speaking to heterosexual males about anomic behavior patterns that broke the Holiness Code so important to the Hebrew culture.

Both the priestly writers of the Hebrew text and the apostle Paul, who was trained in this same law, were admonishing their followers not to participate in these cultural practices, which would have been against the cultic law set forth in Leviticus. To have engaged in these practices would have meant breaking the laws of purity; by making themselves unclean in this way, Jews would have been defiling themselves. Peter Brown wrote of these Toraic prohibitions:

> Sexual codes were made to bear a heavy weight of meaning. The prohibition of marriage to non-Jews; the condemnations of close-kin marriages; the insistence of the careful observance of the codes of purity that governed the woman's menstrual cycle and the man's emission of seed; a carefully nurtured disgust for the promiscuity, public nudity, and homosexual love allowed to the young male in pagan cities: all these points of difference

heightened the sense of separation of Israel from the pagan world (40).

A literal reading of the canon allowed advocates of slavery to use citations from the text (Colossians 3:22-4:1; Ephesians 6:5-9; I Peter 2:18 and I Timothy 6:1-2) in support of their mistreatment of African-Americans, but our nation no longer finds slavery to be acceptable. In the Hellenistic world, athletes competing in Olympic-style events were nude, but we do not subscribe to that ancient standard. The writers of the canonical text believed the earth was flat, but we do not impose that archaic belief upon our contemporary culture. If we were going to apply a literal reading of the canonical text to every modern societal situation, we could find citations that encourage one to gouge out the eyes and cut off the hands of those who yield to human temptation (Matthew 5:22-29). Divorce would be stricken as a legally acceptable way to end a marriage (Mark 10:9-12). Banks and brokerage houses would be bankrupt, because we would not be able to use their services (Exodus 22:25). Any woman who is not a virgin when she is married could be executed (Deuteronomy 22:13-21). Marriage would not impede any man's right to take concubines in addition to his wife or wives (I Kings 11:3). It is easy to see the ways the canon adheres to a long-past cultural reality, and the actual selectivity of proof texts calls them into question.

Finally, *habits of the mind* are so deeply inculcated into the collective unconscious they are "resistant to change and tend to persist even after the material conditions that gave rise to them have disappeared." Just as nudity in Olympic events is no longer a norm, and scientists can show us irrefutable proof that the earth is not flat, so too other contemporary material conditions have displaced the norms that were assumed over time. In the United States it has been many years since women were expected to wear hats and gloves to church. Rigid dress codes prevailed when men wore hats as well; milk was delivered to the front door in glass bottles; the Fuller brush company employed dozens of door-to-door salesmen; thousands of Mom and Pop grocery stores flourished across the nation; attendants at service stations not only pumped gas for customers, they checked the oil and washed the windshield, and, for the most part, the husband and father in the family always drove the one and only family car. The "material conditions that gave rise" to all these cultural habits have changed and we have changed with them, but old norms evoked by canonical stipulations are the most difficult to change.

Sheldrake's hypotheses of morphic fields and morphic resonance also apply. If a culture has been driven by a particular cultural norm, like the necessity for marriage between opposite genders as an ideal, and that norm has been assumed for thousands of years, then long after the material conditions that gave rise to it have disappeared, it is still regarded as the ideal. The ideal then takes on an energy of its own and humans in that culture are expected, by those who subscribe most vehemently to the ideal, to conform to it. The morphic field of energy around such an ideal is a defining aspect of the intensity of debates related to it. That energy gathers around a pattern of behavior until an archetype emerges, in this case, the marriage archetype.

Women no longer need husbands who are hunter-gatherers while they stay home to be sole mother-nurturers, nor do they step outside their front door each morning to pick up milk delivered in a glass bottle. Despite all the myriad changes in the social fabric of the culture, the morphic resonance around a canonical ideal increases the power of this cultural habit of the mind. Conversely, since this habit of the mind is so much a part of our morphic field, great energy is given to supporting its continuation. Even though most women find it necessary to work alongside their husbands to support and sustain their families, a "princess" mentality drives the socialization of girls in our culture. This skewed form of social consciousness would maintain an ideal mother as a stay-at-home one.

Veblen's habits of the mind theory articulates the power of tradition and the snail's pace of social change. Whenever the biblical text is used as proof text for contemporary legislation or policy making, its true purpose is twisted to drive a political agenda. Despite the archaic reality of biblical cultural stipulations, the shadow, fed by the ancient archetypal energy held in the collective unconscious, will use these biblical proscriptions to drive its agenda rather than for spiritual growth. Such mind-soul-spirit manipulation then feeds the collective shadow that seeks out a scapegoat in order to conceal itself. Then the shadow can blame all the problems of the family on women who work outside the home, or onto homosexuals who refuse to be treated as second-class citizens by climbing back into the closets where, supposedly, they had been comfortably ensconced.

Diverse social institutions are intrinsically linked to the habits of the mind that would maintain traditional power without change. Many institutions, like the welfare system or the church, were initiated as positive concepts for social change. These same organizations quickly bog down in institutional stasis when, to continue their existence, they must raise funds necessary to sustain themselves. The soul of any given institution is often lost as negotiations are attempted with those who have the power to determine levels of financial support. Historically, many social institutions, including the government and the institutional church, have been adopted by those who wield financial—and thus political—power. These brokers strive to maintain cultural norms by pushing these social institutions into a static holding pattern, in the mistaken belief that stasis can be equated with cultural stability. A societal addiction to comfortable levels of stability feeds this perception of the *stasis quo*, and its reliance upon the shadow force of refusal is part of this addictive pattern.

Positive change cannot be accomplished in any society where the forces of power link themselves to the shadow forces of refusal as they participate in the process of governing. As the public watches the Congress function in ways that protect old paradigms, old traditions, and old understandings of an ideal, millions of Americans go without health or dental care, day care for children and elders, adequate housing, and food. Because old traditional patterns of power holding and power wielding actively employ the shadow forces of refusal, change can be circumvented and ultimately prevented. Because the shadow force of refusal is the only force old dominant leaders know and trust, it is their weapon of choice in debates around change. It is the power in which authoritarian leaders believe. It is the power they are most likely to use for negative purposes.

Shadow refusal holds everything it encounters in a state of suspended stasis, maintaining negative energies for angry or harmful purposes, while preventing positive energy from entering. The shadow forces of refusal can take any positive teaching or creative concept and twist it to conform to old belief patterns, holding it hostage to tradition. By binding it to old patterns and addictions, the angst of the old ways pulls individuals and the collective right back into its control, to hold them in its bondage.

Nowhere is this bondage more evident than inside the institutional church. Despite the ways Jesus lived in authentic soul relationship with the very Spirit of God, the church has not followed suit. Claiming the teachings of Jesus as unique unto itself, over time the institutional church unconsciously changed and distorted those teachings to inflict a rigid code of behaviors and expectations upon its adherents. The underlying, unconscious shadow dynamic that emerges allows the church to protect itself and to strengthen its institutional organization, so that this organization would ultimately be perceived as necessary.

Despite its vigorous denial, the shadow is wrapped inside the rigidity of many church "eye for an eye" belief patterns and "tooth for a tooth" dogmatic declarations. They define a god who is not one of free will, but of old traditional understandings inculcated deeply within the collective psyche by the shadow forces of refusal. The Judeo-Christian posture of imposing rules, laws, and dogma upon its followers is simply another example of the shadow forces of refusal at work. More harm is inflicted by the church's active use of the shadow forces of refusal than by other negative energies within the realm of human existence, because the church claims to represent the love of God and/or Christ-consciousness, while, instead, functioning from an unconscious place of shadow-refusal.

Because shadow-refusal is negative energy, it will not function in any other way. The feeling of power that shadow-refusal brings can be perceived by the cognitive mind as healthy strength, because it seems to be expressed in that way. It creates an energy obstacle that feels like authentic strength. When one has pushed the shadow so far out of consciousness as to believe that one is capable of functioning only from a rational perspective, this can be the very time that the shadow is most evident. Cognitive thought does not occur in a vacuum. No human being is capable of rational thinking that has not been influenced by the personal and collective unconscious levels of the psyche. The illusion that one is capable of the rarified process of pure, precise rational thought is created by the shadow, which leads the ego into believing that the strength of this perception is both authentic and healthy. This illusion is a closely held human energy perception and is called upon when energy for a negative purpose seems necessary. Because it has a counterpart in healthy refusal, it can be mistaken for its counterpart. By employing it one will feel strengthened by using its negativity, even when such refusal is a participation in the killing of one's own soul or the collective soul. As I have watched George W. Bush function in the Office of President, he invokes this negative energy, believing it is both right and noble.

These same dynamics are operative in corporate situations where groupthink takes hold. Once the negative energy of the shadow is released around an untruth, and it is defended as truth, intensity emerges and is strengthened by its own negative energy as it feeds upon itself. If you consider both the dynamics that preceded and followed the war on Iraq, groupthink was evident. If you consider the ways decisions were made during the Kennedy administration regarding the Bay of Pigs invasion, groupthink was equally evident. In both administrations, the cohesion of the inside group was maintained, while failing to consult with those who would suggest alternatives or oppose the group's decision. The shadow's energies of refusal drove both processes.

Writing on the disastrous Bay of Pigs invasion in the *New York Times* on February 8, 2004, Richard Goodwin indicated, "To his credit, President Kennedy learned from the debacle. He reorganized his intelligence apparatus and brought advisors whose instincts and moral compasses he trusted—including his brother Bobby—into the inner circle of foreign policy deliberation. More important, the lesson that intelligence and military advisers had to be thoroughly challenged guided Kennedy as he later steered the country through the Cuban missile crisis."

Robert McNamara, whose old-age reflections on the reality of this same situation form the basis of self-reflection for the film, *The Fog of War*, spoke to any simplistic view of the Cuban missile crisis. While claiming that all three—Kennedy, Kruschev, and Castro—were "rational" men, McNamara believed that the nation came alarmingly close to nuclear war during that confrontation. If the dominant thinking during the Bush administration had prevailed during the Cuban missile crisis, we would have declared a preemptive strike to be a necessary response, and we would have attacked the Soviet Union. Nuclear war would have been the result.

The collective shadow force of refusal is key in institutions that strive to maintain their organization based on some grand old tradition. Shadow-energy is visibly evident in military academies where rape became an awful fact of life after a government mandate that women may attend formerly all-male institutions. A draft survey published by the Department of Defense "revealed that 80% of all sexual assaults at the (Air Force) academy go unreported.... The same survey indicated that 74% of (one) year's female student body at the (Air Force) academy were victims of rape or attempted rape, and 18.8% were victims of sexual assault" (Bingham, 166). Despite these startling and worrisome statistics, not one male "cadet has been incarcerated for raping another cadet."

Anna Quindlen noted in a Newsweek essay, "A colonel in the Air Force whose daughter says she was attacked by a fellow cadet told the *New York Times*, 'She knew she could have been captured by an enemy, raped and pillaged in war. She did not expect to be raped and pillaged at the United States Air Force Academy'" (72).

On February 7, 2004, Vern Loeb, writing in the *Washington Post*, reported, "A total of 88 cases of sexual misconduct have been reported by the military services over the past year in the Central Command area of operations, which includes Kuwait and Iraq" (A18).

More than a decade after active warfare in Kuwait, Secretary of Defense Donald Rumsfeld issued a directive regarding sexual assaults, indicating that appropriate medical care must be offered. Yet Loeb reported that one senior officer opined, "Most of those cases involved fraternization between male and female service members, not sexual assaults." Kate Summers, director of the non-profit Miles Foundation, which tracks such abuse in the U. S. military, has worked with thirty-eight cases out of this larger total. She reported that seventy-five to eighty percent were rape or attempted rape and noted, "Women have been re-victimized through the filing of charges against them for adultery or fraternization" (Schmidt, 2/26/04).

When a congressional investigating committee, composed of women, took testimony from one male advocate, he told them, "While these friendly fire attacks leave no trail of blood, they leave many damaged souls in their wake."

These seemingly sympathetic words from a male advocate for rape victims are a measure of the psychic inability of males to fathom the degradation felt by women victims of sexual assault. His analogy fails abysmally because there is nothing "friendly" about deliberate sexual assault. "Friendly fire" implies an accidental tragedy. These assaults are a tragedy, but they are neither accidental nor friendly. They are provoked by the deepest primordial notions of women as lesser beings, who must be violently dominated to keep them in their place, and whose bodies can be used like slabs of meat.

When these charges were considered before the Senate Armed Services Committee, the senators were told that 112 reports of sexual misconduct had occurred in Iraq, Kuwait, and Afghanistan during the eighteen months prior to the hearing. In addition, two dozen women at Sheppard Air Force Base in Texas "reported to a local rape-crisis center that they were assaulted in 2002." While the senators expressed "shock" and "outrage" at these reports, David Chu, the civilian head of the Pentagon's personnel and readiness office, conceded that the assault rate against female troopers was "still too high" (Graham, A19). One can only wonder if the same number of assaults against men (subjected to anal rape by their peers) had been reported, how these same senators would have reacted and what action they would have taken.

Those who resent basic changes in the social reality that drives any established culture will deny the violence that emerges to protect old assumptions that are part of its systems. Denial of flagrant violence during the desegregation era is just one example.

Human evolution must support spiritual evolution. Spiritual evolution is the process of surrendering the spirit to the call of divine energy to live in the present moment, while knowing that the present moment impels us forward into an unknown future. This divine energy gives each human the free will to trust that future or to hold oneself in a place of stasis. To break out of old patterns of such stasis is to participate in innovative thinking, where wise free will choices are a reality in every moment.

By protesting that honoring tradition is a primary concern, those who use the shadow's refusal energies most effectively turn this vehement argument into the idolatrous reason for their actions. By worshiping a cultural imperative, the shadow is elevated along with the cultural imperative and both become idols—and, thus, objects of profane worship. The cultural inference of tradition as a positive attribute is an assumption held in the deepest levels of the collective psyche. This cultural *habit of the mind* clings to that notion of tradition's generally accepted definition: *to carry forward*. This habit of the mind is linked to implicit positive connotations of carrying forward a culture's "inherited, established or customary patterns of thought, action or behavior" (Merriam-Webster Collegiate Dictionary, 1251). When tradition is the god that is served, the distortion and elevation of historic norms is a dominant factor in the adulation of historic paradigms.

Despite this energetic loyalty to the past, tradition holds within itself an etymological core of shadow energy. Concealed within its derivation is the Judas aspect of itself. When you consider the etymology of this word, it is derived from the Latin word *tradere*, from which the words *treason*, *traitor*, and *treacherous* are also derived. Thus, it can also mean "to betray" (Ayto, 61).

Tradition is then dynamically and energetically linked to refusing change, even through betrayal. This is the unconscious core—the shadow-dynamic that fosters betrayal. The underlying treachery of social tradition is a dynamic that willingly colludes with the shadow's forces of refusal, giving them energy and intensity. In this way the shadow aspect of tradition is an active participant in the betrayal of soul—individual soul, collective soul, world soul. By feeding upon its energy we live in an emulation of Judas.

Chapter 4

Scapegoat, Ritual, and the Atonement Principle

To understand the dualistic nature of the shadow and its Judas energy, one must understand something about the history of ritual. Contemporary confusion about appropriate ritual leads to shadow extroversion through profane or secular ritual. Historically, ritual has been used in every culture as a means whereby humans could confront and come to terms with the shadow side of the psyche. When the difference between sacred and profane ritual is understood, the dualistic nature of the shadow is illuminated. Then one can further contemplate how surrendering to the divine is a life lesson in acquiring authentic wisdom.

Ritual can be understood in the ways large symphony orchestras begin any performance. The conductor is the last person to arrive on stage. Before his or her arrival, all the musicians have entered and found their seats. They are all focused upon tuning their own instruments. When it is time for the performance to begin, the concertmaster is the one who calls the musicians to attention. The concertmaster, the person who holds the first chair in the violin section, leads the other musicians as they tune their instruments together to the same note. This individual stands and gives a signal for the oboe to play an A. Following this lead, the concertmaster then signals for the woodwinds, and finally the strings, all of whom tune their instruments to the same note. The concertmaster tunes his or her instrument last. It is only then that the conductor appears, coming forward to shake the hand of the concertmaster. Then the conductor bows to the audience, and the concert begins.

Some years ago I attended a performance of the Russian National Symphony Orchestra. Their ritual and discipline was striking in the ways the musicians sat, backs straight, at attention, throughout the performance, and rose to their feet when the conductor came on stage.

A Catholic mass is one form of structured worship ritual. This ritual is designed to draw the worshiper into a deeper awareness of self in relationship with God. If effective, it becomes the means whereby the worshiper reaches a place of changed consciousness and becomes one with God. This change in consciousness is a process of at-one-ment.

To many people with some passing association with Christianity, the word *atonement* implies a connectedness to Jesus as a salvific figure, even if that implication is only fragmentary or lacking in substance. The concept of Jesus as a sacrificial substitute has long been the basic undergirding for atonement beliefs among those who call themselves Christian. Yet, the atonement principle is part of every great religion. Since the notion of human sin is one of the commonalities shared by most religions, atonement for that sin is the means whereby humans are reconciled or brought back to a place of *at-one-ment* with a god.

While the word atonement appears in numerous places in the Old Testament, in the New Testament this word only appears once, and in only one English version of the text. In the King James Version of the canon, the word atonement appears in the book of Romans. In most other English versions of the canon this word has been translated as reconciliation. Thus, down through the years, there has emerged a differentiation between the two words, atonement and reconciliation, with the latter representing the result of the former. By drawing a distinction between atonement and reconciliation, one may understand the unconscious societal and contemporary need for scapegoats, those onto whom we project our unacceptable traits, including anger, shame, guilt, and unacknowledged sin.

In ancient times rituals to embody the atonement principle were common in celebrations that began a new year. The collective sins of a given people were held up to the light of prayerful evaluation, and purging sacrifices for such collective sin were common to worship rituals corresponding with a new year. In the Mesopotamian regions, the Day of Atonement featured a *kuppuru*, an atonement ceremony in which a sacrificial sheep, carrying the sins of the people loaded upon its back, was put to death as the symbolic evidence of atonement (Briffault, 91-95).

Yom Kippur, known to those who adhere to Jewish belief as the holiest day of the Jewish year, was a syncretized parallel of this Sumero-Babylonian kuppuru. The celebration of Yom Kippur centered around an elaborate ritual of purification, which included sending a goat (which had been encumbered with the sins of the people of Israel) off into the wilderness to die. This final symbolic act brought to completion the process of ritual purification and cleansing, of decontamination, known in Hebrew as *kippurim*. The Hebrew word for day, *yom*, added to this, then gives this day of atonement its name, Yom Kippur (Gaster, 138).

Yet the English word atonement is an inadequate substitute for the Hebrew understanding of *kippurim*. This Hebrew word implies a purging, a cleansing of all that has contaminated and kept the people in alienation from God. Its implicit meaning is to purify as an ablution; such purification would, by its very nature, allow for a cathartic emotional release of this accumulated contamination.

As Christianity took its place side by side with Judaism, the notion of atonement by one person, Jesus, was elevated to an ideal. Jesus, whose sacrifice for all believers for all time, became the ultimate blood sacrifice. The notion that the atonement of Christ was like no other allows those who subscribe to this all-encompassing belief to sublimate or even abdicate any responsibility for their own personal soul growth. This concept of atonement created a psychic undertow symbolized by the human need for ritual cleansing in some tangible form and with solid symbolic substance. Such symbolic cleansing allows humans to relinquish their stored psychic sepsis to a god who has the power to cleanse it. It is one thing to know that Jesus is an atoning substitute on some intellectual plane; it is another to internalize the grace implied by that atonement at the deepest level of the soul. The mind may argue freedom while the heart remains in chains. The heart may cry out for the concrete, tangible cleansing of sacramental proportions.

I was never more aware of this contemporary need than when I encountered those who asked to be baptized for a second time. The first time this request was made I was startled by the intensity of this need for cleansing ritual, and because the need was so great, I responded to it by preparing a private ritual to reassure and bless the person who had made the request. But, when more and more people who were struggling with their own spiritual connectedness to God made this same request, I began to reflect upon this tangible Jewish ritual, and its significance. Nowhere in the Christian tradition is there an overt, parallel ritual, and its absence is part of a void in this faith tradition.

The people of antiquity knew at some deep, instinctive level how important it was to participate in cleansing ritual. A cleansing ritual that appears time and again in diverse religious traditions is one of cleansing baths. In earlier polytheistic religions those women who functioned as the *qadishtu*, the sacred priestesses in the temples of Near Eastern goddesses, used cleansing baths after participating in sexual intercourse as part of the worship ritual. These cleansing baths were believed to be hymen renewing; these women were then designated as perpetual virgins, a designation as unlikely as the one for the mother of Jesus.

The Jewish *mikvah*, or ritual bath, was an emulation of this earlier tradition of cleansing baths used, especially in connection with sexual activity. Within the orthodox Jewish tradition, males went to the mikvah before the Sabbath and at the end of the workweek, after they had completed their work. The females, however, were instructed by law to go to the *mikvah* before sexual activity and after their monthly menstruation, since they were viewed as unclean when menstruating and thereafter until they had been cleansed by the ritual bath (Harris, 59 & 137). While these practices were articulated in different ways for males and females, and while this articulation has the certainty of misogynistic overtones, the practice of cleansing baths was one of syncretized ritual, replicating in some ways the earlier practices of fertility cults in the Mediterranean region. In the same way, the symbolism and practice of baptism by immersion evolved out of this earlier syncretized ritual of the mikvah.

Ancient Egyptians used a ram as a sin bearer in the cleansing rituals which were part of their festivals to welcome a new year. Worshipers of the ram god, Amon, the Egyptians gave the children of Israel a perfect example of a sacrificial animal to be incorporated into their Jewish observance of the Passover. The shedding of blood, in sacrificing animals to the gods, was a typical practice throughout the Near East and is echoed in New Testament understandings of shed blood as a norm. The author of the book of Hebrews writes, "Indeed, under the law almost everything is purified with blood, and without the shedding of blood there is no forgiveness of sins."

The Mithraic tradition of worship ritual is another example of shedding blood to initiate new believers into a thought form or belief structure. In the Mithraic ritual a bull was driven up onto a wooden scaffold where the high priest would cut his throat. Initiates would walk beneath the scaffold where the animal was dying to be quite literally "washed in the blood" of the dying bull. This blood bath was integral to the Mithraic worship ritual; it served to symbolize a divine cleansing ablution in the form of a sacramental initiatory ritual.

The paschal lamb of Christianity, whose shed blood became salvific for generations thereafter, also had an earlier counterpart in ancient Chinese sacrificial customs. There, prisoners of war were renamed *Ch'iang*, meaning *Shepherd*, and became the symbolic "sheep" who were sacrificed. The figure of a man with his throat severed by a knife is depicted in the Chinese pictograph for Ch'iang (Hays, 188). Once sacrificed, after death this "shepherd" bore the designation Son of God (Briffault, 100).

A Shinto ritual known as *Ohoharahi* is the Japanese parallel to this same substantive understanding of ritual cleansing. There the collective sins of the people are named and then transferred onto objects like rice stalks and animal hides. Each person also uses a sacrificial doll to represent the self. This doll is named for each individual whose personal sins it represents as it is thrown into a stream of water, there to be carried away to the gods who are believed to dwell in the high mountain torrents (Gaster, 139).

In the Hebrew celebration of Yom Kippur, the Toraic law found in the book of Leviticus called for two goats, along with other animals, to be used in the sacrifices marking this holy day. By casting lots, the priest determined which of the two goats would be used for which function. One of these goats was sacrificed to God as a burnt offering for sin. The other whose lot had fallen to *Azazel* was the scapegoat, the goat upon which the sins of the people were heaped before it was driven into the wilderness. The canonical text indicates this goat was the one consigned to Azazel.

Explanations regarding Azazel's identity are amusing, if for no other reason than the scholarly strain at maintaining dogmatic assumptions of monotheism, since in this context henotheism might be applied more appropriately. There are those who declare that Azazel is a designation of the animal itself as "scapegoat," because of the Hebrew words for "goat that departs." Another explanation is that Azazel was a place, the wilderness place to which the animal was sent. Still another explanation was that Azazel represented a demon that inhabits the desert regions where the goat was sent (Gaster, Int., 325-326).

Yet, the derivation of Azazel could also be a pre-Hebraic god-entity from Syria. A Syrian deity known as "God's Messenger," this god-being was named *Aziz* by his Syrian worshipers (Cumont, 113). It would seem that the Hebrews took this Syrian god-being, perhaps giving him the designation of demon, and each year (on the holiest day of the year) they sent him a sin offering. The seventeenth chapter of Leviticus mentions a goat-demon, to whom the people have prostituted themselves, so perhaps elements of this ritual emerged in reaction to that.

The historical assumptions of Judaic monotheism are called into question by this ritual, but it is as if the God of the people of Israel is clear about their need for offering one sacrifice to a God who represents atonement and/or reconciliation, and another sacrifice to a shadow-being who represents the contamination of sin. In this way they acknowledge and honor the hidden side of God, the shadow side so vehemently denied by the Christian church.

Azazel emerges with a new identity in Christianity. During medieval times, Christian demonologists designated Azazel as one of the leaders in the pantheon of hell. Exorcists categorized Azazel as a possessor, whose "lively, active function" befitted his ancient designation of Hermetic-style "messenger" (Walker, 81).

Each particular ritual of atonement had, at its core, an understanding of ritual cleansing from the contamination of sin as its purpose. The purpose of Yom Kippur was to bring the collective of the people to a place of acknowledging their sin, and to repentance for that sin. The ritual of atonement was the instrument for cleansing the collective of the people, not one individual person. Thus atonement was not operative without a public articulation of sin. Since corporate confession cannot assure that each one among the collective will, indeed, be repentant or will fully confess, the goat sent out to Azazel became the corporeal image who carried a blanket confession for the collective of all the people (Gaster, *Festivals*, 142-143).

This ritual was performed as a purification ceremony that was efficacious for both the temple and its human worshipers, but it did not mean some sort of religious spring cleaning. It was the means whereby the temple was cleansed of spiritual contamination every year, even as it was also the means whereby the souls of the people were likewise cleansed. To participate in such ritual was to participate in a "rehabilitation of impaired holiness." It was the way in which the sacred was revived, so that whatever had been besmirched, or even defiled, during the preceding year was cleansed. Intrinsic to this cleansing was an awareness that it occurred in the presence of God. *God was an active participant, cleansing and being cleansed.*

I have often thought such a ritual would be beneficial, even now, in some churches that I have served. I have entered church sanctuaries that, from the psychic energy emanating from them, needed to be cleansed. When a church has been embroiled in conflict, and its people are clearly focused upon conflict—and upon protecting their own tiny turf rights—the church itself will bear the marks of such contamination. This contamination does not depart of its own accord. It lies in the corners and under the pews. It curls around and into the cracks and crevices; its hidden face is a part of the character and personality of such conflicted congregations.

Theodor Gaster addressed the need for cleansing in these kinds of settings. He wrote, "Where holiness is sullied, there, too, is life itself impaired, and...no continuance can be expected unless and until the taint is removed." The culture as a whole is carrying this kind of contamination; denying the shadow creates such depravation. Our fierce denial of the negative aspects of individual and collective shadow has created an environment, a morphic field, of negative shadow energy. This means that individuals who come into the church are carrying this soul-level cultural contagion inside their beings. While this contamination is carried at an unconscious level, it is revealed when people show a profound lack of respect for each other in rude and hurtful words, accusations, and blaming. Despite American proclamations of collective "Christianity," and the imagined superiority linked thereto, old national deeds that have impaired the holiness of such a claim are stored deeply within the collective unconscious. We cannot deny the ill treatment of those who inhabited this land before we came to it, or those we bound in chains and brought to it to become our slaves, or those who, in our contemporary times, are the scapegoats for our projections of unhealthy sexuality. All these examples, and more, have fed the morphic resonance that swirls around us—holding us in a morphic field of "impaired holiness."

An undertow in this nation has been provoked by centuries of "hell fire and brimstone" proclamations by old-line clergy. The United States was settled by puritanical believers whose rigid, narrow beliefs still hold powerful energy inside many churches. Old-time religion is well known for its castigating pronouncements and exhortations to "Repent and be saved!" Aggressive forms of persuasion are employed to convince listeners that this advice is critical, and dire consequences are promised to those who refuse. When such antagonistic tactics are rejected, the positive aspects of surrendering to the divine are rejected, too.

Repentance, in the original Hebrew understanding of the word, means to turn around or to turn away from. The positive connotations of this word have been lost in the noisy babble from high-visibility televangelists and fundamentalists, whose primary focus is upon New Testament texts. By disregarding the historical balance of the Old Testament and the lessons it teaches, the turning of repentance—as a result of appropriate self-reflection—falls into the shadow contents of the collective unconscious. Few educated, intelligent adults want to hear screaming exhortations to "repent," but a surrendering to divine energy is lost in this rejection and replaced with an empty void, where profane ritual becomes a substitute for holy ritual.

In his explanation of the historical evolution of the celebration of Yom Kippur, Gaster articulates a ritual that has evolved from a concentration upon atonement for evil within the people to a recognition of how human sin contaminates both humans and God. Such an understanding is helpful for recognizing the shadow contamination within both culture and church in this day and time.

All of the world's great religions have understandings of repentance as a necessary part of healthy human interaction and holistic living. Repentance is a way of confronting one's own evil, of looking one's own shadow in the face. When one confronts this hidden side of self, when confession and surrendering are real and authentic, even God is cleansed by it. Sin and corruption are not just impediments to our welfare and prosperity, they distance us from God by contaminating both us and God (Gaster, Festivals, 144). When even holiness itself has been impaired by human actions, conscious or otherwise, we must participate in its healing and transformation.

The American Christian church operates inside a culture that has stepped away from this necessary aspect of healthy soul journey. The American culture has fostered a schizophrenic environment where independence and self-sufficiency are lauded, but blame, innuendo and victimizing are commonplace. Repentance, confession, and atonement are obscured in the nether regions of some religious order, or assumed as a kind of "cheap grace" by those who find confession unnecessary if Jesus died for the world's sins anyway. As the culture moves more and more into a secularized notion of itself, where precious little occupies a sacred space, and as the church begins to mirror this understanding of self and institution, both culture and church reflect the acute and unhealthy nature of such evolution.

The culture and the church are adrift in a sea of old assumptions, primary among them that Jesus has sacrificed all that ever needs to be sacrificed, that Jesus has "paid it all," that "victory in Jesus" makes any surrender or sacrifice on the part of humans a redundant or even anachronistic exercise. Assumptions regarding the dominance of atonement through Jesus are the accepted norm.

If the core of these assumptions is explored, what emerges is something that has been articulated in Veblen's *habits of the mind* theory. Veblen determined that

> ...habits of the mind are not mentally stored in a random or haphazard way but, rather, in consistency with the overall nature of human mental abilities; furthermore, they are organized around a people's particular, usual, and typical activities. They thus come to support, cognitively and emotionally, typical ways of behaving and oppose violations of the usual. In other words, a people's habits of the mind form the basis of cultural norms. Thus culturally normative views of right and wrong, acceptable and unacceptable, are grounded in mental habits that have emerged from repetitive...activity. Once cultural norms emerge, they both form the basic common stock of knowledge of a people and are strengthened as they are passed down to later generations through socialization (Ashley & Orenstein, 373-374).

Any notion of the need for ritual sacrifice would be opposed as a violation of the norm, since the norm assumes such soul-level sacrifice is unnecessary. Jesus was and is the preeminent sacrifice and no soul-level surrendering is deemed important by our cultural habits of the mind. Those habits of the mind fail to recognize that the collective unconscious levels of the psyche are still driven by primitive instincts. These instinctual needs for the sacrificial are part of the driving impulse for the violence in our contemporary world, whether that violence is regarded as normative, as in declared war, or anomic, as in gangland war.

The deep primeval levels of the human subconscious are attuned to blood sacrifice. It is an innate motivator for war between nations. Suicide bombers have embraced the illusion that their death will be glorious, and this delusional anticipation of ecstasy provokes their insane actions. An equally unconscious need to connect with the sacred is revealed in the ways national, territorial war is glorified. Arlington Cemetery is a classic example of a place that has been labeled "hallowed ground" and its glorification of death in battle is part of the unconscious need to sanctify blood sacrifices. These same sacrifices are elevated and magnified in every celebration of Veterans' Day.

This glorification of battle victory came spilling out of the voices of national leaders the morning after Saddam Hussein was captured. Senator Joseph Lieberman was a guest on Meet the Press that morning. When asked by the moderator about how he felt when he received the news that Hussein had been captured, he exclaimed, "Praise the Lord…. This is a glorious day for the American military."

In addition to claiming God as an active participant in this capture, Lieberman went on to wax eloquent about how this was an astounding victory and a great day in the history of this nation. He then politicized its significance by declaring that if one of his opponents for the 2004 presidential candidacy for the Democratic Party had occupied the White House, Saddam Hussein would still be the leader of the Iraqis. More importantly, rolling off Lieberman's unconscious tongue came the "glorious" elevation of war as blood sacrifice.

As the coverage of this event continued we were shown over and over again the reaction of American military troops who were informed that Hussein had been captured. Their reaction? Noisy jubilation. Tom Brokaw followed up one of the countless times the network aired a clip of the initial announcement of the capture by reporting, "That was Ambassador Paul Bremer, President Bush's man on the ground in Iraq."

Later in the same broadcast, Brokaw used a similar designation for National Security Advisor Condoleezza Rice, calling her "President Bush's woman in charge on Iraq."

Here the dominant role of the news media casts a projection upon the Office of the Presidency. From that very public, vocal projection it seems as if everything the United States does in an international arena is a personalized action attributed to its president. The projection crowns the president with royal favor, so that each announcement from the executive branch of our so-called "democracy" is predicated with "The President has decided." Anytime the national media use a term that can easily become commonplace, they model an assumption for middle America. Assumptions of American superiority are fed by these same dynamics. Language is a powerful weapon and the language of blood ritual is more powerful than any other. It feeds the cultural habits of the mind that participate in a primordial, albeit unconscious, worship of blood ritual. When we engage in blood ritual, we tap into the most unbridled, uncivilized, and savage aspect of the human psyche.

Martin van Creveld has written, "So elemental is the human need to endow the shedding of blood with some great and even sublime significance that it renders the intellect almost entirely helpless" (166). The intellect is not the sole motivator when the ritual sacrifice of warriors is unconsciously called out each time a nation engages in warfare. The primordial levels of the psyche are the parallel initiators of such sacrifice. Rarely are battles fought without sacrificial killing. Such killing is endowed with a glorified or deified notion of noble cause and honorable motivation.

When Adolph Hitler held power in Germany, a British psychologist attended a rally where he spoke. Here is the way Roger E. Money-Kyrle described that rally:

> The people seemed gradually to lose their individuality and become fused into a not very intelligent but immensely powerful monster, which was not quite sane and therefore capable of anything. Moreover, it was an elementary monster...with no judgment and few, but very violent, passions.... The monster became self-conscious of its size and intoxicated by the belief in its own omnipotence (Fornari, 151).

Here the contagion dynamic that turns crowds into mobs is evident. When shadow-driven personalities use their charismatic quotient to trigger a primordial reaction from a crowd, such a leader's shadow is the venomous virus that infects the collective psyche of the listeners. Once the collective shadow is triggered, a crowd is changed into a mob with no conscience and functions primarily from the strength of the collective shadow, not the cognitive abilities of the intellect.

The primordial levels of the psyche that demand blood sacrifice are the motivators for violence and blood sacrifice, though such killing is rarely acknowledged as sacrificial.

Years ago Carl Jung wrote,

> The damned-up instinct-forces in civilized [humans] are immensely more destructive, and hence more dangerous, than the instincts of the primitive, who in a modest degree is constantly living negative instincts. Consequently no war of the historical past can rival a war between civilized nations in its colossal scale of horror" (Zweig & Abrams, 159)

Symbolic ritual sacrifice and blood sacrifice are not synonymous. Symbolic ritual sacrifice involves surrendering the soul to the divine, bringing the ego to a new awareness of its need for that which is sacred. Blood sacrifice, in our contemporary age, is the end that justifies the means for exercising overt power over others. When we are at war we participate, however unconscious such participation might be, in the most primitive of sacrificial rituals. We simply deny our participation in such bloody ritual.

In our more sophisticated notions of ourselves we have substituted profane ritual for ritual ceremony previously performed within an established arena for such practices. An evening cocktail hour where spirits are unconsciously consumed in an equally unconscious effort to connect with Spirit has become the substitute for healthy ritual.

Millions of Americans leave work every day swearing, "Man, this has been a day from hell. I really need a drink!"

Ritualistic meetings with friends or co-workers over a beer or glass of wine seem like a perfectly harmless way to end the day. These late afternoon drinking sessions become ritualistic when they become habitual. The setting is immaterial. The evening cocktail hour observed by white collar workers in fine homes where alcohol is consumed from delicate crystal goblets is no different from beer consumed from bottles or cans with a bunch of buddies at the local blue-collar pub. The psyche is driven by the same need in both situations. The ultimate unconscious sacrifice may be manifested years later at a physical level, when the soft organs of the body are injured or destroyed, with the liver lapsing into dysfunction and the heart with it. Both are sacrificed to an unconscious god of spirit(s), but the blood sacrifice is an unconscious one.

Young men and women who unconsciously emulate the warriors of a past age by their violent and often fatal participation in gangs are driven by an unconscious need for ritual initiation and blood sacrifice. It might be assumed that such participation is driven by a lack of healthy role models in their environment, cultural conditioning in their subculture, low self-esteem and/or attempts to fit in with their peer group. While all these factors contribute to their motivations, their impetus is also an unconscious over-identification with the warrior archetype within. Even when their bloody acts of gangland warfare seem lacking in focus, they are functioning from the most primordial region of the psyche, that place where only the primitive is compelling. Lacking healthy ego formation, these children dwell in the land of the collective unconscious, and their days are encompassed by its awful fairytale unreality.

Other indications of our need for healthy rituals are revealed in the unhealthy ritualistic aspects of our addictions, like eating disorders, smoking, and the consumption of drugs, both prescription drugs and their street counterparts. By taking chemicals into the body, we unconsciously attempt a connection with something that represents an ascendancy over that which is merely human and mortal. And still, it is our mortality itself that is revealed in such an unconscious way, for often there is a seeking to connect with some otherness, something sacred, something of the spirit, while at the same time denying the need for the divine.

Again, our assumptions, our *habits of the mind*, have caused us to trap ourselves inside the cognitive cage of a supposed norm, while unconsciously trying to hammer at its door with unhealthy ritual. These habits of the mind illuminate the power of old assumptions. Each of these basic concepts is evident in a culture that has evolved away from a connectedness to sacred ritual, while still unconsciously carrying assumptions that were cast upon it historically by the Christian tradition that Jesus was, once and for all time, a sacrificial substitute. Thus, the soul-searching, the repentance, the surrendering and sacrifice of past Judaic tradition has been set aside as nonessential.

However, the psyche, that formidable unseen entity which drives mind and body, still yearns for appropriate ritual and symbolic sacrifice. Those needs, unanswered, rise from the unconscious in unhealthy rituals that take on a life of their own and, as they continue, begin to gain strength purely because they have become part of our habits of the mind. Even though our society, from its educated stance of Information Age sophistication, believes itself too civilized for barbaric ritual, unhealthy, unconscious ritual has taken the place of older, intentional and more primitive rituals.

These profane rituals are simply not acknowledged.

Whenever I walk down the street of the small college town near my home and see young women or men with a metal ring or stud in their nose, lip, eyebrow or tongue, the underlying and unconscious psychic savagery of such body mutilation is very evident. Americans may speak in mocking sarcastic tones of those who mutilate themselves, but such mutilation is an indicator of the terrible psychic need for healthy ritual.

The evolution away from individual confrontation with one's own individual shadow into a collective diffusion of responsibility, which evolves ultimately into a complete abdication of responsibility, may have begun in part thousands of years ago. There was a paradigm shift, a change in the ritual that was observed for Yom Kippur. In the days when the Temple in Jerusalem provided a sacred space for the God of Judaism, the ritual for Yom Kippur included a prayer of confession in the *first person singular*. The high priest, who sent the sin offering into the desert upon the scapegoat's back, first placed his hands upon it and prayed a prayer saying, "O God, I have committed iniquity, transgressed and sinned before Thee, I and my household. O God, forgive the iniquities and transgressions and sins which I have committed and transgressed and sinned before Thee, I and my household..." (Gaster, Festivals, 147).

Here was a visceral reminder of each individual's participation in, and responsibility for, the collective sin of the nation. When the high priest used this first person singular form of prayer, there could be no denial of individual fault. That ownership of individual responsibility within the collective was integral to the redemption of each person, as a participating penitent, and to all the people who comprised the nation.

After the Temple in Jerusalem was destroyed in 70 C.E. (Johnson, 137), sacrifices were ended, and the prescribed mode of confession was changed to the *first person plural*. Now the older tradition of sacrificing animals was replaced with "a process of personal catharsis, involving the successive stages of contrition, confession, reform and absolution" (Gaster, Festivals, 150). Even though Israel had a different notion of the collective than is now a part of contemporary Western assumption, this change from tangible sacrifice and first person singular confession may have been one of the first steps in an evolution away from a concrete awareness of sacred responsibility. Carried forward in the collective unconscious, even as archetypes feeding the collective morphic field are still carried forward, it may have been part of a paradigmatic shift that fractured the collective unconscious from its connection to sacred ritual.

In the Jewish understanding of collective, the nation "was never elevated to the status of an independent, transcendental entity" (Gaster, Festivals, 150). Each person was part of the collective, in that individual misdeeds and transgressions formed into an accumulation of collective contamination, which ultimately required the cleansing atonement of Yom Kippur. Only when each person participated in the step-by-step process that began with contrition and ended with absolution was the collective redeemed by the totality of such individual participation.

Our culture suffers from an assumption that the collective stands as some sort of entity unto itself, so that our references to "the government," or "the state," or "the nation" fail to acknowledge that we are actively or passively participating in every action we attribute to such an external entity. Our lack of awareness of our own shadow side is a parallel to our failure to acknowledge our contributions, or lack thereof, to the society in which we dwell. When we can stand in some distant psychic place of isolation, claiming to have nothing to do with the collective, we set ourselves apart from the reality of our own individual shadow, and its negative participation in the collective. Our Judas legacy is one of blaming others, of scapegoating, of looking for a target for projection, of comfortable habits of the mind that allow us to wallow in self-righteousness and superior, but false, inflation.

Historically, such inflation and self-righteousness were contained to some degree within the sacred container that was religion or synagogue or church, where confession and repentance were called forth. As confession and repentance slip deeply into the modern morass of contemporary narcissism, the contamination of our culture becomes more and more evident. If there is individual psychic surrendering, it happens more often now in the therapeutic setting of a psychiatrist's or psychologist's office. This may not be a negative aspect of our modern world; it may even be our redemption, if it produces an appropriate understanding of the full spectrum of our soul material.

The atonement inherent in historic practices of ritualistic scapegoating has been lost to a civilization that uses scapegoating as a bludgeon, thus trivializing its previous sacred ritual. Now, scapegoating is practiced unconsciously. Whether it occurs in families, where one member is the unfortunate target for the rest of the family's shadow, or whether it occurs in a public arena, scapegoating is now the primary way in which blaming finds its voice in our society. It is an accepted practice in Washington, D.C. Government officials seem to thrive on scapegoating energy.

Nowhere is this dynamic more evident than in our projection of "evil" onto Usama bin Laden, Saddam Hussein, terrorists, and others who are, most especially, not "Christians" like us. September 11, 2001 gave us a multitude of "evil" others to cast shadow projections upon. The ancient atonement principle is lost from the equation, and only the negative aspects of such scapegoating remain. When we return to positive forms of ritual sacrifice we will encounter, heal and transform our own stored shadow agonies.

Chapter 5

The Cultural Evidence of the Judas Legacy

Our culture is filled with examples of the Judas legacy and its shadow betrayal of the soul. Everything from carefully concealed incest in families to child abuse is part of this legacy. Arrogant American nationalism, racism, sexism, homelessness, ageism, and anti-Semitism are also indicators of shadow-driven dynamics in our culture. Both the historical aspects of anti-Semitism and gender bias can be directly linked to the biblical text and its literal misapplication to contemporary circumstances.

Distorted perceptions of women's roles have been defined for years by using the canon. The biblical text is characterized by the paucity of its stories about women and their lives. The stories of women have been omitted, distorted, or subjected to the revisionist interpretations of Western scholars whose ethnocentric understanding of ancient Eastern customs and cultures is limited by both their gender and their methodology. Yet, even as the twenty-first century has inched its way into our reality, these canonically defined roles are thrust upon women.

When the roles of contemporary women are defined, certain clergy, radio talk-show hosts, and elected officials will haul out old notions of gender roles as they have been articulated in the canonical text. These roles, of course, are part of the "family values" rhetoric. There are those who point to the ideal role of women presented in the book of Proverbs and demand that women function out of this literal Old Testament image. Mothers' Day sermons are filled with this particular imagery. The ideal woman of this text is a metaphor for "Lady Wisdom" or "Hokhmah," the divine connecting point between the finest human cognitive function and God's sacred mind. By describing Lady Wisdom with a multitude of attributes, the original Hebrew author was striving to articulate the vast wealth and extent of God's divine wisdom and its interaction with both the human intellect and soul. The cultural imperatives driving the culture would not allow the writer of this ancient text to name this "the feminine side of God," but Lady Wisdom is a metaphor for these divine characteristics.

Those who turn to Paul's pronouncements in the New Testament often insist they are the ideal and appropriate roles for women. If the totality of these proscriptions were true, every American woman would be dressed head-to-toe in the burqa of her Arabian sisters.

As women are depicted in such a way, men are also locked into roles imposed upon them from unconscious assumptions. Down through the years, stereotypical gender roles for men have been defined by a culture demanding they have a physical body like Tarzan, the sex-appeal of Mel Gibson, the courage of General Patton, the stoicism of John Wayne, and the absolute dedication to work from which workaholism is derived. The last of these was critical, because making money was what men were supposed to do, since they were responsible for providing for the needs of wives and children, in addition to their own.

The puritan work ethic is deeply embedded in these stereotypical notions of gender roles, and addiction to work has become a modern malady as difficult to break as any other addiction. Working hard has been a definitive part of the underlying habits of the mind in this country. Anyone who will not or cannot do so, by default, carries projections of the shadow as the societal stigma related to work as a norm. Historically, men have wielded more power in the marketplace and in the family, but their lives were bound by rigid expectations and limitations as soul-killing as role boundaries for women.

While men and women traditionally had gender roles that were clear in their delineation, now there is no such thing as a clearly defined gender role. This ambiguity is held with no small uneasiness in the collective psyche. Although gender roles for American women and men have undergone tremendous changes in the last decade, the healthy aspects of these changes are often lost in the public arena with its continuing, and quite tiresome, debate about family values.

This collective psychic uneasiness reveals itself in the ways some parts of society have turned around and headed for the hills of nostalgia, where gender roles were more clearly defined, and the head of the household was always male. Out of such nostalgia and uneasiness, more than one new movement has been spawned in recent years.

One organization which has promoted this return to an anachronistic mentality is a men's organization called Promise Keepers. This "Christian" group is predicated upon the understanding that men should be "the head of the household," although that assumption is not always publicly acknowledged. Its reliance upon such Pauline canonical fiats is not only an indicator of the need to use the ancient text of the Bible as a literal rule, but also the equally powerful indicator of the unconscious psychic impetus toward regressive patterns of being. In such regression, the bumbling stepchildren of retrospective and revisionistic memory emerge as nostalgia, but parade as actual historical recollection.

The Promise Keepers were highly visible from their very beginnings because they were founded by a former coach of the University of Colorado football team, Bill McCartney. Over time this organization has acquired a large membership of men who hold that traditional gender roles are the ideal, despite the realities of lives that would indicate otherwise. The notion of keeping promises, to one's wife and to one's children, is surely an admirable one. Why such promises should be regarded as unusual, requiring extraordinary efforts, makes less sense.

The off-setting and off-putting notion that women can be pigeon-holed back into some kind of June Cleaver status is the primary flaw in this organization's assumptions.

Today, according to Maurico Velasquez, CEO of the Diversity Training Group, women business owners employ 35% more people than all the Fortune 500 companies combined. Of the net increase of the workforce between 1992 and 2005, 62 percent are women. Women earned 238,563 of the master's degrees conferred in 1996-1997. Men earned 181,062 master's degrees in this same period of time. Women will not and cannot return to some biblical or idealistic role of full-time homemaker and mother.

This notion of women who "should" be subordinate beings, and its promotion by the Promise Keepers, is an indicator of misusing the biblical text for a political agenda. When the canonical text is used as the basis for rules or for domination of another, what emerges is rigidity and anachronistic patterns of belief. The canon is meant to nourish the soul and to feed the spirit. When it is used to stultify the soul and to harm the spirit, it is obviously misused.

The Promise Keepers, in urging their members to stay connected through local small group work, are promoting healthy interaction between generations of men, grandfathers, fathers, and sons, who need to be communicating with each other. Their goal of promoting better understanding between the black community and the white community is admirable. In a time when racism continues to be an embarrassing dynamic in America, such communication can only help to heal old wounds. These two aspects of this organization are commendable (Bly, 86, 177-179). However, their insistence that women need to be subservient to men, since men must without exception function as "the head of the household," is a shadow perspective on appropriate gender roles in this modern time.

The Promise Keepers are not alone in their regressive attitudes. An action by the 1998 Southern Baptist Convention could have been written by the leaders of the Promise Keepers. It also elevates archaic gender roles set forth in texts attributed to the Apostle Paul, although more recent biblical scholarship shows some of these texts were probably written by one of his disciples. These texts define the ways wives should relate to their husbands. The notion that men should be acknowledged as heads of households, to which their wives should "graciously submit," is inserted into a late-twentieth-century declaration from a large mainline denomination, as if all the subsequent decades of social growth, positive social change, and changes in cultural norms had never occurred.

To pretend that this statement was part of a national concern for the fragmentation of family values fails to address the participation of men in cultural degeneration. This simplistic solution to a much larger and more complex array of problems is a powerful indicator of the shadow side of the church. Judeo-Christian creedal statements and declarations of belief have historically denigrated the status of women and their equal place within both church and culture. To encounter shadow within either culture or church, one can look at the way women, and by default, children, are treated.

African-American women have long held the distinction of being some of the worst treated women in this nation. Their history is linked to archaic assumptions of feudal property rights that allowed white males to rape any black woman they chose, first as landowning slave keepers, and later as males who held this unspoken but clearly assumed sense of entitlement. When Strom Thurmond's elderly African-American daughter, Essie Mae Washington-Williams, announced the identity of her birth father on December 17, 2003, she revealed the absolute hypocrisy lived by a politician who had spent forty-eight years in the United States Senate.

In 1925, when he impregnated Carrie Butler, who was only fifteen years old, he was guilty of statutory rape. Butler gave birth to her daughter at age sixteen. Her daughter, Essie Mae Washington, would be the same age, sixteen, when she met her white father. At that point the statute of limitations would have expired, and Thurmond would have been protected from charges of statutory rape. Never has "toxic love" been more evident than in the strange bond melded between this high-visibility senator from South Carolina and his low-visibility secret offspring.

Thurmond, whose hate-mongering support of white supremacy in a public arena was compartmentalized in private as he funded his African-American daughter's education, declared at a 1948 anti-civil rights rally, "All the bayonets of the Army cannot force the Negro into our homes" (Tresniowski, Dodd, and Morrisey, 78). Yet he knew more than most people about the closest possible contact with "the Negro" in his father's home, contact between a vulnerable fifteen-year old black servant and a white man who dehumanized "the Negro" with every public statement he made. His public dehumanizing words were simply mirrors of his dehumanizing private actions.

Strongly supported by "family values" proponents, Thurmond is a classic example of a man whose rape of a "Negro" was kept secret for many decades, and then discounted when the truth was revealed. Support from the Christian Coalition did not end with this announcement of Strom Thurmond's family secret, although its classic denial was a textbook example of the shadow-driven reason such misconduct has flourished for eons.

Jeffrey Gettleman, writing in the *New York Times*, quoted Roberta Combs, president of the Christian Coalition, who said, "From a moral standpoint, yes, what happened was wrong. That's not the traditional family. That's not how it's supposed to be. But, we're not going to sit around today and criticize Strom. He's helped so many people. He's touched so many lives."

Such a statement allows the Christian Coalition to pretend that its high standards were never breached. The same dynamic is operative in families where sexual abuse is denied and concealed. By denying the gravity of his criminal behavior, this "family values" coalition can continue its admiration of Strom Thurmond "because he helped so many people and touched so many lives." The nobility attributed to Thurmond by this simplistic statement is the same kind of "Let's Pretend" game played by all politicians, including this conservative "Christian" coalition. The ghost of Carrie Butler hovers in the midst of such doublespeak, for it is the same kind of slippery rhetoric that protects the sexual misadventures of men while pretending that these same men actually possess some shred of honor.

When Thurmond's African-American daughter finally told her secret, his family responded by opining, "She seems to want acceptance...." That they were offended by her desire for acceptance is the indicator of the power held down through the generations in this family.

In his *New York Times* article, Jeffrey Gettleman continued, "Ms. Washington-Williams said she has been instructed not to divulge which members of the Thurmond clan have welcomed her to the family. The Thurmonds, once again, are telling her to be quiet" (Gettleman, 1/4/04). And, sadly enough, she acquiesced to the posturing of Strom Thurmond's white relatives.

In a postscript to this story, when Essie Mae Washington-Williams spoke at a fundraising dinner in Columbia, South Carolina, Thurmond's cousin Bruce Elrod came and hugged her, declaring, "She's carrying Strom's torch right now, and I'll tell you Strom would be very proud of her" (Ritch, 2/29/04).

If Senator Thurmond was proud of her, he didn't show it during his lifetime. A man who carefully and cleverly concealed this daughter from public knowledge during his lifetime is given credit for her gracious personality, as if he had taught her how to be gracious. Such a statement is filled with covert sexism and racism. Both racism and sexism flourish when those who are cast as subordinates maintain a silence that becomes sheer fear-filled collusion. Women, both black and white, reap the unfortunate consequences of these historic patterns of behavior. By their acquiescence they foster ancient habits of the mind that continue to drive our culture. Their arrogant partners go on to success, and if women gather to support each other, they are, more often than not, considered a threat.

In November of 1993, twenty-four hundred women gathered in Minneapolis for a conference whose focus was upon "re-imagining" both the image of God and their relationship to this God. Led by clergy and laywomen from a variety of ecumenical backgrounds and mainline denominations, this conference was later attacked with a vicious verbal brutality that was shadow-driven. When the women at this conference looked for and had conversations about an authentic feminine side of God, both male and female conservatives in the Presbyterian Church, U.S.A., called for new governing and doctrinal control over such a lapse in theological perspective.

The General Assembly of the Presbyterian Church, U.S.A. made sweeping statements intended to circumvent this kind of departure from the supposed norm. The fallout from this conference became an excuse for conservatives to cry foul whenever women do not adhere to a carefully articulated party line. In reaction to what conservatives labeled heresy, thousands of dollars of support were withdrawn from the denomination and funneled into the coffers of the conservatives who were characterized most clearly by the noisy untruths they promulgated about this women's conference.

The sad and troubling aspect of this conference that was so roundly trashed by conservative media reports is that it was intended as a forum for addressing the needs of women within the context of their respective cultures. However, most Christian churches, whatever their denomination, do not know how to function in cooperative interaction with women, because the unacknowledged shadow of the church has fostered an environment rich in hatred of women.

Hatred of women who break away from old accepted norms of behavior is not peculiar to men alone. Women who speak out in a public arena know that their worst detractors will often be other women. Quoted in *The Layman*, a conservative Presbyterian newspaper, more than five years after this conference, one woman stated, "It was an extremely difficult experience. I believe it's the closest I've ever been to 'evil.'" The projection of 'evil' onto a target is a dangerous thing, for the notion that exploring matters of the spirit from a new perspective must be labeled evil is a measure of intense shadow denial by those who declare someone else to be what they deny: evil. When bandying this word about, one needs to consider how much of one's own shadow is revealed by its projection onto another.

This women's conference, when compared to the huge gatherings of Promise Keepers has one notable difference: it was a women's conference; and many of the women who gathered in Minneapolis were clergy with the same abilities for exegetical and theological expression as their male counterparts. For the conservative press to later declare that their usage of the word "Sophia" was goddess worship is to deny that this word is the Greek equivalent for *wisdom*.

Writing in a leading denominational publication, Joseph D. Small and John P. Burgess declared, "Wisdom/sophia, both in frequency and formulation, became an alternative employed in distinction from the triune God" (Small and Burgess, 11).

Because the Father and Son male entities within the generally accepted definition of the trinity were not elevated to their usual place of dominance, these male theologians roundly criticized this conference. They also cited the *Book of Order*, the governing rule of law that enjoys an elevation of canonical proportions among Presbyterians, as the arbiter of heresy committed by women at this conference. For the conservatives to hone in on this one word was to reveal the real agenda, one of power. This conference scared male leaders. It showed churches across a broad spectrum of denominations that old assumptions and norms of belief are not static, but God is a changing spirit whose feminine side has been ignored and denigrated for generations by the males who have previously held the sole power of interpretation.

The issue of power, both in leadership and in the interpretation of belief structure, was ultimately the sticking point. The shadow portrayals of this conference were without precedent in many ways, for the positive aspects of this conference were ignored in a yellow-journalistic thrust to squelch the voices of women who hold the same credentials as male clergy. Objections to the "misguided theology" of this conference had little to do with theology, but everything to do with power and with the collective shadow in our culture.

Power is also at the center of the ongoing national debate about abortion. Those who strive to retain power over the bodies of women and the sexuality of any citizen seem to find their way into politics or leadership positions in the church. In the autumn of 2003 the Congress passed, and President George W. Bush signed into law, federal legislation banning so-called partial-birth abortion, even to protect the health of the mother. This legislation was later upheld by the Supreme Court. The problem with a rigid "right-to-life" form of morality is its failure to encompass the ambiguity and inexactitude of life's realities. No ironclad rule, doctrine, law, or carefully articulated policy is ever large enough, or comprehensive enough, to anticipate the unexpected happenstance of life's journey.

Two examples from my own experience leap to the forefront of my mind. One night I received a call from a member of the church asking for counsel, as she struggled with whether abortion was a sin. Her best friend, who lived in Nebraska, was a brittle diabetic who was in the seventh month of her pregnancy. That day her friend's obstetrician discovered that her baby was suffering from a severe disability and could not survive the birthing process, nor was she viable enough to live to the end of the third trimester. The mother's health was so precarious he knew she needed a therapeutic abortion, because she had already been hospitalized numerous times during the earlier stages of this pregnancy. The dilemma? Nebraska had a restriction on partial-birth abortions. To secure a therapeutic abortion, this mother was forced to travel out of state. Her life was at stake, but her doctor was unable to perform this abortion—because of the Nebraska law. Had she not had this partial birth abortion immediately, she would have died trying to give birth to a child who could not live beyond birth. The Supreme Court ruled later against the Nebraska law, declaring that it was too broad and too vague; but that did not help this woman. That law compelled her to seek appropriate treatment in another state.

With the passage of this prohibitive legislation at the end of 2003, Congress made these kinds of therapeutic abortions illegal. Such legislation is barbaric and unconscionable. It gives no credence whatsoever to the real psychological and physical trauma inflicted upon mothers and fathers who must seek out such therapeutic procedures. When President Bush signed this bill into law, not one woman stood among the legislators who surrounded him for the signing. Not one of them possessed a womb, despite their overweening need to control this body-organ unique to the female of the species. Yet politicians strut and brag about protecting life. Such legislation does not protect life, any more than guns protect people.

I was serving as the interim pastor in another parish when I received a call from a young pregnant woman who was a member of that church. She asked if she and her husband could come to my office to talk with me. A petite brunette, she came into my office later that day, looking forlorn and filled with sadness. The porcelain skin on her face seemed drawn in on itself, she was in such despair. She sat beside her husband, a tall, sturdy man who could have been a football player. Together they told me of their plight. That day she had been referred to a specialist because her obstetrician had discovered that her baby was severely disabled. After this visit, it took almost a month for her to secure an appointment with a specialist at a preeminent teaching hospital and another several weeks before she saw still another specialist, a tertiary referral.

All this while the pregnancy was advancing toward that forbidden zone where abortions become partial-birth abortions. Ultimately each of these three doctors, whose specialties qualified them to make such stark recommendations, determined that her baby should be aborted. She and her husband came back to my office on another beautiful spring day to tell me the terrible news. We talked together for a long while. We prayed, too, and when words would not come, we wept in mute incomprehension. Their grief was so palpable, you could have gathered it into a wrinkled mass of utter gray sadness and held it in your hands.

They needed still more time and we left my office to go outside and sit under a small tree. Tiny baby leaves were just bursting forth on the limbs of this sapling as we sat contemplating their awful dilemma. She sat with her hands folded across her swelling abdomen, rocking back and forth. But I will never forget watching her husband; in utter misery, he fell over onto his belly beneath that tree. Lying prone upon the ground, he clutched its slim trunk with trembling hands and gave voice to his abject grief, wailing aloud. His tears watered the root of that young tree as he wept for their daughter, a soul locked inside a tiny body that could not survive the birthing process. This young mother had a therapeutic abortion the next day and their baby was cremated. Days and months passed . . .

Autumn had come and the leaves were sparkling with brilliant color when I climbed with the two of them to the top of a nearby mountain, where we held a private funeral and sprinkled their baby's ashes upon a mountainside. Again I watched as this young father wept in agony over the death of their daughter, and held his tiny wife whose body shook with her own sobs. The sun was shining brightly down upon their young heads, but I felt as if the sky should have been cloaked in roiling black clouds. Their grief was magnified by their own helplessness in the death of their baby.

If the politicians who believe they are omniscient and omnipotent had stepped into either of these situations, would they have voted differently on a partial-birth abortion bill? As I watched their debates on C-Span, I was struck by all the shadow-driven ego pronouncements about the "right to life." Ego inflation is a dominant part of this legislation, and reveals the cultural and collective shadow need to control women. Horror stories and ghastly pictures used to describe the "crime of partial birth abortion" are a form of domestic terrorism, since such procedures are far more rare than the American public or the Congress has been led to believe.

When the church is enmeshed in the legislative and judicial process, taking a rigid right-to-life stance, the church and its clergy are guilty of one of the worst forms of religious persecution. These unhealthy behavior patterns are a blatant example of spiritual, sexual, and psychological abuse. To be terrorized by those who believe they know the mind of God is not Christianity, but a form of domestic terrorism inflicted by those who worship power, while invoking the name of God.

The federal legislators who enacted this legislation seem oblivious to the parallels that can be drawn between their archaic attitudes toward women and the similar attitudes of their fundamentalist counterparts in the Taliban. Are some souls meant to return to God without living long lives in the human realm? In their departure do we learn powerful, albeit bitter, lessons? Our failure as a culture is evident each time such bad legislation passes, for it serves the political purposes of those who seem to believe they own God or know the mind of God. No denomination, or individual community of faith, or nation, can own God. Our society is served poorly by those who believe they must inject their own particular, or peculiar, God-belief into the legislative process.

The more the church is dragged into the middle of the legislative process, the more we risk muddling the very liberties the founders of this nation sought to secure. They were wise enough to incorporate a separation of church and state into the original documents defining the undergirding structure for our government. They were wise enough to leave the work of angels to angels. And they were wise enough to articulate a freedom of religious faith that is at risk in contemporary America.

The Bush administration was not satisfied with simply passing a bill on partial-birth abortion. A few months after this bill was passed, the *New York Times* reported that the Department of Justice issued subpoenas "demanding that at least six hospitals in New York City, Philadelphia, Illinois and elsewhere turn over hundreds of patient records for certain abortions. This egregious intrusion of patients' privacy was being pursued in the name of defending lawsuits against the abortion ban" (NYT, 2/14/04). The *New York Times* editorial concludes, "Americans should see [Attorney General] Mr. Ashcroft's intimidating tactics for the dangerous threat to liberty and privacy they really are." Two weeks later, the *Washington Post* reported that the Department of Justice had issued subpoenas for hundreds of files on abortions performed by Planned Parenthood affiliates in major cities across the nation. This aggressive intrusion into the private lives of citizens had not been thwarted by its patent illegality. The Department of Justice, while seeming determined to pursue the political agenda of the Bush administration at whatever cost, withdrew some of these subpoenas after a federal judge ruled against them. However, the *New York Times* reported that on March 12, 2004, Judge Avern Cohn of the Federal District Court in Detroit "ordered the University of Michigan Health System...to turn over edited abortion records" to the Department of Justice.

William Safire asserted that when George W. Bush ran for election to the Office of the Presidency he declared, "I believe privacy is a fundamental right, and that every American should have absolute control over his or her personal information" (NYT, 3/10-04). Safire also stated, "Medical patients 'no longer possess a reasonable expectation that their histories will remain completely confidential.'"

Safire continued, "But in defending the law, Attorney General John Ashcroft went overboard." If ever there was an understatement, that one qualifies! When the most personal and intimate details of any person's life are held in medical records that used to be regarded as confidential, the obvious and overwhelming need for control exhibited by the Department of Justice was more than stunning. It was a tactic employed heretofore by totalitarian governments that were roundly and aggressively criticized by our nation.

Using the excuse that terrorists employ the Internet as an effective communication tool, the Department of Justice in early 2004 filed a seventy-five-page Federal Communications Commission petition proposing that providers of high-speed Internet service be forced to grant easier access for FBI wiretaps and other electronic surveillance. This same petition suggested that consumers should be required to pay for these changes (Eggen & Krim, A01). With these subpoenas and petitions, the Department of Justice violated standards of privacy that have never before been breached, and suggested that those whose privacy was invaded should pay for the invasion.

The drive to invade the private lives of any American citizen is far more dangerous than any action taken by a branch of the federal government in decades. Why? Because this dysfunctional pattern of behavior is an indicator of the unhealthy thinking that underlies such actions. The impetus for such thinking is pathological; there is no other way to describe it. By breaching appropriate boundaries on privacy, the Bush Department of Justice undermined the long-held standards for personal freedom and privacy that have been a part of this nation's history.

This brazen disregard for the personal privacy of American citizens was evident in the day-to-day suspension of the rule of law. This administration also chose to circumvent the 1978 Foreign Intelligence Surveillance Act (FISA). A law passed in direct reaction to the abuses of the Nixon administration, FISA prohibits the National Security Agency from wiretapping private citizens' phone conversations or conducting other domestic surveillance without a warrant signed by a judge. However, in an action that replicated the egregious ones of the Nixon administration, George W. Bush issued a secret executive order in 2002 that allows this agency to secretly monitor the phone and e-mail communications of private citizens. The administration even bypassed the watch guard group of government attorneys who would usually review such an order and the actions spawned by it.

When these same actions were revealed to the nation in December of 2005, the administration initiated an aggressive offensive against any criticism of them. As Congress scheduled hearings the Bush administration continued its overt criminal activity unabated. Protests by citizens and Congressional leaders were ignored, as if this president and his cadre of advisors had ascended the throne and had no intention of heeding any protest.

By the time the president gave his State of the Union address to the nation on January 31, 2006, the fix was in. By reiterating, that "previous presidents have used the same constitutional authority," Bush cast himself in the company of Presidents Franklin D. Roosevelt, Abraham Lincoln, and Woodrow Wilson. The fact that such surveillance, without benefit of a warrant, was struck down by the Supreme Court in 1972 was ignored. The fact that the 1978 passage of the Foreign Intelligence Surveillance Act was intended to stop such abuses was twisted into the usual pretzel of distract and divide strategy that has been so successful during this administration. The fact that his defense of this strategy was met with a thundering ovation is the most dangerous, disheartening, and thoroughly frightening aspect of this issue. As people across the nation watched those who are supposed to have the intellect and the integrity to lead in the Congress, they saw their leaders applauding defiance of the law.

On August 17, 2006, U. S. District Judge Anna Diggs Taylor found unconstitutional the domestic surveillance program conducted by the National Security Agency. Taylor, of Detroit, handed down a forty-three page opinion indicating that the Bush administration, in defending this program, was claiming that it had the inherent power to violate federal law (AP, the *Roanoke Times*, 8/19/06).

Taylor wrote, "It was never the intent of the framers to give the president such unfettered control. There are no hereditary Kings in America and no powers not created by the Constitution. So all 'inherent powers' must derive from that Constitution."

In reaction to this decision by the court, George W. Bush went before the nation to criticize the ruling. "Striking his finger on the podium to underscore his point," the president declared that opponents fail to understand the nature of the world in which we live. Bush asserted, "I strongly disagree with that decision, strongly disagree. That's why I instructed the Justice Department to appeal immediately, and I believe our appeals will be upheld" (AP, the *Roanoke Times*, 8/19/06).

While the Congress found the time and energy to pass regressive legislation that struck at the core of health care for women, robbing individual doctors and their patients of reasonable choices, it abdicated its role in protecting the nation from assault rifles and easily accessible weapons. While the Department of Justice, the State Department and the Bush White House operated like synchronized swimmers, the Congress seemed to be in a coma. While billions of dollars fluttered away into the debacle of the war in Iraq, the Congress wrung its hands about private health issues that should not be public ones.

Nebraska Republican Senator Chuck Hagel declared, "Congress has abdicated much of its responsibility. It could become an adjunct to the executive branch."

He continued, "Congress is the only thing that stands in the way between essentially a modern-day democratic dictator and a president who is accountable to the people."

Increasingly, the boundaries between public policy and private citizens were breached during the Bush administration. During this same period of time the legislature in the State of Florida opted for an intrusive invasion into the health care of a comatose woman, Terri Schiavo. Schiavo's dreadful plight had been jerked out of a private arena, where it belonged, into public headlines and unmerciful media attention. Relying upon the shark-like frenzy of media attention, Terri's parents, who had clashed with her husband over continuing treatment for Terri, took their conflict to the public. Its shadow energy continued, unabated, with lawsuit and court action after court action. Governor Jeb Bush defended the intrusive legislation known as "Terri's Law." He tried to have a judge who had called this law "presumptively unconstitutional" removed for bias, but was unsuccessful (the *Roanoke Times*, 2/11/03, A-9).

> An editorial in the *Roanoke Times* asserts:
> Though 'Terri's Law' is tailored to apply only to Schiavo, its import is great. With their abuse of power to curry political favor, legislators sent a message that mocks *the rule of law:* If a powerful interest group exerts enough pressure, a law may not necessarily apply to all. When votes are at stake, Florida legislators will selectively override the legal process, the balance of powers, medical expertise and rights of individuals under privacy and death-with-dignity laws (10/30/03, italics added).

So many negative cultural shadow forces were driving this unfortunate scenario. An abject fear of death even when a patient is comatose, a dysfunctional family system, an intrusive legislature, and the hyperactivity of the media are all indicators of the depth and breadth of the shadow's influence in our culture. The dominant fear is the fear of death; it drives huge segments of our economic structure, as well as much of the right-to-life movement.

On March 20, 2005, the Congress and President George W. Bush took a precedent-setting legislative action that shattered all previous Congressional actions. This legislative action came after the Schiavo case had passed through many months of legal processes and federal judges had denied final appeals. In a strange violation of all the rules that govern legislative process, the Congress stepped into a private family situation that should have remained private. In taking an action that essentially ignored the rule of law, another example of governmental intrusion pushed the collective psyche to accept such intrusion as a norm instead of vehemently protesting the ways individual privacy and freedom have been abridged.

This particular tragedy was another example of the extreme extroversion of shadow in our culture. Never before, in the history of this nation, has there been a president or his advisors who have been more driven by the shadow. That makes them and their actions the most dangerous ones this nation has ever had. The unmitigated self-righteousness at the core of such thinking gives the shadow full reign in an environment of anxiety and fear. That environment, created by fear-based daily communications from a White House that consistently employs pronouncements of doom, opens the collective psyche of the nation to believe these shadow warnings. With this clever management tool, the Bush administration uses emotional manipulation like a cattle prod.

The heart of the Schiavo case and its resultant crazed actions revolved around the peculiar patterns of a death-denying American culture. We are terrified of death, even though we do not hesitate to send it overseas where we kill innocent children and women and call such killing "collateral damage." We spend countless hours of news coverage on death, spilling horrendous details of numerous murders into our souls' daily environment. We, a supposedly civilized nation, clutch the death penalty to our collective chest as if it were fashioned of pure gold, but by contrast, our fear of death is absolute.

Our fear of our own mortality is readily obvious in the images cast as ideals in our culture. Pre-pubescent girls and boys are the ideal models in a society that fears aging more than it fears terrorists. Increasingly younger girls are sexualized through media-hype as products are sold using their adolescent bodies for fantasy projections. The specific product is almost insignificant in the marketing ploy. Using scantily clad teens, everything from toothpaste to automobiles is linked to sexualized imagery. The world of fashion also has changed its once elegant images. Now it projects something akin to soft pornography in its inevitable ads, and nudity is so commonplace as to be unremarkable. The image of a female, wearing stiletto heels and nothing else, has become the accepted standard. Very expensive shoes are successfully marketed in this way. We are addicted to our images of youth as an ideal and if they are nude, all the better. The plastic surgeons who prosper in this country contribute to this obsessive pursuit of the impossible, feeding youth-oriented addictions with increasingly outrageous surgeries.

An opposite cultural dynamic of warehousing elderly individuals in isolation completes the fear-filled undertow that denies death as a natural, normal ending to human life. Little old skeletons tied in wheelchairs and lined up, like down-to-the-bone soldiers, against the walls of nursing homes, symbolize this abject fear. From this impetus, elderly, disabled individuals are deprived of contact with the rest of the population. We justify our reasons for such warehousing by claiming that people live longer lives, that our mobile society has lost much of the extended family mentality, and that we are busy with outside activities. The elderly are segregated because they remind us too much of death and we don't want to be reminded of our own mortality. Our most profound fear is of death and the American culture continually strikes a pose against its reality.

We run like terrified rabbits from death, using euphemisms to describe death like "left" or "passed away" or "went to be with the Lord," while refusing to acknowledge the startling prevalence of guns—and thus the easy means to death—in this country. The presence of all types of guns is an accepted part of our culture, but we ignore them until mass killings, like the ones at Columbine and Virginia Tech, remind us of this absolute pathology lurking in our midst.

Nowhere is our continuing game of "Let's Pretend" more apparent than around gun control. We are more in love with violence than with non-violence, and our unconscious shadow participation in the dynamics that promote violence is a fact of life. No other nation in the world has a gun-lobbying group as active, or as powerful, as the National Rifle Association. No other lobbying group is more secure in its financial base. The National Rifle Association's vocal and overt support of guns means that schools in this country have been forced to become locked-down fortresses, just to offer children a safe education. By linking their claims to the Constitution's Second Amendment, the NRA's potent group of gun lovers has been the primary force in creating a culture that is more like an armed camp than a civilized society. We are more attuned to violence than to alternative ways of resolving conflict by peaceful methods. We watch its terrible results on the evening news every night, but still we embrace its savage energy by denying the magnitude of our collective shadow.

Colbert King reported that eighteen children under age eighteen were murdered in Washington D.C. during the calendar year 2003 (1/21/04, A-21). Intimidation has become a major determining factor in our failure to convict thugs who kill without conscience. The cultural implications of using fear to manipulate is evident in the actions of gangs of criminal teens who openly threaten anyone who might testify against them, and thus, they obstruct justice. The same fear-filled cultural dynamics drive the gun industry, support the homeland security defense mechanism, foster a budget-supporting inflated and increased military forces, and continually focus upon the threat of terrorist-centered attacks, going far beyond anything that can be predicted with empirical data. The fear and the guns create an environment that provokes more guns and more fear, while whole industries then build themselves upon both. The cultural morass of collective fear, provoked by the government, the guns, the media, and local criminals, strips society down to the core of its worst expectations and invites more of the same dynamics to emerge in future generations.

When the attacks of September 11, 2001 presented us with an opportunity to do so, we leaped back onto our prideful feet, declaring our dominance in a world where domination has never held positive connotations. It gave us a new focus for our scapegoating habits of the mind. We were ready for attack, and it became our sole focus. When George W. Bush lied to the nation about his reasons for turning away from the original target of Usama bin Laden, our pride kept us from questioning his motives and our shadows sealed the bargain. If going to war with Iraq meant he could have been found guilty of "high crimes and misdemeanors," we were equally as guilty of a passive acceptance of such a war. When President Bush misled the nation about weapons of mass destruction, he was praised by his supporters for his tough stance against terrorism.

When the United States considered the events surrounding the presidency during 1998 and 1999, there were self-righteous declarations and proclamations of moral exactitude. These moralistic leaders vehemently insisted that Clinton's dishonesty had besmirched the Office of the Presidency. Yet there seems to be little individual and collective awareness of our own participation in the dynamic of dishonesty that is evident in our culture in the present moment. As we become more attuned to an atmosphere that promotes lying as a way of life, we allow that dynamic to become the morphic energy we are willing to carry. The more souls who carry untruth, the greater its collective energy in the nation.

When President Clinton stood in front of a television camera and lied boldly to millions of television viewers, he not only spoke from the depths of his own fear, he reflected back to us our own fear-filled shadows in a powerful way. If lying has become a fully operative methodology for those who reside at 1600 Pennsylvania Avenue, the prototype for such dishonesty was evident during the Johnson administration, set more completely by the Nixon administration, and displayed through the clever face of the trickster archetype when Reagan simply could not remember the details of the Iran-Contra affair.

These shadow characteristics, however, are simply the tip of an iceberg. Its far more dangerous bulk is hidden beneath the ocean of denials that allow the entire culture of the United States to continue its game of "Let's Pretend." As the societal currents that swirled around our participation in the Vietnam conflict were filled with the flotsam of dishonesty and the jetsam of lost integrity, a morphic field of untruth was created. At some level the population of this country had to pretend to believe the countless lies that were told by the Johnson administration about Vietnam. Otherwise, how could we psychically endure the hundreds of dead bodies stacked up, like cordwood, at Dover Air Force Base every week? The Bush administration has saved us from this same reality during the Iraq war. Its maintenance of undue secrecy has meant the media has not covered the arrival of caskets from Iraq at Dover AFB. In this way we can pretend those dead soldiers disappear into "the wild blue yonder."

This morphic field of pretense, dishonesty, and lost integrity was also evident during the Nixon administration, as the Watergate scandal burst any remaining bubbles of innocence we might have had. By pardoning Nixon we simply swept the shadow further into a new hiding place and forged ahead, stepping over it to pretend again. The abject dishonesty linked to the Iran-Contra scandal was just another step in the continuing formation of collective national dishonesty. By now we have grown so accustomed to lying to ourselves about ourselves, it has become a thoroughly dysfunctional habit of the mind.

Despite all these realities, there seems to be some sort of collective need for our superior stance, our self-righteousness, for we have driven the shadow even further underground in our attempts at defending ourselves after 9/11. Our national leadership has used this terrorist attack as a new and effective excuse for our false inflation and breast-pounding nationalistic pride. We can then indulge ourselves in the ultimate narcissistic weapon, one of manipulation, manipulation of truth, of circumstances, of almost anything, in order to prevent the disruption of our comfortable self-delusion.

Manipulation has become the defining function of a society that manipulates its government through a particularity of special interest groups, while the government responds to such manipulation through its own counterpoint manipulation of laws that respond to polls instead of reality. All this manipulation becomes the means whereby we both defend and betray ourselves. Over time even the manipulation becomes a pattern to which we are addicted, like so many of the other addictions that drive the marketplace in our culture. Addiction is a familiar aspect of our lives, since we are addicted to believing our nation is superior, as well as to a multitude of other addictions about which Anne Wilson Schaef has written so eloquently in her book, *When Society Becomes an Addict*.

Our addiction to overusing fossil fuels is a primary example of one that can neither be defended nor acknowledged as anything but an aspect of our collective shadow energies of refusal. These same elements of refusal drive our failure to develop solar or wind power for extensive use. Many Americans act as though fossil fuels are unlimited, and cognitive dissonance flourishes. Many entrepreneurs and businesses try to develop alternative sources of energy, but find their efforts hampered.

Confronting the shadow in this nation is a multi-faceted task, encompassing numerous aspects of our cultural reality. Doing so is now made far more difficult because we have a high-visibility focus for our angst. When those planes crashed into the World Trade Center and the Pentagon, the collective shadow in the United States found a new enemy target. Finally we had a defined enemy again. Even better, we had the ambiguity of terrorist enemies, with no particular country of origin or national identification to single them out. This ambiguity has allowed our leaders to create "an axis of evil" by redefining who would be cast in the role of enemy.

Despite all the hand-wringing and loud rhetoric about evil, the one thing we resist most is collective self-reflection upon our own individual and collective evil. We don't want to look into the mirror at our own history, for it reveals the hidden face of our collective shadow. An odd counterpoint to our fear of self-reflection is our obsession with narcissistic and incomplete self-reflection. The

Judas legacy colors a culture that has begun to function increasingly as collective victim, as others become our blame-targets. Down through the history of any nation, the so-called masses have blamed kings, queens or leaders for their troubles. Each political party blames the other for the same thing, but never before has this blaming been so powerful—nor has it been so pervasive. Perhaps it is an indicator of our nation's lack of maturity in a world where other nations are much older, or even ancient. Perhaps it is, instead, a natural cyclical pattern of national evolution.

Whether linked to a particular generation or to coming of age in the global arena, the underlying factors for such perceptions lie within the shadow, and the archetype of victim. As individuals, the shadow would have us believe the bad things that happen to us can be blamed upon someone else. The shadow is exceedingly clever at persuading us it is someone else's fault when things do not go our way. And, if we buy into that psychic persuasion, we will always deny our own shadow participation in the events of our lives. We are even addicted to denial.

We are addicted to so many things: alcohol, drugs, sex, money and its accumulation, work, worrying, religious fixations, food and nicotine, just to name a few. During the last twenty-five years or so, it has become increasingly acceptable to seek out therapeutic help. This therapy may be found in the office of a psychologist, a psychiatrist, or even a pastoral counselor. Group therapies abound in such groups as Alcoholics Anonymous, Overeaters Anonymous, and Gamblers Anonymous. Support networks are as accessible as the nearest computer modem. Counseling and its group counterparts can be found in every city, around every corner. Counseling has lost its 1950s stigma; it has acquired a more contemporary face of acceptability. As James Hillman has pointed out, now we are even addicted to endless psychoanalysis.

More and more individuals are focusing upon events and hurts from their past, ones that are supposed to be healed by the therapeutic work done with therapists or in group settings. But an increasingly evident and odd shadow dynamic of this therapeutic process is emerging. The shadow side of analytical therapy is a victim mentality that takes hold and becomes a permanent part of the personality of the analysand. The victim mentality takes the process of analysis and uses it to become amazingly adroit at manipulation.

This victim declares, "If you don't feel sorry for me because I was abused as a child, then there is something wrong with you! I feel as if you are abusing me all over again!" Here "feel" is always the operative verb—since the thinking function has been suspended in favor of the feeling function, so that the victim mentality flourishes in a sea of feelings.

The victim continues, "I feel that you don't understand why your treatment of me has hurt my feelings so much, but then perhaps you haven't dealt with your own past."

In essence, the unspoken message here is actually, "I intend to use my unhappy childhood as an excuse to indulge in narcissistic actions, ones which include manipulation as a subtle instrument for achieving my own self-focused needs. I will then demand that you honor my methods, even my manipulation, for, after all, I was abused as a child." In reaction to this kind of conversation, most people then apologize to the victim and walk away from such an encounter wondering what just happened. What has happened is this: the shadow in collusion with the victim archetype has successfully finagled an apology in response to its own manipulation! In addition, the shadow of these victims takes a little verbal knife and, by implying that listeners have not dealt with their own pathology, thrusts that knife right into the ego to bring the negative projection to completion.

Couple these dynamics with the opposite tendency of those others who need to find healing in therapy, but refuse it. These people unconsciously perceive themselves as victims, but deny it. The unfortunate result is a nation with a large percentage of people who perceive themselves as victims. Such perceptions feed a nation which denies shadow, because the only way to remain a victim is to deny one's shadow. And in the very denial of shadow, we feed its strength and become a nation of shadow people.

While we have all this evidence of an apparent desire for healing in our culture, there are odd indicators that people are not so much interested in healing as in the process of analysis as an endless shallow focus upon themselves. In his 1992 book entitled *We've Had a Hundred Years of Psychotherapy and the World's Getting Worse*, James Hillman offers a tongue-in-cheek look at this American pastime. Analysis provides the perfect environment for a narcissistic nation to indulge in its narcissistic need to gaze at its collective navel. If the gazing ended at an appropriate time, after deep self-reflective work, then analysis can be beneficial. But when it becomes a way of life, it needs to be examined, for its shadow is like a soiled petticoat showing below the hemline of our collective dysfunction.

That thousands of individuals, while supposedly seeking health and wholeness through therapy, have lapsed into viewing life through a child's eyes is indicative of our failure to confront our own personal and collective shadow. These adults, while protesting how much they want to grow, are driven by the archetype of the child. Their perceptions of life, and their interactions with others, are all predicated upon their wounded childhood, one used as a psychological cudgel to manipulate situations, events, and other people for their own purposes.

Such is the sweet wounding that has become a part of our collective consciousness. We have taken all these hours of therapy and instead of arriving at a healthy place of solutions, we have used what we have learned to become cry babies. We either cry for a past colored by revisionist memory, or for someone to blame for both the present and the past. As our foreign and domestic policy careens out of control, we are forced to contemplate our own darkness within, both the individual darkness lying inside each one of us, and the darkness at the heart of our society. Now we must look ourselves in the face and claim our demons, for every aspect of our society is colored by this undertow. Like the nation, the church needs to look at itself and address what it has become and what that represents. Those who leave its institutional spaces often turn toward New Age concepts to comfort themselves.

I have been intrigued with the tendency of the New Age movement to take a similar direction, of denying its shadow. It seems to have fallen into the same pit, focusing upon all that represents light and purity and peace and goodness and global unity, while unconsciously repressing and denying the shadow side. Participation in conferences, workshops, or gatherings of those who espouse a New Age belief may leave one feeling overwhelmed with a mawkish aftertaste.

My first encounter with the soft, sweet persona of New Age thinking came when I trained at Jungian events or educational institutions. In these encounters I found an inflated notion of superiority seemed to color the conversations, despite the focus on spirituality and visionary notions of a world where peace would reign supreme. Behind the perfectly closed faces and spoken declarations of "We are all one" was an undertone of moralizing that implies how right New Age thinkers are in comparison to all those other hateful, ignorant folk who haven't found Jungian theory or New Age thought. Hidden behind the intellectual facades of polite platitudes lurked the very heavy, hidden viscosity of denied shadow. Denied shadow is the same, whether that denial is given voice by right-wing politicians, left-wing liberal atheists, clergy espousing either left- or right-wing views, or New Age gurus. Positive change does not come from hiding the shadow under the cloak of a "we love everybody" theme. Fundamentalism is not the exclusive domain of those Christians we have labeled in this way; it can infect any collective of people. Positive change requires an unflinching encounter with one's own personal shadow, because a fanatic is a fanatic, no matter what thought form is espoused.

The New Age fundamentalist may substitute a goddess as the object of worship in place of Jesus or God, and a ritual using crystals may take the place of the sacrament of communion. But a system of belief that assumes only the good, the lovely, and the light are worthy of attention is an out-of-balance belief system, whether it is centered in the institutional church or in the contemporary New Age movement. Both will follow the same cyclical pattern of deterioration, because the denial of shadow is inherent in the process of degeneration.

The shame of owning the shadow is key to its denial. If the church and the New Age movement are both supposed to be places of love and light and compassion, but people are feuding with each other, to claim such conflict brings guilt and shame. After all, being good must mean one is not in conflict. It is the shame of owning shadow that keeps shadow carefully concealed and denied.

Our tendency to delude ourselves permeates every facet of our lives. It sits upon the shoulders of adults who are parents, and becomes the model for the kind of learning children assume is the norm. Kurt Wiesenfeld, a physicist who teaches at Georgia Tech, has written of the way these dynamics have invaded university classrooms. Students no longer seem to understand that grades are a direct correlation of applied effort. Wiesenfeld writes:

> What alarms me is their indifference toward grades as an indication of personal effort and performance. Many, when pressed about why they think they deserve a better grade, admit they don't deserve one but would like one anyway. Having been raised on gold stars for effort and smiley faces for self-esteem, they've learned that they can get by without hard work and real talent if they can talk the professor into giving them a break. This attitude is beyond cynicism (16).

These students have, in some respects, learned one lesson well. They have learned that cynicism is one of the dominant attitudes driving the culture in the present moment, and their acceptance of this cultural imperative is no different from any other acceptance of a socialization pattern.

Writing in the *Washington Post*, William Raspberry cites statistical data that shows, "A poll of more than 3,000 students listed in 'Who's Who Among High School Students'—the cream of our scholastic crop—revealed that 80 percent had engaged in academic cheating and thought cheating was commonplace. Moreover, most saw cheating as a minor infraction" (11/22/99).

On October 15, 2006, *Parade* magazine published a poll taken by the Josephson Institute of Ethics. In a survey of more than thirty-six thousand students, the poll showed that 61% had cheated on an exam during the past year, 28% had stolen from a store, 23% had stolen from a parent or a relative, and 39% had lied to save money. These students have learned such lessons from examples set by Enron and Tyco, that dishonesty is accepted as a means to get ahead in an increasingly competitive world. These students are products of an era of mass cynicism, one in which our habits of the mind have been formed by the societal tendency to foster cognitive dissonance. That cheating should be regarded as a minor infraction reveals the thought patterns of a generation of children growing to adulthood in an era of falsehood parading as truth. They are the same children who watched as a president was applauded for breaking the law, and then defying those who questioned it. Metal detectors in doorways and guns carried into schools have become an accepted norm. Compared to guns, knives, or bombs, cheating would seem mild by comparison. Another human being is not murdered when one cheats, but cognitive dissonance swirls around us daily.

Cognitive dissonance is portrayed in rare form when politicians declare themselves the sole arbiters of morality. They would even contend that the attitudes of the students described by Wiesenfeld are the direct result of our lack of so-called family values. These days it becomes increasingly difficult to separate the family values espoused by the Christian Coalition, the Republican party, or the Democrats. Each of these vocal and very influential entities is busily defining and articulating their notions of moral values. In this way, all politicians (the Christian Coalition included) try to influence—through manipulation—voters, who are disenchanted with political games and have no reason to believe their elected officials are interested in their personal lives.

The same levels of illusion fuel our disregard for the social problems in our country. An industrialized nation with the resources we have should not have more than three million women, men, and children living on the streets and sleeping on steam grates to stay warm. Statistics from 2004 show that more than one million of these homeless are children (Washington Profile, 04/19/04). Our treatment of the elderly and the homeless marks a nation more in love with shadow pretense than with realistic efforts to address social problems appropriately. We continue the dance with the shadow by imperiling every facet of our social structure.

The Greek philosopher Aeschylus once wrote, "In our sleep, pain which cannot forget falls drop by drop upon the heart until, in our despair, against our will, comes wisdom through the awful grace of God." Thus we are reminded—we are ultimately and awfully human, and as such are "frail children of dust and feeble as frail."

Chapter 6

American Shadow Symbols

Events in recent history have given us targets for individual and national shadow, whether that target is an unknown cadre of terrorists without easily identifiable countries of origin, or Usama bin Laden, or Saddam Hussein. In the same ways, events in past history also provided us with scapegoats, enemies we could hate. As we enter the twenty-first century, it is as if the culmination of a cultural acceptance of untruth for truth has produced an administration that functions outside the rule of law, outside the previously accepted parameters of public accountability and private freedom, outside the democratic principles that have been vital to the health of the American republic. Sadly enough, there is a vast lack of awareness that the shadow is the driving energy in this administration. On the one hand we project our collective shadow onto those we label terrorist, but on the other hand we delve down into the shadow not only for our response, but to defend our response. The result is a shadow dance of dangerous proportions. The players seem incapable of taking responsibility for their individual and collective motivations for bloodshed, whether they are part of the Bush administration, or terrorists, or proponents of Christianity, or proponents of Islam.

President George W. Bush has surrounded himself with a group of leaders driven by political ambitions, rather than civil servants who understand they serve the people and the Office of the President. Their fierce loyalty to one ideology-driven individual makes a mockery of historic understandings of the Office of the President. By carefully holding both the press and the people they serve at bay, they operate in an environment of secrecy and loyalty to partisan aims and purposes.

A president who held his first term in office by a judicial sleight of hand (enabled by the Supreme Court) acted as if he had been elected with a huge mandate by a vast majority of the American public, when the opposite was true. When the Supreme Court issued its decision, awarding the Presidency to George W. Bush, the Court opined, "None are more conscious of the vital limits on its judicial authority than are the members of this Court, and none stand more in admiration of the Constitution's design to leave the selection of the President to the people" (Bugliosi, 44).

When the Court chose to take this case, reversing the decision of the Florida Supreme Court—instead of allowing an appropriate recount of the votes in Florida—it violated the very Constitution it claimed to uphold and stripped the people of their rights under this same Constitution. Whether this decision was made with partisan aforethought can surely be questioned, but it was about as subtle as a sledge hammer.

David Cole, a Georgetown University law professor, declared, "[The Court] created a new right out of whole cloth and made sure it ultimately protected only one person—George Bush" (Bugliosi, 45).

Akhil Reed Amar, a Yale law professor, stated that the five justices who held the majority opinion "failed to cite a single case that, on its facts, comes close to supporting its analysis and result" (Bugliosi, 46).

Vincent Bugliosi, former District Attorney for Los Angeles County, articulated with careful precision the legal contortions performed by the Court as they reversed the decision of the lower court. Noting the bankruptcy of the "equal protection" rationale used by attorneys for Bush, Bugliosi stressed, "The Court, in effect, was saying its ruling 'only applied to those future cases captioned Bush v. Gore. In all other equal protection voting cases, litigants should refer to prior decisions of this court'" (59). He reflected the underlying dismay and disbelief of legal scholars nationwide when he wrote, "The fact that the Supreme Court deliberately departed from the position it had taken on equal protection cases throughout the years is just further evidence that its ruling only had one purpose—to appoint George W. Bush president" (72).

Supreme Court Justice Stevens, writing in his dissent, lamented, "Although we may never know with complete certainty the identity of the winner of this year's presidential election, the identity of the loser is perfectly clear. It is the *nation's confidence* in [this Court] *as an impartial guardian of the rule of law*" (Quoted in Bugliosi, 61, italics added).

In early January of 2001, an unprecedented action was initiated by more than five hundred law professors, renowned legal scholars of this nation, who took out a full-page ad in the *New York Times* denouncing the Supreme Court's stay order. They stated, "We are professors of law at 137 American law schools, from every part of our country, of different political beliefs. But we all agree that when a bare majority of the U. S. Supreme Court halted the recount of ballots under Florida law, the five justices were acting as political proponents for candidate Bush, not as judges." They continued, "It is not the job of the courts to polish the image of legitimacy of the Bush presidency by preventing disturbing facts from being confirmed.... By taking power from the voters, the Supreme Court tarnished its own legitimacy. As teachers whose lives have been dedicated to the rule of law, we protest" (94).

The action of the Supreme Court was the first in a long line of dubious distortions of the rule of law that would follow during the Bush administration. Those assaults on the rule of law have provoked anger, and sometimes rage, but scorn is also cast upon this president. In a scathing pronouncement published in *The New Republic*, Jonathan Chait declared, "Bush is a dullard lacking any moral constraints in pursuit of partisan gain, loyal to no principle save the comfort of the very rich, unburdened by any thoughtful consideration of the national interest" (Chait, quoted by Samuelson, A19).

Bill Clinton represented a classic shadow persona of aberrant sexuality, and Mike Tyson represents an athlete's shadow persona filled with violence. George W. Bush represents the American cultural aberration of one-sided religious zealotry without concomitant "moral constraints," so that he seems to perceive himself above the law, and acts from this form of egomaniacal entitlement. All these shadow personalities are indicators of a culture more driven by falsely inflated ego than by rational thinking. Such ego inflation rejects critical, reasoned thinking, even when it perceives itself as functioning from authentic intellect. Furthermore, these same characteristics apply to the institutional church driven by its noisiest and most fanatical adherents, instead of by those thoughtful, spirit-attuned folk who function out of the public eye and ear. If the history of the last thirty years is factored into the equation, the accumulated emergence of this shadow energy would be predictable.

This shadow emergence did not happen overnight. The environment inside the beltway inculcates a dangerous sense of self-importance in government leaders. By the very nature of their isolation, these government leaders foster a culture in which the collective shadow is nurtured, expanded, and denied. It is denied most vigorously by those who participate in governing from that very level of the psyche. The history of the American nation is littered with the silent bones of shadow at work, even when those bones have been scrupulously concealed before they were carefully buried.

Knowing where the shadow began to hold its collective power is a subjective projection at best, but the Civil Rights movement was certainly a deciding factor. The assassination of John F. Kennedy was also a factor in the collective shadow's emergence. The impact of the Vietnam War upon the national consciousness became a fencing match of complex psychic proportions, as those who favored the war wrangled with those who opposed it. Veterans who returned to American soil were often spat upon and ridiculed, adding wounding to the already unimaginable wounding they carried around in their psyches. As these bloody war scars hang upon the nation's conscience—never having been healed—we create more wounds to the nation's soul as the war in Iraq continues. Now the collective psychic defense mechanism is jaded by our tenacious history of denial. We distract ourselves in countless ways, and that distraction is cleverly employed by those who use psychological manipulation in the place of truth. A form of national shadow paralysis invokes a sigh when our response should be "en garde."

When the Johnson administration shamelessly lied about the Gulf of Tonkin incident, dishonesty became a defining undertow, allowing more and more lies to be promulgated in a public arena. By the time Bill Clinton lied about the foolish stupidity of a personal sexual encounter, this dishonest atmosphere was deeply ingrained into the assumptions that are evident inside the beltway. Clinton simply tapped into the prevailing ethos that had been perfected during the Nixon years and its Watergate debacle. Reagan's military manager, Oliver North, proudly claimed his own version of truth when questioned about the Iran-Contra affair and the tradition of speaking untruth as fact was similarly evident. The Bush administration has widened and deepened this dishonesty by its very failure to acknowledge its own humanity, and the concomitant human error that cannot be subtracted from it. Lying to the public was neither invented nor initiated by President George W. Bush. It was simply honed to a finer edge, while invoking the name of God.

Whether the collective psyche is lulled into a sense of false security, as before 9/11/01, or an elevated sense of personal insecurity, as after 9/11/01, the shadow functions in similar ways. The shadow lapses into archetypal pronouncements about loyalty as a critical attribute, one held as superior to critical thinking. When loyalty is elevated in this way, despite all indicators to the contrary, it fosters the same atmosphere that led the people of Germany into the ignominious defeats of World War II. The implication of such loyalty is a suspension of reasonable public discourse and healthy opposing interaction. Without the balancing alternatives of a "loyal opposition," the shadow becomes a defining player in the governing process, and its most dangerous component. From such one-sided loyalty, suspension of reasonable opposition, and the failure of appropriate interactions among our governmental system of checks and balances, an unacknowledged evil slips into the game, for the shadow is capable of hiding evil quite effectively.

In *People of the Lie*, M. Scott Peck described evil personalities in this way: "By their nature the evil inspire in us more of a desire to destroy than to heal, to hate than to pity. While these natural reactions serve to protect the uninitiated, they otherwise prevent any possible solution" (127).

The denial of internal shadow allows evil to emerge, while reactions of passivity infuse the collective with an impulse for more and more shadow actions. When the collective shadow is triggered, solutions for its negativity seem beyond reach, just as Peck has noted. It is the very unconscious and unacknowledged nature and power of the shadow that makes such situations most disturbing. Passive, psychically paralytic reactions to the shadow's powerful energy are predictable. Historic examples bear this out.

While claiming Jesus as his role model, Bush actively chooses a leadership style more like the warrior mentality of Genghis Khan, not an emulation of the Christ, the Prince of Peace. His style is more dictatorial than cooperative, more tyrannical than egalitarian, more grounded in unremitting expectations of total loyalty than in cognitive analysis, diplomatic process, or mature adult-to-adult engagement that would encourage accountability.

A feature article in the *Roanoke Times* reported that in an experiment conducted at Emory University, Professor Drew Westen and Associate Professor Stephan Hamann determined that emotions drive political decisions and loyalties. Cognitive mental processes, through which rational and reasonable conclusions emerge, were not the determining factor in partisan loyalties. This research project found that "committed partisans will reach emotionally biased decisions, hearing those things that reinforce their beliefs and rejecting information that contradicts them."

Professor Westen declares, "Once a person's political attitudes have calcified, an emotional bias takes over and a person is looking for information to 'stamp in' or reinforce their view" (AP, 1/31/06).

Westen also concludes that the Republicans have been "far better at capitalizing on emotions" in their campaigns. This strategy was evident in the mid-term election in 2002, when the Republicans managed to divert attention away from internal domestic chaos, focused upon the war on terrorism and claimed their superiority in making the nation safe. That continuing strategy was a dominant and determining factor in the 2004 presidential campaign. Senator John Kerry never seemed to understand that he was outflanked by the Republican Party's insistence on national security as their domain. His intellectual reasoning did not take into account the psychological factors that were used to drive the Bush campaign. Karl Rove successfully manipulated the national psyche in these campaigns, although he learned that using this same manipulation during the mid-term elections for 2006 did not work. Finally the voters of this nation stopped believing every lie propounded by the White House. Even though this strategy did not succeed in 2006 elections, it is still employed by the White House. Psychological manipulation is the dominant methodology of the Bush administration, and the shadow has never been employed more effectively. The tone of the 2007 State of the Union Address, before the Congress and the American public, was cast from the same fear-provoking consciousness.

Back on December 18, 2000 Bush met with the four Congressional leaders who hold the majority and minority posts in the Senate and the House of Representatives. During that meeting he actually telegraphed his intentions to the nation, although his message was laughed off as a witty sound bite. Bush declared, "I told all four that there are going to be some times where we don't agree with each other, but that's okay. If this were a dictatorship, it would be a heck of a lot easier, just so long as I'm the dictator" (Suskind, 8). With this supposed quip, George W. Bush set the tone for a presidency that would thrive on untruth and innuendo to destroy political opponents. He created a White House that would steamroll any objections to its methods, or purposes, or the means employed to accomplish its end results. From a stance of righteous self-aggrandizement, the president, with one statement, revealed his true character and his shadow personality.

Scott Peck uses a four-point argument to articulate the personality that functions from the shadow, a personality type he labels as "evil." The first characteristic of such personalities is their "consistent destructive, scapegoating behavior, which may often be quite subtle" (129). From the first day Bush stepped into the oval office, he chose scapegoating as a way of achieving the political goals to which he aspired. Ron Suskind's book, *The Price of Loyalty*, clearly shows that Bush came into office prepared to initiate a preemptive strike against Iraq, since Saddam Hussein is obviously Bush's scapegoat for his own powerful shadow.

At the first meeting of the National Security Council, on January 30, 2001—ten days after he took the oath of office—and eight months before planes would crash through the Pentagon and World Trade Center—the focus of the meeting was set in this way. Bush opined, "Sometimes a show of strength by one side can really clarify things." Then he turned to Director of National Security Condoleeza Rice and said, "So, Condi, what are we going to talk about today? What's on our agenda?"

Her response? "How Iraq is destabilizing the [Middle Eastern] region, Mr. President" (Suskind, 72). Two days later, on February 1, 2001, the National Security Council met again. The articulated purpose for this meeting? "To review the current state-of-play (including CIA briefing on Iraq) and to examine policy on how to proceed" (83). Under the purpose for this meeting were items including an "Executive Summary: Political-Military Plan for Post-Saddam Iraq Crisis (interagency working paper)—SECRET," a "Summary of United States Sanctions on Iraq," and "Iraq Sanctions Regime," State Department, for use in public statements." This meeting set the singular, obsessive focus for the Bush administration's foreign policy agenda and occurred months before the nation was thrust into terrorist-driven panic because of the events of September 11, 2001.

Scott Peck's second distinction for an evil personality type is "excessive, albeit covert, intolerance to criticism and other forms of narcissistic injury" (129). When Suskind's book was released the White House was incensed, and one anonymous official told CBS news that they were simply prepared to discount anything former Secretary of the Treasury Paul O'Neill said or did "because everybody knew he was crazy." Writing in the *New York Times*, Paul Krugman, noted,

> Administration officials have attacked Mr. O'Neill's character but haven't refuted any of his facts. They have, however, already opened an investigation into how a picture of a possibly classified document appeared during Mr. O'Neill's TV interview. This alacrity stands in sharp contrast with their evident lack of concern when a senior administration official, still unknown, blew the cover of a CIA operative because her husband had revealed some politically inconvenient facts (1/13/04).

Early in the initial days of Bush's first term, it became a well-known practice for the Secret Service to marginalize anyone who was protesting the president's administrative policies or actions in a public arena. When Bush spoke in public forums, the Secret Service pushed anyone carrying an opposition sign into an area away from camera-range or earshot of the president, so that they were effectively prevented from voicing or exhibiting any disagreement with the administration. The publicly articulated reason for these actions? The president's safety. These practices continued during the presidential election campaign of 2004.

The White House stance was one of absolute intolerance for anyone who disagreed with it. Verbalizing this stance, any and all opposition was labeled as "unpatriotic" in a time when the nation was "fighting a war on terrorism." When its secret wiretapping of private citizens was revealed at the end of 2005, the Bush administration turned itself into another corkscrew of distorted thinking. In a striking example of the duplicitous motivations that typified the Bush administration, the Department of Justice launched an investigation into the source of the leak of this information to the public. Once again there were cries that revealing this information to the public was a treasonous offense. Once again the president declared that the war against terrorism had been damaged by revealing this information to the public. By focusing upon the leak as the unlawful aspect of this debacle, the president and his cohorts again adopted a pathological perspective, and functioned from it. Every time unlawful or covert actions were revealed, the Bush administration launched an investigation to divert the public's attention from the actuality of its own unlawful conduct. Each time its appropriate accountability to the Congress or the American public was questioned, the Bush administration scoffed at such questions, claiming some imagined, even delusional, monarchical powers because of the war on terrorism.

Scott Peck also defined the "evil personality type" as having a "pronounced concern with a public image and self-image of respectability, contributing to a stability of life-style but also to pretentiousness and denial of hateful feelings or vengeful motives" (129).

On Friday, January 16, 2003, President Bush installed Judge Charles W. Pickering Sr. to the Fifth Circuit Court of Appeals during a Congressional recess. While this is a legal device that has been used by other presidents, this appointment, which bypassed the legislative process—was described by Senator Charles Schumer as a 'finger in the eye' for all those seeking fairness in the nomination process" (NYT, 1/17/04). Senator Schumer did not call this appointment what it really was, revenge. In appointing Judge Pickering, Bush declared, "Today I was proud to exercise my constitutional authority to appoint Judge Charles W. Pickering to serve on the United States Court of Appeals for the Fifth Circuit" (Lewis, 1/17/04). Bush indicated that he "was forced to do so because a minority of Democratic senators has (sic) been using unprecedented obstructionist tactics to prevent him and other qualified individuals from receiving up-or-down votes. Their tactics are inconsistent with the Senate's constitutional responsibility and are hurting our judicial system" (NYT, 1/17/04).

As he appointed only the second Congressional recess judge to the bench during a twenty-year period of time, Mr. Bush seemed stricken with a singularly short memory. When Bill Clinton occupied the White House, the Republican-controlled Senate rejected 114 of his nominees to the bench. Even when urged to approve judges because the judicial system was being harmed by their actions, the Republicans used both vote and procedural obstacles to set aside Clinton's judicial nominations. Yet Clinton only exercised this executive appointment during a Congressional recess once, for an African-American candidate (Judge Roger Gregory) to the Richmond, Virginia appeals court. This judge was later approved by the Senate, when Bush also nominated him after he came into office.

Finally, Scott Peck characterizes the "evil personality type" as one of "intellectual deviousness." Nothing is more devious than the ways the environmental laws and policies of this nation have been stripped of their effectiveness by an administration that "opens national forests to destructive logging of old-growth trees, and labels it the Healthy Forest Initiative. A policy that vastly increases the amount of pollution that can be dumped into the air is called the Clear Skies Initiative" (Gore, 1/16/04).

While battleground casualties may be quantifiable, what is not quantifiable is the environmental damage to the planet. On January 28, 2006, the *Los Angeles Times* reported that the Environmental Protection Agency "has become an agency that too often ignores science…and *prevents other public agencies from moving forward to protect the environment* [italics mine]."

Former Vice-President Al Gore, speaking to an audience in New York City on January 14, 2003, asserted,

> I have noticed a troubling pattern that characterizes the Bush-Cheney administration's approach to almost all issues. In almost every policy area, the administration's consistent goal has been to eliminate any constraints on their exercise of raw power, whether by law, regulation, alliance or treaty. And in the process, they have in each case caused America to be seen by the other nations of the world as showing disdain for the international community (Herbert, 1/16/04).

Gore continued,

> They devise their policies with as much secrecy as possible, and in close cooperation with the most powerful special interests that have a monetary stake in what happens. In each case, the public interest is not only ignored, but actively undermined. In each case, they devote considerable attention to a clever strategy of deception that appears designed to prevent the American people from discerning what it is they are actually doing.

Dr. Robert S. Norris, Senior Research Associate with the Natural Resources Defense Council, reported that the Bush administration formally withdrew from the ABM Treaty on June 13, 2002. He continued,

> They have refused to ratify the Comprehensive Test Ban Treaty (though there are no plans to resume nuclear testing). They have refused to find solutions to verifying the Biological Weapons Convention and the Missile Material Cut-Off Treaty. They let the START II Treaty wither on the vine after the Senate ratified it.... Beyond the arms control area they have refused to join the Kyoto agreement, the International Court and thumb their nose at various torture standards set by the Geneva Treaty.

A nation that built its governmental structure upon accountability at the highest levels of government watched as the Bush administration advanced its causes by any means possible. As it abrogated actual responsibility for its own obvious duplicity, this administration functioned from every aspect of the negative energy of the shadow. Dr. Norris noted that "the current Attorney General said in January, 2002 that the Geneva limitations were obsolete and its provisions 'quaint.'" He concluded, "Under the generally held standards, international treaty obligations are binding as U.S. law and thus by not adhering to them the President is saying he is above the law. We have seen this imperial stance in such domestic areas as wiretapping" (E-mail to the author, 4/19/06).

Dr. Justin A. Frank, in his remote but careful psychoanalysis of George W. Bush, asserted that the president has the personality traits of a paranoid megalomaniac. He wrote, "The megalomanic personality's blurring of reality is ultimately self-serving." The negative side of the shadow always blurs, distorts, and creates a fog of confusion inside the psyches of those who are driven by it. This blurring of reality not only serves to comfort the falsely inflated ego, it also provides a measure of insulation so vitally important to this type of pathological personality.

Dr. Frank wrote, "In the end, what Bush is driven to avoid at all costs is the pain of self-recognition."

Dr. Frank opined, "Bush is tremendously invested in the illusion of his inner goodness, which he can maintain only by externalizing his considerable capacity for destruction." Ultimately this practicing psychiatrist and professor at George Washington University drew this conclusion about President Bush: "He is forced to annihilate any recognition of himself as impotent or as a failure, by defining and then extinguishing external persecutors" (208-209). The sticking point is that George W. Bush regards anyone who does not completely agree with him as some form of persecutor.

George W. Bush used the shadow's energy of refusal when he declared emphatically, "I won't negotiate with myself. It's as simple as that" (Suskind, 117). By making this bald pronouncement, Bush revealed his inability to engage in the appropriate self-reflection of any mature adult or the process of critical analysis that is assumed in most corporate arenas. His sense of entitlement is so profound, he cannot think or reason beyond his own need for absolute control on his terms. That need to control is a classic example of dry-drunk behavior patterns. Internally, Bush has himself on a tight leash. That leash is tightly woven with the iron threads of his own profound fear.

Forty years ago, Erich Fromm noted the ways evil kills the human spirit. Fromm's definition included "the desire of certain people to control others—to make them controllable, to foster their dependence, to discourage their capacity to think for themselves, to diminish their unpredictability and originality, to keep them in line" (Peck, 43).

Fromm's description characterizes the day-to-day practices of any totalitarian regime, but most disconcerting is the accuracy of this description for the Bush administration. By shutting out intelligent discourse that would reasonably question its practices, this administration actively participates in stultifying the soul of America. Negotiation is not part of the Bush nomenclature, where a frantic and fanatical adherence to the White House propaganda line displaces appropriate governing dialogue or process. Conservative ideology drives the executive machine, so that it operates like a cross between a sledgehammer and a steam roller.

By emphasizing how much our lives have been changed by 9/11/01, vocal leaders imply that social change is frightening or, at the very least, anomic. Social change is neither, but those who hold powerful positions in government have a stake in implying that it represents something harmful to families. Their stake in maintaining the stasis quo is only outstripped by their even greater determination to foist regressive social mores upon the populace.

Change is a normally occurring factor of human, animal and plant life. Every organism changes daily in some way. So, too, global systems, cultural dynamics, societies and social institutions are forced to change. The Bush administration has chosen regressive, militaristic thinking patterns as its model for policy-making. Chosen over new models of cooperative endeavor, collegial discourse with other government leaders, or collaborative focus with other nation states, the Bush White House seems to have stepped out of a 1940's time warp. Such regressive actions and thought patterns are held as ideal by those who support fundamentalist beliefs, systems and policies.

In a speech on April 7, 2004, Sen. Robert C. Byrd offered this forthright opinion on the practices of the Bush White House: "Questioning flawed leadership is a requirement of this government. Failing to question, failing to speak out, is failing the legacy of the Founding Fathers." Our collective failure to question or to speak out has allowed the President and his cadre of worker bees to give full reign to their pathological impulses. If their dysfunction was limited to their personal lives, it would be sad, but it would not have the catastrophic impact it has had already upon millions of people in the world.

We are no longer living in a protected global arena where our American foreign policy can be predicated upon isolationistic notions of independence. The whole planet is an interdependent organism. Our nation and its people are participants in that interdependence, whether we want it or not, whether we like it or not.

Chapter 7

The Christian Church in America: The Link to the Judas Legacy

The strange melding of marketing ploys and popular culture into what passes for religion in the United States in the earliest years of the twenty-first century results in an unpalatable recipe for contemporary pseudo-Christianity. A popular series of books written as fiction but hyped as canonical truth are the means whereby evangelical Christian writers inculcate fear into masses of ill-informed and biblically illiterate Americans. This "Left Behind" series tells the story of an apocalyptic event, the Rapture, that fractures families, ripping mothers from babies, as its fear-inducing narrative declares the metaphorical writings of the canonical book of Revelation to be factual. Initially written in a fever of millennial anticipation, its authors no doubt expected the Rapture they predicted to occur at the dawning of the changing millennium. When the world did not erupt into a cataclysmic Armageddon at 12:01A.M. on January 1, 2000, this book and its successors were marketed to a still-fascinated audience. The Rapture would have fulfilled their prophecy. Yet, maybe the money derived from book sales trumped even that, since CBS reported that sales of these books "exceeds $100 million in annual revenue" (60 Minutes, 2/8/04).

When interviewed on 60 Minutes a number of years after the publication of their first book, the authors of this series declared their allegiance to their form of fiction, defending it as if it were nonfiction and employing it as an instrument for patriotic fervor.

One of the authors, Tim LaHaye, asserted, "I think if you cut us, Jerry and I would bleed red, white and blue. We believe that God has raised up America to be a tool in these last days, to get the Gospel to the innermost parts of the earth."

CBS reported, "At the Watermark Community Church in Dallas, Rev. Todd Wagner tells his flock that the books may be fiction, but they are based on hard facts. Non-believers are doomed."

Interviewed by the *Washington Post* for an earlier article written in November of 1999, one manager of a Christian bookstore opined, "The actual [Left Behind] book itself is fiction. However, to me, it's fact. It's the story...of what's in the Bible" (Murphy, 11/28/99, C-1).

The lack of biblical scholarship in such fiction is exempt from appropriate assessments within the scholarly arena, simply because it is marketed as fiction. While marketing terror-filled fiction that has been given the elevation of biblical prophecy, the authors can use the very fact that these books are works of fiction as their armor against criticism. Fear has become the means whereby huge segments of the population are exploited by both government leaders and the Christians who write these books.

During his 60 Minutes interview LaHaye declared, "I think 9/11 was a wake-up call to America. Suddenly, our false sense of security was shaken. And we're vulnerable. And that fear can lead many people to Christ."

In the waning years of the twentieth century and continuing into the present time, many liberal Christians abdicated the voice of the church in America to their more aggressive conservative counterparts. During these years, the vocal fundamentalists of Christianity became the public face of religion in American.

Former President Jimmy Carter, a man whose moderate Baptist Christianity is a defining part of his personality and lifestyle, pointed out the problem with fundamentalist Christianity, or any other fundamentalist movement, like the Taliban or Al Qaeda. In his book entitled *Our Endangered Values: America's Moral Crisis*, he indicates that intense forms of fundamentalism have five prevailing characteristics. They are invariably led by authoritarian males with "an overwhelming commitment to subjugate women and to dominate their fellow believers." While subscribing to the past as superior to the present, "self-beneficial aspects of both their historic religious beliefs and the modern world" are used for their own narrow purposes. Carter also said fundamentalists are "convinced they are right and anyone who contradicts them is ignorant and possibly evil." They "are militant in fighting against any challenge to their beliefs," and exhibit aggressive behavior patterns of anger, and "sometimes verbal or physical abuse." Finally, President Carter declares that fundamentalists have an isolated narrow worldview characterized by rigidity. They "view change, cooperation, negotiation, and other efforts to resolve differences as signs of weakness" (Carter, 34-35).

If these characteristics are applied to the public persona of the Bush administration, from the first day of its inaugurated power until the present day, they present a clear distinction between this administration and previous administrations. The American public is duped daily by a White House cadre of pseudo-Christians, and by public leaders, like the Tom DeLays of this nation, who wave their Bible with one hand while picking voters' pockets with the other one.

Since liberal Christians seemed more uncomfortable with loud proclamations of an extreme stance, that discomfort has meant that fundamentalist, highly assertive Christians became the loudest voices for the church. The media listened to this particular right-wing version of Christianity because it was the simply the most vocal. To find its opposition required work the media was apparently unwilling to do. Then the media made assumptions that this fundamentalism was, in fact, the defining faith for an entire nation. Jerry Falwell received far more airtime and television exposure than liberal theologians who were his counterparts. By their reticence, most liberals have abdicated a vocal, defining role to those who were determined to publicize their belief in the inerrancy of the gospel despite the many places where the canon contradicts itself. And, by their acquiescence, the nation's media offered right-wing conservative Christians a public forum to air unequivocal beliefs and prophecies of doom.

By the time George W. Bush managed to secure his place in the Office of the Presidency, right-wing conservatives had established a dominant presence in many social institutions in America. After the elections in 2004, conservatives declared that a mandate for their beliefs, values, and political stance had been achieved.

By the end of 2004 it seemed as if the religious right had a chokehold upon the Republican Party. When old-line conservatives, like the Barry Goldwaters of the world, were articulating authentic conservative values, this party had been wise enough to step back from mixing religion with politics. The value of the separation of church and state was considered an integral aspect of political interactions. That boundary was first breached, then later blurred into ambiguity, when the Moral Majority became an organized, vocal force in the political arena. Reflecting the beliefs of its founder as if they represented statesmanlike honor and integrity, this organization, and its first cousin, the Christian Coalition, hacked away at the very separation of church and state that had always been part of the underlying, well-defined structure for the national government.

When the Bush administration came to power, the line between the practice of religion and the function of government became more and more blurred. Invoking the name of "our" God, the United States launched a war against terrorists and those who had been defined as evil.

One highly visible commander in that war wears the invisible badge of American Christianity stamped upon his forehead, as if to repel "the anti-Christ" represented by other nations with other religious beliefs. Appointed by former Secretary of Defense Donald Rumsfeld to the position of Deputy Under Secretary of Defense for Intelligence, General Jerry Boykin preached his beliefs from pulpits as if he were a latter-day messianic leader proclaiming the nation's only hope. Speaking from the pulpit of First Baptist Church in Broken Arrow, Oklahoma, Boykin projected an enlarged photograph onto a movie screen. Taken in Mogadishu, Somalia, after the failed Blackhawk Down mission resulted in the deaths of eighteen Americans, this photo included his defining image of "Satan." Showing the congregation an image of a huge shadow in the background of this photograph, he declared this "strange dark mark" to be "the enemy."

Flashing this image onto the screen, Boykin declared, "Ladies and gentlemen, this is your enemy. It is the principalities of darkness.... It is a demonic presence in that city that God revealed to me as the enemy" (Arkin, 1).

General Boykin is reported to be "an intolerant extremist" who has spoken openly about how his belief in Christianity has the power to defeat Muslims and other non-Christians in battle. When confronted with questions about those of the Muslim faith, Boykin contemptuously asserted, "Well, you know what? I knew that my God was bigger than his. I knew that my God was a real God and his was an idol" (5). Boykin believes, "Other countries have lost their morals, lost their values. But America is still a Christian nation."

General Boykin is just one example of those who have been appointed to lead by the Bush administration. Extolling Bush's leadership as a "man who prays in the Oval Office," Boykin declares, "George Bush was not elected by a majority of the voters in the United States. He was appointed by God." He tells a congregation in Oregon, "Ladies and gentlemen..., I want to impress upon you that the battle that we're in is a spiritual battle."

When Boykin's tendency to preach about his beliefs was criticized by adherents of the separation of church and state, the Christian Coalition responded by calling Boykin's critics "an intolerant liberal mob" and declared, "most Americans agree with President George W. Bush when he said of the radical Islamic creed, as represented by the Taliban and Usama bin Laden in January 2002: 'We're taking action against evil people' and '...Our war is against evil. This is clearly a case of good vs. evil, and make no mistake about it: Good will prevail'" (www.cc.org).

Their statements supporting Boykin unconsciously deny their own internal shadow by declaring that the United States represents the good as opposed to our enemies, who represent evil. If the enemy is all evil, we get to be, by contrast, all good. By drawing that harsh contrast, the president of the United States verbally isolates this nation even further from healthy dialogue with other nation states in a global environment made small by advances in technology. That General Boykin holds a senior administrative position is not only disconcerting, it is a prime example of stereotypical ethnocentric arrogance in a global arena. Our actions and words create immeasurable conflict and provoke unknowable negative consequences that no subsequent diplomacy will repair. Our continuing declarations of the inerrancy of Christianity reflect the depth and breadth of our massive denial of the wrongs we have committed in the name of "freedom." Impervious to the ways our policies and institutions are reflections of fanatic religious obsession, corporate greed, and sheer recklessness, we publicly claim that we are liberators, while at the same time serving anti-war protestors with federal subpoenas under the stark provisions of the Patriot Act (Davey, 2/10/04).

The personal and collective grandiosity driving the nation led by a man who defines himself as "a war president" is wrapped around our shadow refusal to admit our own human fallibilities and failures. To cast the war with Iraq into alignment with the practice of religion is to cast it into some modern Western parallel with the Crusades of early Christianity. However, the unmistakable parallel with the religious fervor of Al Qaeda operatives and their fanatical leader, Usama bin Laden, more swiftly comes to mind.

In a global environment of instant communications and the international availability of dialogue with any other language or people, the notion that "God Bless America" should be the hymn of the moment is both ludicrous and lamentable. When George W. Bush repeats, over and over again, "Anyone who is not with us is against us," he believes every ideological syllable of this statement. For President George W. Bush, there is only one God, a God whose divine focus is particular to the United States, whose singular benevolence is intended only for Americans, and whose only church is peculiar to the American culture. By creating a skewed perception of Christianity in a public arena, religion and patriotism become synonymous in the minds of uninformed citizens, who begin to meld national patriotism and religion in the deepest levels of the psyche. More often than not, any resultant reactions are then shadow reactions.

For a number of years I specialized in interim ministry. This simply means that I went into churches or agencies of the PCUSA denomination to work with them during the period of time between installed or permanent pastorates. One of my contracts entailed working as an interim executive presbyter (somewhat like a bishop, though without the power of a bishop) in a regional office that was the resource and arbitration center for more than eighty churches.

One day I left a meeting of a district committee and, as I turned onto the main street of the little village where the meeting was held, I encountered the local men of the Ku Klux Klan wearing their full-dress, white-hooded regalia. At three-o'clock in the afternoon on a bright, sunlit autumn day, the leader of their pack stepped out in front of my car as he led his marching cohorts in their overt statement of white racism. His hood was thrown back away from his face, as if he claimed this affiliation with pride. His followers, however, were faceless; each one had a hood covering his face.

When I spoke of this incident at a meeting of another presbytery, a pastor—who had worked within the presbytery where the KKK was active, vocal, and visible—protested that he had never heard of any KKK in that region. Furthermore, he declared, he did not believe there were any KKK members in the presbytery about which I spoke. His own shadow threw up the cognitive dissonance that allowed him to face me in a public arena and call me an outright liar, and to do so with a perfectly straight face! The shadow happily participated in his untruth.

My own experience inside the institutional church has colored my reaction to both Bush and Boykin, since I have watched the Presbyterian Church, USA evolve from a denomination that held moderate to liberal views on life, theology and the role of church into one where conservatives have become the vociferous provocateurs, questioning all things "Presbyterian." In that evolution away from a more moderate stance marking this denomination thirty years ago, the soul of this denomination has been lost to the noise of conservative agitators. The shadow is a major player in these evolving dynamics.

The shadow's influence is so much a part of the church it cannot be avoided. Money has become the prime means for shadow manipulation within many churches. When I held the position of staff financial officer at the regional level of my denomination, I developed a hypothesis that many of those who opt to become treasurers in individual churches are people who could be categorized as stereotypical misers. These latter day Ebenezer Scrooges opt for this office in the church because they have some inborn need to control and manipulate, and money is an ideal tool for both.

After working in eight different regions of the Presbyterian Church, USA, I reached a point where little surprised me, since the shadow is denied so vigorously at the center of the institutional church. That denial feeds its secrets. In one of the regional offices, where I was working in an interim executive position, I was the advisor to the committee charged with determining how mission funding would be spent at the regional level. As I sat in one meeting, where the committee made plans for a mission trip and acted to fund this trip for the small number of people who were going, I saw more than $20,000.00 earmarked for a trip taken by fewer than fifteen people. This money paid for "mission vacations," in essence, despite glib protests to the contrary. It paid for travel and other expenses for those traveling down the East Coast to a mission station on the border between Mexico and the United States. When I asked if the designated purpose of this funding was going to be reported to the full presbytery (comprised of all the clergy and representative elders from every church in the presbytery), the group demurred. Later I took my concerns to the executive board of the presbytery, only to have the chairman of the committee in question whirl on me and call me a Pharisee! When the executive board smiled and passed it off, I knew I was fighting a losing battle. Yet the shadow untruth that these trips functioned as "mission" was deeply ingrained in the motivations for using these funds in this way. If the small number of participants and the total amount of funding had been revealed to the full presbytery, a hue and cry would have arisen, and should have.

The church in America has countless stories such as these in its carefully protected and concealed archives. Many of the worst memories would never have been recorded, but are carried as a toxic imprint within the souls of individuals. Idealistic projections of a majority of the members onto the institution, or onto its clergy, create an atmosphere where the denial is as strong as the idealistic projection. There is a direct correlation between the denial of shadow and the idealistic projection of most people. This projection is a form of idolatry, not unlike the unconscious drive in the United States to project a kind of pseudo-divinity onto this country and its leaders. Patriotism is seen as synonymous with Christianity and the flags found in most churches only serve to create this mistaken notion of a parallel.

When the members of a church project the perfection they believe characterizes God onto the church and/or its clergy, they slip into idolatry, focusing upon the tangible, instead of on an unseen God. Many members are in love with the building itself, and spend huge amounts of money and time in maintaining this structure. Some church consultants call this an "edifice complex." Church members are comfortable with focusing upon building repairs and maintenance. They are less comfortable with opening themselves and their churches to radical change, whether in programming or the people they welcome into their worship service.

Racism is a powerful shadow energy in our culture. This prejudice is revealed in the ways Native Americans are still perceived, and in the continuing debate over Affirmative Action for minorities of any race. My own personal experience as an interim executive occurred when I was working in a state north of the Mason-Dixon line, not in the Deep South, where the Ku Klux Klan is supposedly more entrenched. I have found deep-seated racism is no longer overt in the churches I have served, but occupies a subtle corner of the interactions between people across a broad spectrum of occupations and income levels. That subtlety is sublimated behind a shadow pretense of acceptance that is far more dangerous than the overt racism of the past, because it is denied behind the fervor of unacknowledged games of "Let's Pretend."

When I worked as an interim pastor with a cross-cultural congregation I discovered the covert aspects of contemporary racism. When I interviewed for this position, I was led to believe that this church was a shining star of racial equality and egalitarian standards. When I arrived and became acquainted with the congregation, I discovered that far more Africans from a number of different countries were members of this church than were African Americans. Many of the Africans were refugees, but there were also members who were part of the diplomatic corps, so a broad spectrum of Africans was represented in this church. It was an ideal place for cross-cultural dialogue and healthy global interaction, except—such dialogue was minimal to nonexistent.

The white majority of this congregation wore its cross-cultural status like a badge of honor upon its sleeve. They overtly boasted about the ideal church the previous pastor had created over more than three decades, but failed to understand why it was important for them to actually interact with the African members in their midst. While they had been generous in their financial support of certain African members, they seemed incapable of moving beyond that paternalistic, condescending stance. They were sophisticated enough to be unfailingly polite, but they did not know the names of their African members, nor the names of their children.

When I suggested that the African women in their church be invited to host an evening dinner event, the more overt aspects of their hidden racism emerged. In the classic management style of every Presbyterian planning process, this suggestion was referred to a committee. When I sat with the committee and we talked together about my suggestion, one woman declared that the white women in that church had never been invited to host a dinner event. This blatant untruth hung in the air like an awful bird of prey hovering over a carcass, but not one person confronted the lie that had been spoken. When this event was announced, it had been morphed into "an international dinner" where everyone was invited to bring food that represented their native country. White folks sat with their white friends and black folks did the same. Interaction between races was so minimal, it was not only discouraging, it was heartbreaking. The collective shadow refusal was so palpable, you could have plucked it out of the atmosphere, formed it into a body of denial and pretension, and set it upon their fine white tablecloth as an accusatory witness. Their masterful game of "Let's Pretend" was never more evident than on that night.

In the Presbyterian Church, USA, conflict on a national level has evolved into open verbal warfare over recent decades. A conservative faction began to rise to the surface during the years of the Reagan administration. It gained further strength during the first Bush administration, and now has the kind of big-money backing typical of these movements during the present day. This conservative offensive, and the accompanying conflict with those who take a more liberal view of theology and religious practice, became so pronounced that the church attempted reconciliation through a committee appointed for that specific purpose.

This committee was singularly unsuccessful in its attempts at productive conversation. Never mind reconciliation—these people were hard-pressed to maintain even a facade of civility. The attempt at reconciliation failed because an inflexible stance was adopted by both sides; thus, negotiation of any kind became impossible. In essence, this battle is one of control, nothing less and nothing more.

Lest it be said that Presbyterians give up too easily, as the continuing conflict waxed and waned throughout the denomination, it was determined that another attempt must be made toward resolution of some kind. In the summer of 2001 a Theological Task Force on Peace, Unity, and Purity was appointed by the General Assembly to "address issues of contention facing the Presbyterian Church, (USA)." Composed of twenty-one members from across a broad spectrum of churches and agencies in the denomination, this task force was assigned a virtually impossible task.

While the sons and daughters of this nation are dying in the streets, where guns are as numerous as the televisions to which we are addicted, the church argues over who will articulate its stance and define its theological doctrine. We argue with strained courtesy over who will define "tradition." Many elderly adults lie in the urine stench of nursing homes, but we focus, instead, on "addressing contention" in the church. Millions of homeless Americans struggle to survive one more frigid winter season, but the church pours its energy into deciding who is worthy of church affiliation and the privilege of church office. Presbyterians have not embarked upon a singular or unique journey. No denomination is exempt from this current dynamic. Every mainline church in the nation has spent countless dollars and hours of wasted spiritual energy on this "contentious" phenomenon during the last several decades.

The denial of shadow, and its concomitant idolatrous projection, are part of an underlying abdication of responsibility by the collective in most churches. The membership abdicates its responsibility for both its own individual and collective shadow and for nurturance of the soul and spirit. The members of the clergy are expected to provide these critical spiritual components. At the same time the institution and its clergy-leaders are expected to be without shadow, without a dark side of any kind, even though such a thing is humanly impossible. The resultant unleashing of unconscious shadow is made much more powerful by these ever-present dynamics.

This shadow denial began when the first books of the New Testament were written. Those who wrote of Jesus, beginning their work in a political arena from an apologist's perspective, wrote of Jesus in a particular way. While on the one hand they wrote of his humanity, they stripped that humanity of its full depth and breadth by claiming that Jesus was perfect and without sin.

Jesus was surely a man whose humanity was different from other humans. He embodied a full awareness of divine consciousness, even in his youth. Yet when he was very tired, his shadow showed through. The perfectionistic descriptors used by biblical writers, however, forced the image of Jesus into an illusory mold where shadow had no place. And yet, shadow always is present, whether it is owned or denied. The denial of shadow within the institutional church began more than two thousand years ago. Due to its long history and traditional character, the energy of this shadow denial has taken on gigantic proportions. It has become a habit of the mind with great energy, because it has been part of the unconscious assumptions inculcated both inside and outside the institutional church.

The people who make up the church, while on the one hand claiming they do not expect their pastors to be superhuman, on the other hand unconsciously demand an extreme level of perfection of these same leaders. But what sort of Jesus is the pastor to represent or emulate? Is it the real Jesus whom the text reveals as fully human, with a temper and frustration and fatigue? Or is it the emasculated "gentle Jesus meek and mild" of legend and nineteenth century piety?

These assumptions of perfection are the meat of shadow denial. They foster unconscious projections of perfection within the institutional church, and outside it, too. Very few people who claim to be disinterested in the church are actually disinterested. More often they are disenchanted with a social institution that functions like every other major corporation. Yet, the more the expectation of something beyond human, something more perfect than human capacity, especially from the human institution that is the church, the more the shadow is evident in every facet of the church and among its detractors, and the greater the shadow's power. Those inside the church and those outside it are bound together by one defining characteristic, a denial of shadow. Churches where mistakes and fallibility are accepted as part of being human find ways to have reasonable conversations together when conflict arises. These churches are far healthier than those where idealistic projections are tossed about.

Church professionals have tried to describe healthy churches for many years. Using many theories and resources, church consultants strive to define what a healthy church looks like, and how its members act. Often when pastors are searching for a new position, they will have a conversation with an executive or bishop who will describe a particular church as a "healthy" church. The only "healthy" church would be one fully capable of acknowledging its shadow side. Since few people are able to do so, few churches are able to do so. The ambiguity of the collective stands as a prohibitive obstacle to such psychic movement.

The church, in its focus upon all that is bright and shining, upon Jesus as "Light of All Light" has, for more than two thousand years, been in love with an ideal. The ideal does not exist. It lacks a shadow side. The shadow side of both God and the church is vital to the creative life of spiritual development, for the ability of the church to interact authentically with those who pass through its doors is predicated upon how honest it is with self and other.

For many years, the denied shadow in the church has also meant the church denied its own wrongdoing, heaping insult upon injury. The sexual abuse in the Catholic Church described by Jason Berry in his book, *Lead Us Not Into Temptation*, has been a known fact since the mid-1980s. One Catholic clergyman reported that "no one believed him in 1985 when he warned Roman Catholic leaders that resolving cases of sexually abusive priests could eventually cost the church more than $1 billion" (AP, the *Roanoke Times*, 6/10/05, 1A).

One archbishop declared with more than a little arrogance, "No one's ever going to sue the Catholic Church."

Yet, on July 17, 2007, the Los Angeles Archdiocese announced that it had reached a landmark settlement of $660 million to be paid to victims of clergy sex abuse (AP, *The International Herald Tribune*, 7/17/07). According to the *New York Times*, this settlement involved 508 plaintiffs in cases that dated from the 1940s. This settlement was only reached after four and a half years of negotiations. It made the 2003 settlement of $85 million by the Archdiocese of Boston seem paltry by comparison.(Reuters, the *New York Times*, 7/17/07; also Goodstein, NYT, 7/17/07).

Matthew Fox tells the story of a parish priest in Manhattan who decided to offer a midweek workshop of reconciliation to people who had been wounded by the institutional church in the past (Fox, Tape 1). The priest set about formulating his plans, advertising this workshop as a time when people who had left the church because of such wounding could come and talk about what had happened to them in the church. Using the average number of people attending regular mass as his baseline, this priest assumed he would have about thirty-five participants. Instead, more than 450 people showed up, far more than he had ever had at mass. Such is the magnitude of the church's shadow, historically, and in the present time.

There was a time when the hierarchy of the institutional church could keep a lid on its scandals and shadow secrets. But those who worked on its fringes, in highly visible televised arenas, were those who revealed the shadow of Christianity at its worst. The ugly little secret lives of the Jim Bakkers and the Jimmy Swaggarts of televangelism infamy became a kind of watershed, a breaking point for church in society. No longer could the institutional church deny the visible and embarrassing shadow aspects of itself. Yet, in spite of an outburst of negative information from the evangelical strand of the church, mainline denominations were struggling mightily to conceal their warts.

Two definitive books about sexual misconduct, one by an investigative journalist (Jason Berry) and one by a woman pastor, Marie Fortune, had a marked impact on the positive public-relations campaigns of the institutional church. Jason Berry's book, *Lead Us Not into Temptation*, is a soul-rending description of the magnitude of sexual misconduct within the Roman Catholic church, soul-rending because Jason Berry is himself a Catholic who mourns for his church, and for his faith. Even as he reveals information about numerous incidences of inappropriate and unethical behavior by clergy and those within the hierarchy who later protect clergy, Berry wants his church to be healthy. The salient issue, again, is the intensity of the denial. Berry wrote,

> I had come to see the molestation cases as symptomatic of a larger breakdown in ecclesiastical life. If there were

four (as reported) or six (now certain) priest-child molesters, that was a question of degree. Playing musical chairs with such men stemmed from a denial mentality I was only beginning to fathom. The church's contorted views of sexuality folded into a mind set that tolerated both pedophiles and sexually active gay priests.... Secrecy was the glue that bound priests together when the church was under attack—while other priests vented their outrage by leaking information to me (135-136).

Secrecy has always been the glue that bound the church together with certain of its clergy and its membership, for secrecy is a code of honor in churches where the shadow has flowered and produced progeny. For clergy working within such churches, revealing these secrets will most often bring condemnations of a failure to honor so-called "confidentiality."

Accusations related to breaking confidentiality are the verbal bludgeon most often used to maintain this unhealthy secrecy. Berry's book unleashed a torrent of further denials and condemnations, even before its publication. He wrote of a priest whose principal vocation was counseling, since he held a degree in psychiatry. A highly effective speaker and negotiator, this priest told a conference of Canadian and American bishops, "The Christian church has had an exclusive focus on the genitals as comprising all of human sexuality.... The chasm between the biological sciences and theological sciences continues to cause, rather than heal, much human suffering" (203-204). Yet this priest had his own secret, his homosexuality, something he chose to conceal right up to the time he died of AIDS. After his death, colleagues spoke with candor about his homosexuality; it was the typical church secret that was not a secret.

Berry opined, "As a psychiatrist-priest, he found exalted status in a clerical culture primed on therapy as a new confession. Penance still existed, but the examination of conscience was readily adaptable to patient-therapist dialogue in a larger search for causes and effects of psychological pain" (197).

A decade later, as reports of the enormity of the misconduct in the Catholic church were released to the public, Anna Quindlen wrote in a *Newsweek* essay, "Cardinal Edward Egan of New York, who somehow managed for a long time to contain his public outrage at pedophiles in the priestly ranks, decried the notion of same-sex marriage and referred to 'the desecration of something sacred.'" (68). Quindlen continued, "To characterize this sort of devotion as desecration is reprehensible. Anyone who defines marriage largely in terms of what happens in bed has never been married. Which may explain the Catholic Church's official reaction."

Penance may still exist as a part of the Catholic tradition, but like its reformed counterpart, its value has been tempered by the impact of the culture upon the church. Acknowledging shadow is one of the purposes of confession. The prayers of confession in the Protestant tradition differ from the confessional of the Catholic Church. Watching to see the widespread reluctance or absolute refusal to participate in such prayers can be a stark reality check for pastors in churches where these prayers are an accepted part of the worship service. The weakness of the reformed understanding of confession may be in its lack of tangible penance. No particular action is stipulated, no intentional participation is called forth, and no restitution is required.

The Roman Catholic tradition of exacting a tangible act of repentance, a penance for sin, has been replaced in the reformed tradition with a brief liturgy of atonement, often called "The Assurance of Pardon." This brief assurance has been trivialized into a trite, rote answer, evoking no unique reaction from those who are supposedly blessed by it. Appropriate psychic sacrifice is necessary, and the pale substitute in the reformed tradition is an inadequate ritual.

Still greater numbers of people have no forum for confession or repentance, even if they are members of the institutional church. Many churches have dispensed with prayers of confession altogether. They concentrate on praise, adoration, and elevation of Jesus as the perfect son of a perfect father whose perfect heaven will be shared with others who hold identical beliefs. I will claim this as my shadow pronouncement about a certain worship style, but such entertainment-based worship services promote even more denial of shadow. They foster the notion that Jesus has already done all the work. The popularity of that old gospel favorite "Jesus Paid It All" is an indicator of this notion among many Christians. If Jesus paid it all, then that must mean repentance is unnecessary. Such ways of denying shadow simply allow it to go underground, where it flourishes in secret, for secrecy in churches is the rich and fertile garden where the shadow blossoms with vigor.

Marie Fortune, in her book entitled *Is Nothing Sacred?* wrote of a Protestant pastor who dabbled in sexual misconduct with a complete lack of respect for the soul-wounding of those women who were his targets. Ultimately, six women filed charges of professional misconduct against him. Fortune's book details the abuse of power in the institutional church once these charges were brought. She wrote,

> Institutions also share a pattern of response to the misconduct of an authorized representative and to the public disclosure of that misconduct. An institution acts first on what it perceives to be its self-interest. Seldom does it identify its self-interest to be the same as the interests of the people it is supposed to serve. Thus it tries to protect itself by preventing disclosure of professional misconduct. It prefers instead to shoot the messenger, that is, to denigrate whoever had the courage to tell the secret (p. xiv).

Shadow extroversion thrives in secret. The one who is bold enough to reveal such secrets is the one who will often be forced to face the formidable and dominant opponent that is the larger institutional church. The notion that the church represents a place of sanctuary, some sort of celestial environment, where one is both safe and cared for with compassionate love, is an illusion. On the contrary, the church is that place where clergy shadow is safest, for it is the place where clergy and laity alike have historically refused to claim either individual or collective shadow.

Many of those who become clergy do so out of a profound shadow need. Sometimes "the call" to ministry is a shadow impetus to address unacceptable, even monstrous, psychic aspects of one's self. As clergy unconsciously strive to resolve that which rises out of the deepest primordial murk of the psyche to force them to look into its wart-filled face, they enter the ministry as a way of running away from the shadow. There they find a safe haven, for the church is the place where shadow is denied, and "being good" is valued far more than being honest with self or others.

On Friday, January 30, 2004, NBC television in its Dateline program featured the story of a family profoundly harmed by a Catholic priest. This priest had an affair with their mother, who ultimately committed suicide in his presence. When she lost consciousness, he left her nude body in her home and went for a walk to ponder the situation, only calling for emergency care when it was too late to save her life. The story of this mother's anguish was heart-rending; it included years of desperate depression, confinement within a psychiatric facility, a surgical lobotomy and the birth of two children who were fathered by this priest. For thirty years the diocese maintained secret records related to this situation, and her four children did not know the truth about their mother's death until they were able to secure secret documents held for decades by the Catholic Church. The final disposition of this case was a monetary payoff by the church, though no amount of money can heal the wounds inflicted on this woman or her children.

The vehemence with which the institutional church denies the reality of human sexuality is the yardstick by which its shadow can be measured. The Roman Catholic Church is not the only branch of the Christian church where issues of sexual misconduct have presented themselves. Two highly visible men, both presidents of well-known Presbyterian seminaries, have been charged with sexual misconduct in recent years. Both men left their high-profile positions. In one case, the Board of Trustees apparently knew the reason for the abrupt early departure of the president (of the seminary from which I graduated), but did not reveal this information to "the seminary community" from whom it solicited funds for a festive going-away dinner with its accompanying accolades. A year later, the true reason for his departure was finally disclosed to those from whom these funds were solicited and garnered.

Some readers might think that this example, since it only includes two men, is inadequate. The weight of this misconduct hinges upon the fact that both these men were presidents of well-known, high profile seminaries where Presbyterian and other denominational clergy are trained. Their influence was potentially far greater than that of one clergy person in one church. Their misconduct, with more than a few students, created untold negative influences on those they preyed upon, and the congregations those clergy would subsequently serve.

On February 9, 2004, more than ten years after Jason Berry published his book on sexual misconduct within the Catholic Church, the Associated Press reported that the Roman Catholic Diocese of Orlando had paid out $4.2 million to three dozen victims who accused twelve priests of sexual misconduct with children. These payments, all covered by insurance, were reported as part of a national survey to determine the extent of sexual abuse within the church since 1950 (the *Boston Globe*, 2/9/04; the *Roanoke Times*, 2/9/04, A-4). These twelve priests had been removed from the ministry. The same cannot be said of some of the clergy who commit sexual misconduct in my denomination.

When Pope John Paul II died in the spring of 2005, the Vatican sent a shadow message out into the global arena when former Cardinal Bernard Law was appointed to celebrate the fourth Mass of mourning for the pope. This church leader had been forced to resign from his position in Boston because of scandals related to more than four hundred claims of child sexual abuse by priests who were pedophiles. When Pope John Paul II died, the Vatican ignored protests by American Catholics asking that former Cardinal Law not be given this visible role in official ceremonies related to the pope's funeral. This cardinal, who had been appointed to the Vatican position of Archpriest of St. Mary Major Basilica after he had left Boston, was taken under the protective wing of the Vatican hierarchy and given a position of honor and authority.

My experience in the Presbyterian Church, USA leads me to believe there are numerous pastors who are equally as guilty of heterosexual misconduct who are sheltered by the good-old-boy network that prevails as an undertow in every denomination. I personally know of men who were previous pastors of "tall steeple churches" (i.e. sizeable churches) who have admitted having "numerous" liaisons with women in their congregations. How would "numerous" be defined? When confronted, both of these married men admitted to more than thirty affairs with women in the parishes they had served. I know this to be true, because I confronted one of them, and a colleague confronted the other. Yet both are "honorably retired" from their last parishes without a shred of scandal. If they admitted to that many encounters with women outside their marriages, the real number would have exceeded that figure by at least twenty percent. My informed guess is that it was double the number to which they admitted.

Sexual misconduct among clergy is marked by the innumerable ways it presents itself, the shadow excuses that are offered for its extroversion, and the ways it is denied by power brokers. For example, the Associated Press reported that a pastor who was charged with four counts of sexual misconduct with an underage girl, or statutory rape, had been appointed to the national Faith-Based Initiative Commission in Washington by Senator George Allen when he was Governor of the State of Virginia. While this pastor came from the evangelical strand of American clergy, I watched the ludicrous drama that evolved around another member of the clergy, a "tall steeple man," as it was played out in my own denomination.

In one of the eight presbyteries where I have worked, I attended a presbytery meeting where I was handed a huge stack of evidence gathered about the sexual misconduct of a pastor who served one of the largest churches in the state. The irrefutable evidence of his professional and personal misconduct, detailed in page after page of sordid information, was distributed to all the commissioners in the presbytery. Was he stripped of his ordination? Was he terminated from his position? Was his salary reduced or was he required to pay a fine of some sort? No. The answer to all of these questions is—No! He was brought before the presbytery and rebuked. This rebuke took the form of a verbal smack on the wrist and a caution to be good in the future. Did he stand alone to receive his wrist smacking? No, again. He was surrounded by eight elders, all male members of his governing board, who "stood with him" during his thirty second rebuke. He returned to his tall steeple church and continued in the same capacity as its senior pastor, drawing a salary that had exceeded six figures for many years.

Did he heed the advice of those who counseled him with such concern for his well-being? No. Less than ten years later, this same man was again accused of sexual misconduct. This time he simply renounced the jurisdiction of the denomination and retired, to receive the high-dollar pension that had been funded by those who continued to adore him. Civil charges were never filed against him. Despite his lack of professional integrity, he retired with full pension benefits. Despite his failure to exhibit a shred of compassion for either his wife or the women with whom he had liaisons over many years, this man retired to a comfortable income, guaranteed for life. Of course, the other tall steeple pastors to whom I referred earlier did the same thing; they were never charged with misconduct. As long as the institutional church pretends that its shadow teachings and ecclesiastical embarrassment about human sexuality are not a massive problem, this immense problem will persist.

A number of writers, Catholic and non-Catholic, have written books urging major changes in the Catholic stipulations about an all-male priesthood and its required celibacy. James Carroll, writing in a book entitled *Toward a New Catholic Church*, advocates sweeping changes that more nearly reflect the reality of a twenty-first century world, including women clergy and a relaxation of the stringent rules governing divorce, celibacy, and birth control. Carroll is a former priest who speaks from an informed and credible stance (Ostling, 7/26/03, C-8). However, celibacy is not a part of the Protestant tradition; but its pastors are not exempt from the same shadow extroversion that overtakes Catholic priests, and Protestant churches struggle with sexuality as much as do Catholics. It simply reveals itself in different ways.

One source of the problem is the institutional church's inability to consider sexuality in healthy, balanced, or appropriate ways. Some members of the clergy, as well as denominational resources, like to refer to sexuality as "God's good gift to humankind." But the historical undertow of thousands of years of the church's embarrassment about the body and its sexuality has created a morphic field of resistance to authentic dialogue about this "good gift." The reader will find a more complete exploration of this topic in Peter Brown's book, *The Body and Society: Men, Women, and Sexual Renunciation in Early Christianity*. My book *The Magdalene Legacy: Exploring the Wounded Icon of Sexuality* also discusses the historical dynamics of the church's aberrant views of sexuality. The current trend toward a more conservative view of God colors the morphic field of energy where churches function. This trend feeds old habits of the mind and creates an environment for more shadow secrecy. The historical repression of healthy sexuality enables the shadow extroversion of sexual misconduct by clergy.

An interesting correlation between financial malfeasance and clergy sexual misconduct is something I cannot substantiate with statistical data, but in investigating clergy misconduct I have found that there seems to be a correlation. A colleague who has worked on committees that investigated misconduct agrees with my concerns. She has also found that often there are questionable financial practices in the same congregations where clergy were subsequently found guilty of sexual misconduct.

The February 26, 2007 issue of *Time* magazine features a story on financial malfeasance in the already beleaguered Catholic Church. The Roman Catholic diocese in Palm Beach, Florida sent in auditors to a parish in Delray Beach. These auditors estimate that two different priests misappropriated $ 8.6 million over a period of forty-two years (Padgett, 46-47). Internal financial controls in Catholic parishes were so lax that one survey found that 85% of seventy-eight dioceses reported embezzlement cases.

A day later, the Associated Press reported that the Roman Catholic diocese of Richmond, Virginia had found that one of its priests had embezzled $ 600,000. This same priest had retired and was living "with a woman and three children," but was not married to the woman, even though he had referred to her "his wife" for the past decade.

In the matter of sexual misconduct, the final report of the National Review Board, conducted by the John Jay College of Criminal Justice in New York and using the Catholic Church's own numbers, reported that more than 10,000 minors were violated by more than 4,000 priests in a time period between 1950 and 2002. Of these abuses, most of those who were perpetrators were never prosecuted because few of these abuses were ever reported, and 95% of the abusers were never charged with any crime ("The Facts." the *Baltimore Sun*, 3/9/04).

In response to this report, James Carroll lamented:

> Catholics cannot hear this news the way other people do. For us the devastation and anger involve also a measure of personal remorse. It is not only that our entire church stands indicted—from its system of authority to its clerical culture to its tradition of secrecy to its basic teachings about morality—but also that each of us has reason to feel implicated. I am not talking about a generalized corporate guilt here, nor do I mean to take away from the particular responsibility of individual perpetrators. *But this massive failure could not have happened if we the church had not enabled it* (the *Boston Globe*, 3/27/04, italics mine).

James Carroll knows the Catholic Church as well, or better, than I know the Presbyterian Church, USA. Those inside the political institution that is "church" know its warts from the inside, and if one is willing to suspend personal integrity in favor of loyalty to this political institution, one can advance along a career track with relative ease. To speak honestly about the underbelly of the church provokes an opposite reaction.

As James Carroll continued his articulation of grief over the stark statistics reported about the fifty-year history of abuse in the Catholic Church, he wrote:

> When we cooperated in the climate of dishonesty that pollutes the church's teachings about sex, not making an issue, for example, of the absurd birth control prohibition, we were shoring up, in Garry Wills's phrase, the "structure of deceit" on which abusive priests depended. When we declined to hold bishops accountable for their excessively autocratic exercise of authority in small matters (forbidding girls from serving at Mass) and large (closing parish schools without consultation), we supported the power system that bishops were protecting in protecting abusers. When we failed to make an issue of the unjust discriminations against women embodied in the male-only priesthood, *we were part of what allowed patriarchal clericalism to reach its present state of calcified corruption.* When we passively accepted the hierarchy's refusal to implement the Vatican II reforms aimed at empowering the laity, we gave the abusive priests a place to hide and their sponsoring bishops a way to keep them hidden (the *Boston Globe,* 3/27/04, italics mine).

This eloquent lamentation is an equally eloquent accusation of the "calcified corruption" that bedevils the Catholic Church. Despite these numbers, when one diocesan official was questioned about this same report, he opined, "They did good ministry, they were good to their people, they were kind, compassionate. It was that era of the 60s.... The whole atmosphere out there was, it was OK, it was OK to do" (Sniezyk, 21). Never has one person verbalized the way the shadow feeds cognitive dissonance more clearly.

When asked for clarity about this seemingly relaxed and permissive atmosphere, this same official "clarified that sexual misconduct in any context is unacceptable." But, his shadow answer revealed the depths of denial still evident in the Catholic hierarchy. The only difference between the levels of corruptive calcification in the Catholic Church and its Protestant counterpart is that such sexual misconduct usually occurs between clergy and adult in the Protestant ecclesiastical strand. Furthermore, the well-documented tendency of perpetrators of sexual misconduct to seek out multiple victims, just as do pedophiles, is part of the "dirty little secret" kept carefully tucked into the bottom drawer of the Presbyterian Church, USA. A large majority of these Protestant members of the clergy are never charged with misconduct, because the system mediates against it. These male clergy prey upon women who seem to acquiesce in such liaisons, often functioning from a victim's simplistic, childish attitudes of trust and an accompanying tendency to idolize pastors. Here I refer to women who are victimized, since most of the sexual misconduct charges brought in any presbytery are brought against men.

On February 22, 2007, the *Roanoke Times* picked up an Associated Press report on molestation inside the Baptist church. One woman reported that she was raped by her pastor at age 15 and later impregnated by him at age 18. When the pregnancy was discovered, she was verbally mauled by church leaders, who "forced her to go before the congregation and ask forgiveness as an unwed mother." The pastor, who had moved on to another parish, has "acknowledged that he had a sexual relationship with (her) and was the father of her child."

Yet, these same men profess an innocence that pretends to be unaware of their own tendency to seek out women or children to comfort themselves. When a male pastor tells me, in what he believes is a guileless protest of innocence, that he has sought out a female physician from his own parish to be his personal doctor, I know he has no concept of appropriate boundaries. If he does have such a concept, he has apparently pushed it so far back into the outer reaches of his psyche as to make it inaccessible. When he then admits to having a sexual escapade with this same person, he is revealing the extent to which he functions from his shadow.

As he laughingly declared, "Well, I went in to have a physical, and she got physical!" he discounted his willing participation in getting physical.

When both of these married professionals protest the innocence of their liaison, they are declaring the delusional levels of their day-to-day interactions, and revealing their shadow personalities. As he joked about the requirement for nudity in a physical examination, he pretended to be the victim and named the doctor the aggressor. His passive aggression was an active player in the foregoing scenario, and his claim to being a victim was the patent shadow lie he told himself as he played "Let's Pretend" with himself and everyone else. His blurred boundaries were symbolic of so many blurred boundaries in our culture. Blurred boundaries are very much a part of the shadow undertow inside the church.

In my work with more than a dozen churches I have found that churches where boundaries were breached were the unhealthiest churches. They reflected the family systems of dysfunctional families with no appropriate boundaries. Those who assumed they could open the locked door to the pastor's office and rummage through the desk were also those who carefully concealed their own family secrets from the public eye.

The blurring of the line between religion and politics is similar to the blurring of appropriate boundaries inside many churches. The ambiguity created by this blurring of boundaries, and the resultant lack of understanding of its dynamic energy, thrusts aspects of religion into every facet of public life. Fifty years after "under God" was added to the original Pledge of Allegiance it emerged again as part of the unending debate about church and state. When this original document was written, it did not include this phrase, since the separation of church and state was assumed to be an integral part of our democracy. This phrase was not added until, during the Eisenhower administration, fear clamped itself around the throat of hearings chaired by McCarthy. The negative energy created by Senator Joseph McCarthy caused public leaders to feel compelled to assert their belief in God, so that they would not, by default, be accused of ascribing to Communism. If you weren't part of the God believers, you were suspect, and obviously sympathetic to the Communists. Fear of McCarthy and his cronies provoked this change in a national document.

As America shifts into the twenty-first century these same scare tactics have crawled out of dusty closets, rat holes, and secret places where they have been waiting for an opportunity to pounce on the God-beliefs of ordinary citizens. By using fear as their "sword of righteousness," right-wing aggressors have taken the national wounding at the heart of the events of 9/11 and used it as "emotional currency," spending it with vigor and aforethought. By emphasizing danger and terrorism and the dreaded potential for another terrorist attack, these "spiritual warriors" drive fearful souls into the corral of their rigid belief structure, herding them with their "us against them" thinking patterns, and branding these same trusting souls with emphatic pronouncements about "good and evil." After corralling their audience, the fear-filled message continues unabated, for as our president would remind us, "If you're not with us, you're against us." That blatant, fist-in-the-air declaration sets the tone for denying the shadow with more vigor and negative energy than was evident during the Red Scare of the McCarthy era.

Lest the reader despair of ever finding hope in any form among the pages of this book, it will be explored in depth beginning with chapter ten. Beginning with individual shadow, ways of healing this energy will be explored. The shadow is so powerful and misunderstood that I have included this multitude of explanations on its character and energy in our culture. Such explanations have been necessary before finding ways to address positive changes in this same powerful dynamic.

Chapter 8

The Money Factor and Judas

The currency of the kingdom is an insistent symbol of class and status, whether in a contemporary culture or during biblical times. Money is a dominant defining aspect of the shadow and part of a long historic line of shadow symbolism. In the gospel of Luke, Jesus tells a parable of a woman who, at losing one of ten silver coins, lights a lamp and sweeps the house, searching carefully until she finds it. Upon recovering the lost coin, she calls together her neighbors and friends, who rejoice with her. They celebrate because she has found this one seemingly insignificant coin.

This story has been interpreted as a parallel with the parables told in the preceding and succeeding verses (Luke 15:3-7 and Luke 15:11-32), and for generations commentators have seen only the parallel aspects of this story. When writing their commentary on the text of the lost coin, its significance is usually sublimated into the parables around it. The particularity of its meaning is lost to a focus on the parables which surround it, most particularly the parable of the prodigal son. This lost coin parable is also linked to one in which a shepherd searches for one lone sheep out of a flock of many. This story is symbolic of the biblical stories of women and their historic roles. By thrusting a shadow interpretation upon this text, the significance of this woman's story is lost.

The story of the woman and the lost coin appears only in the gospel of Luke. This may have been because Luke, among the gospel writers, tended to explore the stories of women. The generally accepted scholarship on this gospel implies that the Lukan accounts are more sympathetic toward women than the other three. Theologian Jane Schaberg refuted this scholarly assumption when she declared, "Even as this Gospel highlights women as included among the followers of Jesus…, it deftly portrays them as models of subordinate service, excluded from the power center of the movement and from significant responsibilities. Claiming the authority of Jesus, this portrayal is an attempt to legitimate male dominance in the Christianity of the author's time. It was successful. The danger lies in the subtle artistic power of the story to seduce the reader into uncritical acceptance of it as simple history, and into acceptance of the depicted gender roles as divinely ordained" (275).

When studying the parable of the lost coin, the reader would find that the ending of this story does not make much sense, if accepted scholarship is accurate, because the celebration that ensues seems to be an overreaction to what has occurred. Most commentators write of this woman as poor, and of her search as significant because this one coin represents a ten percent loss of her meager savings. These *coins, however, symbolize her marital status.*

During this time in Jewish history, it was customary for women who married to receive a headband. Presented to them on their wedding day, this headband was a gift of symbolic importance. Elaborately embroidered, sometimes with silver or gold stitches in a pattern of filigree, this headband was decorated with ten silver coins. The number of coins never varied; there were always ten coins attached to the headband, their number perhaps symbolizing the Decalogue—the Ten Commandments. If this woman had married into a working-class family, the ten silver coins might have been Roman denarii. If she married into a more affluent family, these coins would be Tyrian shekels or Antiochan staters.

No matter what coins were used on this headband, it symbolized the woman's status as a wife and mother in Israel, a status which was the highest any Jewish woman could attain during that time. The headband was then worn so that the ten coins were suspended across the front of the woman's forehead when she went out into public. Any married woman who appeared in public was bound by this clothing norm; she could not go out unless she was wearing her headband with all of its coins in place.

If a woman was accused of adultery, and found by the rabbis who sat in judgment to be guilty as charged, one of the ten coins from her headband was removed, as a symbol of her guilt. By removing the coin, the rabbis sealed her fate. No married woman could appear in public, at any kind of function, religious or social, without her headband. To appear with a coin missing was a humiliating, public admission of a rabbinical sentence of adultery. In this culture, stoning those who had been found guilty of adultery was a common practice. To wear this headband with a coin missing into a public place was to invite death by stoning.

When Jesus tells this story, he implies the woman has lost the coin through carelessness. Finding it provokes a celebration, because finding the coin is critical. This missing coin restores her reputation for virtue, and her status in the community. In this one coin, missing from her headband, her very life hangs in the balance (Hatcher, 23).

Not one of the seven commentaries I consulted, all written by male theologians, explores this hidden cultural piece of the parable. One commentator, with more than a small touch of arrogance, wrote, "Perhaps the coin was part of a headdress of coins; there is no law against such an interpretation" (Butterick, 268). Yet this parable is a story about a woman who will be put to death unless she retrieves this lost coin.

Another commentator opined, "The money would appear to represent the woman's savings or dowry, and it is often suggested that the ten coins may have been worn on a string as a headdress (cf. Kel. 12:7; Jeremias, Jerusalem, 100; Parables, 134f.); but there is no proof that this was so (Klostermann, 157)." (Marshall, 603) Here, in a convoluted stretch at scholarship, this commentator rejects three sources of "proof" in favor of one source who discounts the validity of such proof. In actuality, there is precious little proof for numerous details in the canon, yet they have been perceived and presented as truth for eons. The virgin birth, which Catholic theologian Hans Küng called "a collection of largely uncertain, mutually contradictory, strongly legendary stories," comes quickly to mind (Kristof, NYT, 8/15/03, A-29).

Still another commentator declared, "The main figure is a poor woman who has lost one of her ten drachmas. Luke may intend to depict her as miserly. In any case, she serves to portray divine initiative in seeking out what was lost..., the sinner" (Fitzmyer, 1080).

If Jesus told the parables (found before and after this one in the Lukan text) at the same time, they might have had parallel meanings. Even if this parable serves to form a triptych, it stands alone. It was not included in the other synoptic gospels, so to force it into a parallel takes some exegetical strain by commentators who fail to note its absence from the synoptic texts. This story is one for women about women, a story that speaks to the status of women. That status has been defined for generations by the culture in which they live. In it, morality is locked around the significance of losing that one coin, because the ten coins were symbols of a moral norm. Jesus is telling his listeners that this woman, by carelessly losing the coin, was unwittingly thrust into a situation that called her virtue into question and sentenced her to death.

The Judas legacy emerges when twentieth-century, male biblical scholars take a simple story told in a different culture, in a different historical context, and imbue it with a contemporary pietistic and symbolic meaning. Exegetical methodology, the process of translating and explaining the biblical text, has been fraught with this problem. Religious sentimentality has been thrust upon exegesis for eons. The deeper, richer meaning of this story has been swept away in a sea of religiosity, as commentators mistakenly discount the unique qualities of this parable.

By missing the symbolic importance of the coins in this story, the symbolic, sacred aspects of money are unconsciously demeaned. Perhaps we would benefit from knowing its ancient significance. In ancient times the Roman mint was located in the Capitoline temple of the great Mother Goddess, Juno Moneta. The word "money" apparently originated from the name of this goddess. Whether manufactured of silver or gold, the value of this currency was derived from the inherent blessing the goddess cast upon it inside her sacred temple. Later, popes who wanted to appease those who held a profound remembrance of this sacred aspect of money began to bless Christian amulets and holy medals, since both were used in trade in the place of money (Walker, 667). These same popes denigrated the sacred significance of money by selling indulgences. Martin Luther's vehement disagreement with this profane commerce in the church ultimately provoked the Protestant Reformation.

These sacred strands of money's history are forgotten in a contemporary culture that elevates someone like Paris Hilton to the status of celebrity, not because she has ever accomplished anything in her self-absorbed lifetime, but because she is the inheritor of some portion of her family's wealth. Money may be the reified coinage of Marxist theory, or the implied symbol of contemporary success, but to live in a money-based economy is to recognize its power. Money has become the shadow god worshiped by a nation that idolizes it above all other gods. Manipulating with money is one of the powerful ways the shadow gains and holds control in any culture.

Unhealthy attitudes related to money are one of the more visceral and visible aspects of the Judas legacy. Judas will always hold a place of archetypal significance because of those thirty pieces of silver. Canonical accounts vary. One New Testament author declares that he returned the bribe. To have taken it in the first place was the more damning piece of the story. This memory is held at the deepest psychic levels of the collective unconscious. Judas betrayed for money, and that betrayal was a betrayal of God among us.

Every time a congressional politician attaches a large pork barrel appropriation to an unrelated piece of legislation, shadow betrayal is evident. Every time a federal-tax rebate results in an unbalanced federal budget, shadow betrayal has been an active participant in the cognitive dissonance and distorted thinking that pushed this bill to passage. Every time military budgets are increased exponentially, while social programs benefiting education for children or care for the elderly and/or the homeless are dramatically decreased, the shadow has been effective in its delusionary tactics.

One of the most powerful ways the shadow reveals itself around money is evident in the institutional church. In my life experience, I have found the surest and most accurate way to find the individual or corporate shadow in any church is to watch for the ways people manipulate (or try to manipulate) with money. Our culture manipulates with money more than in any other way, and those who are part of the church are no exception in this practice.

My experience as the pastor of a church where the treasurer played unceasing games with the church's money supported the hypothesis I had developed years earlier. There I was supposed to be paid on the first of each month. When I first arrived in the parish, I thought the treasurer simply wanted to visit with me. When I was invited to drive out to the country to pick up my check every month, a social visit usually ensued. Then it became increasingly apparent that this was a mind game, a game where the treasurer overtly exercised control. My chain was being jerked. At times I would wait to see how long it would take before this officer of the church would offer to pay me. Finally a call would come, somewhere around the middle of the month.

Echoing from the receiver would be a shrill voice, "Well, you must not need your money at all this month, you haven't even called to come out here to get it!"

Most reasonable people would assume the salary check would have been left on the desk, or in the mailbox, on the first of the month. Few people in the corporate world would wait more than two weeks for their regular salary check. There should have been no cat-and-mouse games about driving out to a financial officer's house to pick up the check. This person's need to be controlling about money was part of a dysfunctional personality pattern revealed over succeeding months. Its pathology became more and more evident with the passage of time and events.

At the time, I was also contributing to a tax-deferred savings account. To deposit funds to such an account, the employer must sign paperwork empowering their financial officer to withhold the stipulated amount from the employee's salary. These withheld funds are then deposited to the tax-deferred account. This particular treasurer withheld the funds for this purpose, but failed to deposit them monthly. If the church had been struggling financially, this lag in depositing would have been understandable, but this was a heavily endowed church where money was not a worry. Yet the need to manipulate with money meant that funds were habitually deposited late enough for substantial losses in my earnings to occur.

This church was not a rare exception, but was similar to another church where the collective shadow was a powerful force. When I was interviewed for the position of interim pastor, the governing body tried to negotiate a deal for the amount of salary I would collect. Their proposition was this: if I could do my job well enough to raise receipts by fifteen percent over a period of three months, they would pay me the same salary they had paid the previous pastor. I declined their offer, indicating I would accept only the rate of salary paid to the previous pastor. They realized this was a non-negotiable issue and paid what I demanded. The odd and laughable aspect of this incident came three months later when I realized receipts had risen more than fifteen percent in that time period! Money was, however, a dominant shadow issue in this church, as it is in many churches.

When it was time for the annual review of the financial records, I received a call from the treasurer of the church. In gathering data to be turned over to the review team, three accounts (for which there were no records) showed up in the 1099s received from the bank. When the bank was consulted, these accounts were discovered to be ones started by a member of the church, using the church's name and its federal tax-exempt identification number. This person, however, held no office in the church, nor did this individual have the authorization of the governing body to use its name and tax-exempt identification number. The bank did not hold the corporate resolution required by law for establishing such accounts, since all these accounts had been established in secret. Held for approximately thirty years, an accumulation of thousands of dollars in interest income had been sheltered from federal and state income taxes, without the governing body of the church knowing of their existence.

In consultation with both the regional and national offices of the denomination, the church was advised by the general counsel for the national denomination that their tax-exempt status was jeopardized by these accounts. No one church within a denomination stands alone in its tax-exempt status, but any fraudulent act by one church can potentially jeopardize the tax-exempt status for the entire denomination. This attorney advised the church to direct the bank to freeze these accounts, in order to explain options to the member who had been committing tax fraud. Two options were offered: either the funds could be signed over to the church in whose name they had been held for all those years, or amended income tax returns must be filed for the period of time in which these accounts had been held under the name of the church.

The denominational attorney failed to recognize the power of small town politics. He could never have predicted that the bank would simply release the funds to the member who had initiated the accounts, despite the church's directive to freeze the accounts.

With two meetings of the board, one where the culprit was confronted and one at which this same person was rescued, the underlying collective shadow in this church was set off and turned loose. It roamed at will, even as historically it had been a potent part of the history of this congregation. The member who had committed tax fraud stopped coming to church, and through blatant and subtle innuendo implied that I was the culprit. As the pastor of record, I became the convenient scapegoat onto whom projections of shadow could be targeted. It was highly energizing, because folks were unaware of how much energy can be derived from the shadow.

Groupthink became the order of the day, and the denial implicit in such groupthink was astounding. The peer pressure to achieve group cohesion at the board table was the most obvious and overt that I had witnessed in my lifetime. Irving Janis would have been fascinated at the unhealthy cohesion that emerged around this issue, simply because it fit his theoretic base so superbly. The members of this board, as if they had been collectively programmed from one dominant mind, suspended their individual capability for rational thinking and critical evaluation in order to maintain group cohesion. Absolute and unquestioning loyalty to the group's understandings of the collective self was the applied rule.

Protecting the group or tribe at all costs, in this case one small church, was clearly the determining factor. The intellectual self-censorship which occurred, along with their tendency to share stereotypes of anyone from outside their group as "enemy" and an immense pressure to conform with the group, meant that even those who clearly had misgivings felt that any dissent they might offer would be stifled. The collective shadow chose a scapegoat and I was it.

When I spoke of scapegoating at a board meeting, one vocal and very aggressive woman elder laughed in my face and declared, "Well, of course, you are going to be the scapegoat. After all, you're the outsider. We've known each other all our lives!"

When the regional office of the denomination failed to report this incident to the IRS, I reported this matter to the State Corporation Commission, the FDIC Field Office, the Internal Revenue Service Field Office, and to the Internal Revenue Criminal Investigation Division. My shadow covered all the bases. I did not file charges of any kind. I simply reported the illegal usage of the church's name and its federal tax-exempt identification by an individual who held these accounts for personal purposes and without the appropriate authorization of the church.

The governing board had voted to take no action in the matter once the funds were released back to the person who had held the accounts in the first place. Under the rule of law, every one of the members of this board could have been charged with conspiring to conceal tax fraud. I was the executive corporate officer of record when these accounts came to light. Thus, I would be culpable under the law, for the same reason and despite my opposition to the board's inaction. That was a very tangible concern on my part. But my shadow also demanded its pound of flesh. That impetus for my actions cannot be discounted or denied.

Subsequent events were a continuing reminder of the power of the shadow in our culture today. The governing board learned of my action one day later. Ordinarily, the postal service might take a week to deliver a letter from one part of the state to another. But, in this case, I learned that the bank had been notified by the State Corporation Commission of my letter on Friday, after I had mailed the letter on Thursday. My board had a copy of this letter by Tuesday, and the vocal aggressors on the board were almost apoplectic, because the board had voted not to take any action related to this matter. I was not bound by their action and that was the sticking point. At the next meeting of the board the following week, they spent more than an hour verbally abusing me, although when I invited them to fire me they refused and later insisted on renewing my contract!

Equally as interesting was the reaction of the agencies that had received the letter. The State Corporation Commission, the agency charged with examining the records of state-chartered banks, acted as if it had no reason to be concerned, except to advise the senior bank officer in question so he could cover his own back. The FDIC wrote a letter of response, abdicating all responsibility, since the bank was a state-chartered bank. The original bank kept asking when somebody was going to sue, so they could square off against someone in court. When the object of the exercise was not a lawsuit, they did not know how to respond, except with corporate belligerence.

Each one of these agencies exhibited the most astounding indicators of collective shadow as this event unfolded. The bank of record had erred under federal law when it had not required a corporate resolution for initiating these accounts in the first place. It then took on an attitude of obfuscation and bellicosity when the board sent the letter requesting the funds be frozen. Ultimately, the bank thumbed its nose at the church, indicating that a similar case had been thrown out of court. Its sarcastic message, sent by way of the secretary of the board, was "Go ahead, sue us. We'll tie you up in court for years. You don't have enough money to sue for as long as we can continue this case!"

The underlying assumption of litigation was a dominant characteristic of conversations about this issue, as I was advised repeatedly to seek the advice of an attorney. A worried representative from the regional level of the denomination called in agitation, indicating that the member who had held the fraudulent accounts was threatening to file a libel suit against me and the denomination. I was urged to hire an attorney. When I responded that I would meet that felon in any court in the land and expected the denominational attorney to represent me, the response was a shocked rejoinder that I would need my own personal attorney. The assumption of litigation was a powerful player in these dynamics, but I never hired an attorney because this person didn't have the courage to take an obvious felony into open court.

The bank had already released the funds to the perpetrator, but the bank officer with whom we had contact subsequently told the State Corporation Commission the funds had not been released, even though this money had been turned over to the offender less than a week after the church had sent its letter requesting a freeze on the accounts. The shadow was triggered in profound ways at every level of these interactions. The State Corporation Commission seemed to be most concerned with protecting its own reputation, since its representatives had never found these accounts in all the times they had supposedly examined this bank. Their call to the banker in question was a prime indicator of the good-old-boy network at its worst! He was notified so that he could cover himself; a letter I received from the SCC later confirmed this.

The FDIC acted like so many government agencies these days, and immediately moved to a stance of shadow habeas corpus. While declaring itself without responsibility in this matter, the FDIC also advised that I seek legal counsel. The assumption throughout, and without exception, was that a legal action was contemplated. If anything was going to be resolved it was, by default, going to occur within some courtroom somewhere! The Internal Revenue

Service, however, did act—by requiring this individual to pay past due taxes with interest and penalties.

I encountered similar attitudes related to the shadow energy of money across a broad spectrum of regional areas and the presbyteries that served them. In another presbytery I encountered a tall-steeple pastor whose elders had always provided a secret slush fund for his personal travel and/or discretionary use. Thousands of dollars were fed into a secret fund that exceeded the amounts agreed upon in his "terms of call," the salary and benefit package reviewed and agreed upon by the full congregation. Whenever this fund dipped below a certain level, it was replenished by the elders, who had apparently decided to project "god" onto this mere mortal. The fact that this fund was secret was the key to its shadow status. Whenever secrets are kept about money, such secrets are driven by the shadow.

In another region a church, small and poor by comparison to the other one, not only gave its pastor an automobile when he retired, they also gave him a fat purse filled with cash. Another church with whom I consulted had developed an internal nomenclature for all the men who sat on its finance committee. Designated as "super elders" among themselves, they maintained a tight and unaccountable control over the money in this particular church. The Presbyterian, USA Book of Order has no such "super elder" nomenclature. Nor does it use the term "senior pastor," despite the daily use of this term in churches where their tall-steeple status has been embraced with vigor. These so-called super elders approved a loan of $50,000 in church funds for the pastor during his tenure, but never reported their action to the governing board of the church. When this pastor was asked to leave the church, he still owed a major portion of this secret loan. At that time they came to me for advice. I was asked if they could simply forgive the loan and send the pastor on his way with their blessing. When I told them that they must report this gift as taxable income, and he must declare it in the same way, it provoked vocal protests and angry confrontations with several of these super elders.

Finally, I simply told them to consult any attorney who specialized in tax law and they would learn the same thing. When the attorney gave them the same advice, one of their cabal of super elders was forced to inform the entire congregation about this secret loan, and that an amount of approximately $40,000 was still outstanding. At the time I told them their secrecy around money was not only unhealthy for their church, it was in direct violation of the financial disclosure practices stipulated by the denominational rule of law, the *Book of Order.* Yet I wonder whether financial disclosure is any more transparent in that church today than it was when they frantically cast about for a way to cover their super-elder tracks.

We need to ask ourselves: how much does the modern marketplace intrude upon our sacred spaces? Have our contemporary moneychangers, those who reward and punish with dollars, become the driving force in the national government, major corporations, and inside the institutional church? Based on my life experience in the business arena and inside the hierarchy of the church, the answer to this question must be yes. Are these people the ones who determine the direction of both church and state, who define the message articulated by both? In my experience this is, unfortunately, true.

The influence of money within the Judas Legacy is at the heart of this phenomenon. It feeds the magnitude of the national debt. The extent to which we are willing to betray ourselves, while denying such betrayal, was revealed in the ways the Congress abdicated its appropriate oversight of the budget during the Reagan administration. When a large deficit was racked up during those eight years, it was either ignored or protected by doublespeak and the spin that has become familiar in the political arena. This same failure was a monumental aspect of George W. Bush's successful raiding of the hard-won surplus of $2.5 trillion he had inherited at the close of the Clinton administration.

For a brief moment there, we had a balanced budget. According to Sen. Robert Byrd, it had taken seventeen years to finally achieve this $2.5 trillion surplus (*Losing America* . . . 27). At least we thought we had finally balanced the national budget, no mean feat after decades of pretending that it did not matter. Then along came 9/11 and we leaped into military conflagration with abandon. We allocated billions of invisible dollars we did not have to support a war with Iraq we did not need. We added to this already insane scenario a federal tax cut we could not afford any more than we could afford this singularly blind attack on Iraq. The abdication of Congressional responsibility only served to strengthen the dangerous actions of the White House.

It is ludicrous to run for election by promising tax cuts when tax increases, or cutting spending, are necessary for achieving a balanced budget. Yet, this is part of a continuing illusion perpetuated inside the Washington beltway. It is a critical part of our collective betrayal of self and nation. When a national leader will prostitute himself to the message-manipulators who manage his image, the message is clear. Such individuals betray themselves to achieve the narcissistic goals of power and greed, and will participate in the Judas Legacy at any cost.

What are the people in America doing while billions of dollars are allocated for warfare? We seem endlessly fascinated with the political process, drawing pathetic vicarious thrills from complaining about it, while acquiescing to its inevitable delusions. It is as if our intellects are on permanent disability, and our minds are unemployed. If we are not watching the Congress wrestle with its own incompetence, we are glued to televised football games, where players are paid as if every pound of muscle were, indeed, worth its weight in gold. And no one stands up and yells, "This is insanity, and we are all part of it—the inmates are running the asylum, and we are all confined to its worst locked-down psych unit!"

The value of money has become so distorted, we have no real sense of what an honest day's work is worth. AT&T can lay off forty-thousand employees, but continue to pay its chief executive officer millions of dollars a year. Back when Jimmy Johnson replaced Don Shula as coach of the Miami Dolphins, at a salary of two million dollars a year, he became the highest paid coach in the history of professional football (the *Washington Post,* 1/12/96, B-

1). Now such a salary seems like peanuts compared to the salaries demanded and received by high-visibility athletes.

A newscaster, in an interview with some of the men who played for Miami when Johnson was hired as their head coach, was told, "Jimmy Johnson is a great coach; he will bring discipline to this team, and the work ethic."

This is not the work ethic; this is an obscene derangement of real values. Ten years after Jimmy Johnson was offered a multi-million dollar salary to coach professional football, the coach at Virginia Tech, a state university in Virginia, was given a $750,000 raise in one year. On October 26, 2005, the *Richmond Times-Dispatch* reported that his salary exceeded two million dollars annually. His contract included a termination provision that would require a payout exceeding ten million dollars if he were fired. The football coach at the University of Virginia signed a contract for $1.7 million dollars, an amount which could increase to more than two million dollars by 2009. His contract contains a similar golden parachute.

These financial obscenities do not end there. They are the bulwark of the film industry, the election process, the military-industrial complex, and the corporate endorsement field. In a nation where children are made into baby icons, immature children like Britney Spears are used like puppets by talk-show hosts and the media. What mature adult with reasonable intelligence would be interested in her statement that Bush is the president and we should just go along with the war in Iraq, because he is the president and knows what's best for us? While inane statements such as these are broadcast by a media that wastes its energy upon them, the real needs of children across this nation are neglected and discounted by a Congress which ends welfare assistance to single mothers without considering training programs that will allow them to find employment.

During the heyday of the dot-com expansion, when money seemed plentiful and flowed easily, William Raspberry asked, "What is wrong with a society whose still-vibrant economy spawns new billionaires at a record pace, but whose principal political debate involves deciding how much to cut income and health benefits for children and the elderly poor?"

The undertow created by special interest contributions to politicians is far more powerful than we are willing to acknowledge. A Web site, www.opensecrets.org, lists astounding statistical totals for such contributions. The blatant pro-life ideology expressed by the Bush administration is understandable when you find that pro-life groups donated $4,579,029 to the Republican Party between 1990 and early 2006, but only $233,706 to the Democratic Party. Party-line votes on any hot-button issue in our American culture can be predicted from these political donations. This same Web site shows that $15,282,082 was donated to the Republican Party by pro-gun activists, but only $2,678,870 to the Democrats.

If those figures would startle the average American citizen, support by corporate health organizations and doctors could easily cause a migraine. These same statistical data show that Democrats received $235,670,502 in political donations from health-related sources, including insurance companies, physicians, dentists, and pharmaceutical companies. The Republicans received $ 345,607,324. Of these totals, $23,658,977 went to Republicans and $17,790,822 went to Democrats from health insurance companies, which were categorized as "health services/HMOs" in the survey.

It is highly unlikely that this nation will ever do anything about universal health care as long as contributions at this level are rolling into both party coffers. The political arena has become so corrupted by the funding it receives from special-interest groups that it could only be decontaminated by major reversals in campaign fundraising. For example, www.opensecrets.org has this disclaimer: "These figures do not include donations of 'Levin' funds to state and local party committees. 'Levin' funds were created by the Bipartisan Campaign Reform Act of 2002." Even campaign reform does not work when the patients are in charge of the psych unit. Congress is notoriously poor at policing its own ethics or spending.

No wonder Vice President Cheney gathered corporate executives from large oil companies around him to discuss his energy goals for the Bush administration. $251,909,571 was handed to the Republicans between 1990 and the beginning of 2006, while $107,021,290 was donated to the Democrats by these same oil-related groups.

However, when energy-related funds totaling $358,930,861 are contributed to both political parties who control the government in this nation, it is easy to see why neither party is interested in encouraging new or alternative forms of energy. We will never end our reliance upon fossil fuels as long as politicians and energy corporations collude in this continuing co-dependent process. Our focus upon the oil-rich Middle East is evidence of the power of this relationship between the government and big oil.

Oil prices in the United States jumped dramatically during the last four months of 2005, and stayed elevated into 2006. Oil rigs in the Gulf of Mexico, damaged by Hurricane Katrina, were reportedly the dominant attributing factor in this dramatic price increase. The war in Iraq had exacerbated an already volatile oil market, and the damage incurred by this one storm added insult to injury. On January 30, 2006, the *New York Times* reported that Exxon Mobil Corporation had posted record profits, more than any other U. S. company had ever documented. This oil company posted a profit of $10.71 billion for the fourth quarter and $36.13 billion for the calendar year 2005. A stock market analyst for Standard & Poor's, Howard Silverblatt, indicated that this was "the largest annual reported net income in U. S. history" (NYT, 1/30/06).

When Hurricane Katrina devastated the Gulf Coast, swamping the city of New Orleans and low-lying areas in Mississippi, the projected cost for recovery was phenomenal. When floodwaters destroyed these areas, the national government proved just how unprepared we were for any national disaster. Despite the fact that this hurricane had been predicted with startling accuracy and detailed information, the White House claimed they had insufficient advance warnings. Many months after Katrina had taken its terrible toll, the White House "rejected the most broadly supported plan for rebuilding communities while offering nothing to take its place" (NYT, 1/30/06).

In the midst of this chaos, ordinary citizens carried on with their day-to-day lives. Despite claims that American lives had changed dramatically since 9/11/01, we were still addicted to celebrity watching, as if the lives of most celebrities warranted such attention. We continued our focus upon the spending habits of the so-called rich and famous. The press offered us stories on the Donald Trumps of the world, and we wasted valuable time and spiritual energy consuming them. Trump had once celebrated his fiftieth birthday by announcing the construction of a five-story, four-hundred-thirty-foot yacht. Even the yacht seemed insignificant when you heard him compare himself to Alexander the Great and Napoleon in a televised commercial that sold what this country may have begun to symbolize: nothing. On such facile aspirations and inflated notions of self is a shadow nation born. Trump is obviously a master at marketing himself; that much is clear from his ability to wrangle a reality television show which focuses upon the only thing he values beyond money—himself.

Quoting Trump's biographer, Wayne Barrett, another reporter opined, "The guy churns through management personnel. He's an extraordinarily demanding, abrasive man. Sometimes that goes with success" (Lipton & Stoynoff, 64).

And sometimes it doesn't. All one has to do is read about a man whose center is clear and certain, despite his great wealth. Warren Buffett is the diametrical opposite of Donald Trump. He is gracious and charming in interviews, and his humble manner is endearing. He laughs easily, and his honor and integrity are integral to the public persona he presents to the world. When he tells an audience something, it is believable because it is honest.

We are so used to absorbing the media message about ourselves and our society, we no longer look at what is hidden beneath the message. A decade ago Chevrolet did not symbolize "The Heartbeat of America," but every time we allow such symbolism to creep in through the osmosis of commercial overload, we allow spiritually empty claptrap to become the substitute for authentic symbol, ritual, and honest meaning.

These days, ad copy for everything from automobiles to credit cards has an ethereal quality about it. It is as if we have taken some kind of verse from esoteric literature, lifted it out, and sold it to all the ad agencies in America. If you look at the ads run from the late nineties into the earliest years of the twenty-first century, you will find an undertow of fuzzy family coziness implied in them. One such print-ad claimed, "Nothing binds us one to the other like a promise kept" (*Time*, 9/9/96). This ad, for "The Blue Chip Company, Mass Mutual," makes it seem as if these insurance folks are in the spirituality business. In the same magazine, just on the next page, an ad read, "At Toyota, we know trust and confidence are things that must be built over time." Now, if we could just get our politicians and church leaders to be as trustworthy as Toyota!

These ads, and dozens more like them, reflect two kinds of thinking. They mirror the need to project a kind of distorted spirituality onto things that have no capacity for carrying that kind of projection, simply because these things have no transformative qualities about them. If a Chevrolet is not symbolic of the heartbeat of America, an insurance company cannot symbolize a rarified place where promises are never broken during the course of human interaction. Secondly, these ads are a contorted effort to appeal to, and accommodate, the loud rhetoric about family values.

Insurance companies have been advised by marketing consultants that women value "relationship." Such advice is apparent when ads for various and sundry companies speak of their desire to have a strong relationship with their clientele. The word itself implies an intimacy far beyond the generally accepted notion of insurance agent to client. "Relationship" is a classic example of a trigger word used to subtly indicate levels of trust that exceed a usual business interaction, making it into something more, something personal, something to be cherished. This is a bald way of sending a subliminal message that will hook anyone not wise enough to see through its transparent basis in greed.

Yet our fascination with the media, its message to us, and its detail of those we elevate through fame continues unabated. In the spring of 1996, the estate of Jacqueline Kennedy Onassis offered for auction those items her children had rejected. Their rejects were gaveled away for some of the most exorbitant prices ever received by Sotheby's, the premier auction house which conducted this auction. There, a bundle of magazines (including copies of *Time, Life, Newsweek, Modern Screen,* and *Ladies Home Journal*) was sold for $12,650, a stack of three frayed cushions brought $25,300, and a three-strand, fake pearl necklace netted $211,500 (Adler, 29).

Lynda Rae Resnick, vice-chairman of the corporation that purchased the pearl necklace, was quoted as saying, "It's the thing that symbolized the beauty of this woman, the dignity of this woman, that she could wear pearls that were not real and everyone thought they were" (Adler, 29).

If a symbol of beauty and dignity is a fake anything, then the integrity of the symbol is broken, leaving it as empty and void of meaning as the fake itself. To take fake pearls and elevate them to a symbolic level is the problem. We have lost our connectedness to real symbolism and authentic symbols. We have forgotten that a true symbol points to something transcendent beyond itself. We have been gullible enough to substitute for a symbol the pale and pathetic possessions of a woman whose fame came from our national obsession with projecting royalty upon our president and his family.

One writer noted, "Her formerly priceless reputation now has a price tag—almost $30 million, the difference between the $4.6 million Sotheby's calculated as the intrinsic value of her belongings and the $34.5 million that they brought from people swept away by the giddy rush that comes from spending large sums of money irresponsibly" (Adler, 30).

Neither Sotheby's nor Christie's have been able to imagine the extremes that will characterize sales of celebrity possessions. After Katherine Hepburn's death, a painting she had created was valued at $3,000 by Sotheby's, but was gaveled in at $36,000. "No trespassing" signs from Hepburn's house were sold for a total of $3,600. When Christie's handled the auction of Marilyn Monroe's estate, they estimated that her pots and pans would bring $800, but they sold for $25,300. Her salt and pepper shakers sold for $17,250 (Cerio, 66-67).

Therein lies the problem with making mere mortals into icons. While the one-time possessions of Jacqueline Kennedy Onassis or Katherin Hepburn or Marilyn Monroe do not symbolize anything in particular, the projection of value onto these possessions is an example of the collective shadow in America. Those who purchased things which once belonged to these celebrities endowed them with historical and psychic value beyond their worth. Such an endowment comes from the shadow and feeds the shadow. But, money (and those who represent it) is such a powerful part of our culture, we seem incapable of understanding the ways we invest it with godlike powers. Mixing God and money does not mean "rendering unto Caesar that which is Caesar's." Instead, by melding the two, the human psyche carries the distorted notion that the two are not only synonymous, they should be.

Those who invoke the name of God while serving in public office may sublimate the real purposes beneath their motivations. When they have gained enough power they are prone to shift into grandiose ideas of themselves and begin to cast their public persona from such inflation. When the district court in Travis County, Texas issued a warrant for the arrest of Congressman Thomas DeLay, it offered the public a look at a man whose tendency to hide behind a Bible is as odious as his utter lack of ethical conduct. Charged with money laundering and criminal conspiracy, DeLay, the House majority leader, strode up to the microphones of an eager press to protest that these charges were politically motivated. Indicted by a grand jury for using corporate contributions in the 2002 elections, DeLay proudly announced his innocence with such vocal fervor he could have been heard without a microphone. Even this indictment by a grand jury did not cause him to modify his behavior. He flew "to his arraignment on money-laundering in the style to which he had become accustomed as House majority leader: on a corporate jet...owned by the R. J. Reynolds Tobacco Co" (the *Washington Post*, 1/16/06, A-16).

Like his friend George W. Bush, Tom DeLay turned from a

youth of alcoholism to proclaiming his born-again Christian status as a man of superior ethics and remarkable integrity. The first House majority leader to be indicted in more than a hundred years, Tom DeLay continually protested his innocence, despite evidence to the contrary. It was reported in *Time* magazine that a trip to Britain—where DeLay stayed in a luxury hotel in London, ate at the most expensive restaurants, and saw the hottest shows on the West End—was financed largely by funding that came from the Choctaw Indian tribe (Tumulty, *Time*, 4/18/05). These funds had been funneled through a conservative nonprofit foundation, the National Center for Public Policy Research. The arrangements for this trip were made by his close buddy, Jack Abramoff, a lobbyist whose high-roller status on K Street made him the darling of the party circuit in the nation's capital.

In an interview with a *Time* magazine reporter, Jack Abramoff was asked if he considered Thomas DeLay a close friend. Abramoff answered, "I do." A secondary question caused him to declare, "Tom DeLay is a dedicated public servant. I was drawn to Tom DeLay because of our shared interest in the Bible and like political philosophies. He's a man fortunate enough to have a loving and devoted wife who shares his faith and philosophy" (Zagorin, *Time*, 5/2/05).

Christine DeLay, this same "loving and devoted wife," was reportedly paid $115,000 to contact members of Congress "to find out their favorite charity" (Schmidt & Grimaldi, A-01). That one-question survey would equal more than $200.00 per member.

DeLay's close ties to the lobbying firm run by Jack Abramoff were an example of his willingness to participate in corrupt practices. When Jack Abramoff finally pled guilty to tax evasion, fraud, and conspiracy to bribe public officials, he made a deal to provide evidence against an unknown number of members of Congress. Then, and only then, did DeLay step aside from his position as house majority leader. During the six months between the time when these corrupt practices were reported and DeLay's final acquiescence to the reality of his situation, Congress and the House Ethics Committee, in particular, seemed to be in a coma. Even after Abramoff's plea agreement, members of Congress refrained from asking DeLay to resign, which would have been the ethical thing to do. The Democrats, the silent minority in both houses of Congress at this time, seemed stricken with the same muteness as their colleagues in the Republican Party.

Thomas DeLay slipped into gross denial, circling his own psychic shadow wagons as he told the Fox News channel on January 8, 2006, "I am not a target of an investigation" (Weisman, A-02).

When DeLay finally resigned from his position in the House, he only did so after he had raised enough money to pay his legal fees. John Feehery, who was a former aide to both Dennis Hastert, Speaker of the House, and to DeLay, said, "He needed to raise money for the defense fund. That was the bottom line. He wanted to make sure he could take care of himself in the court of law" (Smith and Weisman, A-01). Since federal election law does not prohibit the use of campaign funds for this purpose, any funds raised for reelection can be used "to pay legal fees stemming from official duties." DeLay's love affair with his own shadow is evident in his careful manipulation of this situation. DeLay is a classic example of a shadow-driven personality.

Jack Abramoff's public statements are also an example of the way the shadow convinces the ego that actions taken are ethical when the opposite is true. The shadow functions best in the midst of delusion. The underlying shadow dynamics of these money transactions is one of the most powerful aspects of corruption in the government of the United States. When Abramoff pled guilty, he also carried the reputations and potential indictments for more than one member of Congress in that plea. He has the key to unlock dozens of conspiracy charges against an equal number of Congressional representatives. Lobbying is a huge industry in Washington and the times that ethical rules are treated with a wink and a nod are too numerous to count.

When these indictments of both DeLay and Abramoff were front-page news, the corrupt culture in Washington was appallingly evident. Stepping into the breach was a man who himself had paid a fine of $300,000 to settle a 1997 ethics case. Newt Gingrich, former speaker of the House, opined, "I think as this thing unfolds, it'll be so disgusting, and the Republicans will be under such pressure from their base, that they will have to undertake substantial reform" (NYT, 1/8/06). That this paragon of virtue had the arrogant temerity to make pronouncements about the morals of current leaders is as unpalatable as the corruption to which he refers. Why would anyone be interested in his shadow opinions? He is a shadow personality whose denial of his own internal darkness is as profound as DeLay's or Abramoff's.

For all the posturing by the DeLays and Gingrichs of the public arena, the infamous use of lobbying funds by members of Congress continues. Adamant declarations of major reform have slipped backward into the shadows of yesterday's news, and neither of the political parties seems very interested in creating ethical standards or enforcing them. The influential free-flowing dollars that undergird the lifestyles of the members of Congress continue to flow, like a vast river. Their shadow-driven purposes are denied as often as reform is promised. Neither denial nor promise changes the deeply embedded culture of corruption in the government of this nation.

While the nation was focused upon the misconduct of political leaders in Washington, the *Roanoke Times* reported, "New academic research suggests that the war in Iraq could cost America up to $2 trillion" (1/15/05, A-20). On October 8, 2007, *Time* magazine reported that, "according to a joint analysis by a Nobel-prizewinning economist and a Harvard scholar, the war in Iraq was costing $500,000 per minute, an amount which could provide health care for more than 400,000 children (24)."

The shadow god in America wears a green face, like the money it represents. Money is never neutral, despite our protests to the contrary. While this chapter has included a wide variety of examples of the ways the negative shadow of money drives our culture, it is intended to show that money is interwoven into the very fabric and texture of this nation. Our souls were better off when bartering was a more dominant form of exchange. If these examples seem extreme, or even redundant, they are simply a means for showing how powerful the shadow of money has become. This chapter could have been two hundred pages long, had it included a more comprehensive view of the shadow aspects of money in America. If these examples make any reader uncomfortable, or even a bit queasy, then I have done my work. Contemporary moneychangers lurk in dark corners, like spiders with hungry faces. The god we worship is not the god of Christianity. It is more often the god of the currency we elevate and to which we pledge our allegiance. Money always carries the weight, the denseness, and emotional baggage of our personal and collective attachments to it. Money cannot be subtracted from the ways we respond to others. And, all the while, the moneychangers spin their webs, wrapping us in the gossamer webs of illusion we continue to embrace.

Chapter 9

The Shadow Side of God

Trying to describe the image of the divine, or to define the being of God, is like trying to draft a map of the planet from the perspective of an earthworm. We have no arms to encompass the magnitude of a God-Spirit, nor fingers to even hold the pencil. We have no words that can adequately wrap themselves around the unlimited nature of a God being. Nor do we have the cognitive ability to perceive the boundlessness of such a God, no matter how expansive our imaginations.

Jungian analyst and prolific writer Marion Woodman declares, "Without an understanding of myth or religion, without an understanding of the relationship between destruction and creation, death and rebirth, the individual suffers the mysteries of life as meaningless mayhem alone." The opposites of the shadow side and the creative side of God are part of such perceptions. We do not gain a balanced perspective on the fullness of a God being until we can perceive the relationship between these opposites, for they are held in tandem and in tension with one another. Neither end of the spectrum exists without the other. Neither exists in some idealistic vacuum devoid of the other.

Our inability to perceive the boundlessness of a God/Spirit is predicated upon the historical notion that God resides in some nether region, often the sky, far distant from the human realm. This same God has been presented, over and over again, as external to us, almost as if there is no commonality of language or thought form. The problem with this habit of the mind is that it has been held as truth for so many eons, it is almost impossible for us to allow ourselves to perceive God as internal, rather than external. After death, when we enter into some form of a spirit realm, the God whom we encounter may be an external presence, but in the human realm, our awareness of and connection to the being we call "God" is internal.

The more we encounter God internally and consistently, the more we have an awareness that God's Spirit energy is fully present within us. Our imaginations want God to be like us, so if we are told we are made in God's image, we are also equally creative about making God in our own image. George Bernard Shaw once wrote, "All great truths begin as blasphemies." When a concept, such as the external being of God, has been fully inculcated into the global habits of the mind for many centuries, moving beyond that old mind-habit is not some simple task. God, as an internal force, is not easily ignored. A God who is "out there somewhere" is far easier to forget.

With these same mind-habit limitations, Jesus has been described in small ways. To define the biblical Jesus as "gentle Jesus, meek and mild" is to foist upon him the legendary and illusionary attributes of perfection that more accurately reflect a human need for him to be something he was not than to describe something that he was. This appellation for the personhood of Jesus carries centuries of perfectionist projections linked to it, and changing that energy may take equally as long. When such spun-sugar sentimentality is applied to Jesus, he is emasculated into a pitiful caricature without feeling, passion or sensuality. A man who has also been called the "King of Kings" cannot function in the realm of the spirit or the realm of humanity if he has been stripped of his masculine energy.

These descriptors for Jesus not only rob a vital, remarkable human of his humanity, but they also thrust him into a mold which does not fit. By turning him into some unnatural model of purity, humility, and passivity, Jesus has been stripped of his potent masculinity and cast into the role of a simpering, pietistic pretty boy, whose face is perpetually wreathed in the sweet smiles painted upon it by generations of artists. Few paintings of a weeping Jesus hang on the walls of churches, but literally thousands of prints of a Caucasian Jesus with up-cast eyes and a tentative, tender smile, can be found in places of prominence. Hands perpetually folded in prayer, this Jesus is portrayed as legend would have it, the symbolic icon of pure, unadulterated goodness.

By presenting such imagery as the ideal, the God image is pushed into a place of pure goodness, where no shadow can exist. This new one-sided God is a figment of New Testament legend and myth. The God of the Old Testament was presented as a god of war, who charged with the armies of Israel into ferocious battle. This same God was also depicted as the opposite soft mothering God who comforted as if all the tribes of Israel were her children. Thus, the God of the Hebrew nation was a multi-dimensional being with both destructive and compassionate characteristics.

Whether these seemingly opposite characteristics can be viewed as attributes depends upon one's perspective. To emasculate such a God is to knock the world and religious understanding off-balance, into a one-sided denial of shadow—in self, in God, and in the world. Yet, the Christians who invoke the name of God as protector and defender in times of war are actually identifying with a warrior God and not the person who was Jesus.

When we worship a one-dimensional God, we have a tendency to discount the multi-dimensional aspects of evil as well. Writing on the subject, Scott Peck asserted, "Human evil is too important for a one-sided understanding. And it is too large a reality to be grasped within a single frame of reference" (39). So, too, is the dark side of God, which also appears with great clarity in ancient religions of other nations.

One of the more remarkable passages in which God claims a dark side through the verbal projections of a human author can be found in the book of the major prophet Isaiah. Here God speaks with authority, and humankind is told, "I form light and create darkness, I make weal and create woe; I the Lord do all these things" (Isaiah 45:7).

These are words without equivocation or apology; here is a God who claims a dark side. The light is not formed to stand alone; it has a counterpart in the darkness. Joy has its dark side as well, for despair is also part of life's reality. Weal (or well-being) is the sister to a brother whose name is woe. Evil is the opposite of good, surely, but neither exists in a vacuum; one does not preclude the other, for both are parts of a normal and natural world.

The God of Judaism is the god of monumental proportions who, having named the children of Israel as "the chosen people of God," and having led them out of Egypt, is described by the author of the book of Exodus (Exodus 32:7-10) as a "jealous God." This writer describes a God who orders the slaughter of the entire nation of these chosen ones because they have worshiped a golden-calf idol.

As the conversation with Moses ends, God demands, "Now let me alone, so that my wrath may burn hot against them and I may consume them...." Here God's dark side prepares to exact revenge. The text depicts a frantic Moses trying to placate this angry God, pleading on behalf of the people, begging God to reconsider. When Moses returns to the camp, he demands that the people choose. It must either be God, or it will be an idol. Those who do not choose to follow this fierce God are put to the sword. Three thousand people died that day, and God's dark side was never more palpable.

Moses, the reluctant leader who has brought the quarrelsome people of Israel out of Egypt, has gone to the mountaintop to speak with God while the tribes of Israel wait at the base of the mountain for his return. High in the rarified air of the divine presence, he demands to see God's face. He asks to see God's "glory." Implicit in his request is his desire to understand the being of this powerful God. He is told that such a thing is impossible; it would be too much for a mere mortal to experience. Instead, he is told that God will place him in the cleft of a rock, and as God passes by, Moses' face will be covered by God's hand, for he must not see the face of God. To do so would be the equivalent of grasping a high velocity electric cable with wet hands. When he comes down from the mountain, Moses' face has taken on some sort of odd appearance.

It frightens his followers so thoroughly that he is then compelled to cover his face with a veil.

The Hebrew connotation of "face" in the biblical text is more complex than its English equivalent. In Hebrew tradition, *to hide the face* or to *turn the face away* expressed displeasure. To *set the face against* expressed hostility. To *make the face shine upon* was an indicator of blessing or of friendly acceptance. Each of these phrases was used to describe God's attitudes over time toward the fledgling nation of Israel. When Moses came back from his mountaintop encounter with God, he had been changed forever. It showed in his face.

All sorts of strained explanations for this phenomenon have been offered historically by commentators, but the Hebrew word in the original text is the word *qaran*. Translated as "shining" in many English translations of the text, this word is derived from the Hebrew word *qeren*, a word rarely used in the Old Testament. This word, *qeren*, may be translated as "horn," but it may also be translated as "radiant." The New Revised Standard Version of the Bible uses the word "shining," but the Hebrew Bible more commonly used in Jewish circles uses the word "radiant." Seemingly opposite words ("horn" vs. "radiant") make for a splintering of translation, partly because many modern translations of the text are tertiary, coming after the original Hebrew was translated into the Greek Septuagint and then translated back into Hebrew. It was clear that the people of Israel were afraid of Moses when he came down from the mountain. If he had grown horns, the people would have had just cause to feel fearful. If he radiated with the glory of God, they might have had even more cause to fear the suprahuman characteristics mirrored in his face. Who knows how his face actually appeared? Whatever its appearance, Moses was forced to cover his face because of his followers' fear. What if his face had melted as if made of wax that had been placed too close to the heat of a roaring fire? What if it had frozen as if subjected to extreme cold?

Annie Dillard in *Teaching a Stone to Talk* asks a critical question, "Why do people in churches seem like cheerful, brainless tourists on a packaged tour of the Absolute?" (40-41). If we understood the powerful length and breadth and height of God's energy, we would be well-served to ponder Dillard's question and her subsequent counsel. We would "be wearing crash helmets" and the ushers would be prepared to "issue life preservers and signal flares; they should lash us to our pews." Then Dillard concludes, "For the sleeping god may wake some day and take offense, or the waking god may draw us out to where we can never return."

The Bible describes a God who annihilated the entire Egyptian army, drowning them and their chariots and horses. These poor soldiers had been sent by the Pharaoh to force the people of Israel to return to their enslavement in Egypt. This same God had "hardened the heart" of the Pharaoh, resulting in the death of all the first-born males in the land of Egypt. Having one's heart hardened by the divine strikes at a very deep core of human psychic misfortune. Pharaoh's actions were driven by the shadow side of God and thus Pharaoh was exercising an absolute lack of control. This is an action beyond cognitive reason, and stands outside rational patterns of thought. Yet this God does not seem to be attuned to such legalistic thought forms, and surely is not bound by them, if the Old Testament has any veracity at all. When later scribes and theologians attempt a polishing of this God-image into perfection, the dark side of God is thrust, like that of the human, into the vast abyss of unconsciousness that houses all that seems unspeakable and unacceptable.

A God who marched with the warriors of Israel when they battled the armies of Amalek, and whose power was a deciding factor in victory for Israel, is not a God without a dark side. When God tells Moses, in Exodus 17:14, to "Write this as a reminder in a book and recite it in the hearing of Joshua: I will utterly blot out the remembrance of Amalek from under heaven," this is a deity with an unquestionable shadow.

The writer of the book of Isaiah also places these words in God's mouth: "See it is I who have created the smith who blows the fire of coals, and produces a weapon fit for its purpose; I have also created the ravager to destroy" (Isaiah 54:16). No one can call this

God "meek or mild." The dark side of a ravager-God is the same characteristic that dominates the traits of the Goddess Kali.

The dark side of this same ravager-God allows, or even causes, Saul to falter and fail, as events open the Hebrew journey for the time when David will become king. When Saul is first anointed to lead the unruly tribes of Israel, he is *not* anointed *melek*, the Hebrew word for *king*. The old self-absorbed judge, Samuel, anoints Saul as *nagiyd*, which would be translated as *captain*, or *prince*, or *leader*. In doing so, Samuel strips Saul of his rightful designation as melek/king and creates an undertow that will eventually play itself out in a sad life, followed by an even more tragic death. The powerful shadow-projection from Samuel taints the anointing of this first leader of the nation of Israel, and God does not intervene or force Samuel to change the anointing. Perhaps Samuel's shadow was too powerful to hear any word of intervention from God. To read the poignant story of the ways David baited Saul, while Saul scurried to and fro trying to please Samuel, until ultimately David inherited the throne, is to read of the striking ways the shadow is a major player in this tragic story.

When King David has committed adultery and murder, again the canon describes a God who exacts an awful price. The child born of his lust for Bathsheba dies, in spite of David's pleas for mercy. The God of the Old Testament surely has a dark side, and it is not the characteristic personality attributed to a non-violent Jesus.

The Old Testament prophets sometimes acted out of their own personal shadows, invoking the name of this God. Certainly Samuel, the last judge over Israel, is a prime example of a shadow-driven personality. In the book of II Kings (II Kings 2: 23-24) Elisha's reaction to taunting by "small boys" who jeered at his bald head is to curse them "in the name of the Lord." The text then declares, "Then two she-bears came out of the woods and mauled forty-two of the boys." God's name is invoked from the shadow, and used for a shadow purpose. God, then, emerges as an instigator of both noble and ignoble actions.

The human shadow has been an influential participant in the

formation of a one-sided mythology of a New Testament God who is only good. Only by acting out of the human shadow could such legendary pureness be extracted from the multidimensional reality of a larger, less-limited God. If that which is unacceptable, that which is rejected, is cast into the shadow, then a God who is a ravager, warrior—anything but pure and good—must possess a celestial shadow that would dwarf the human shadow in indescribable ways. By striving to mold a perfect God into the human imagination, a mold of shadow-less purity and absolute perfection, humans have unconsciously created a God whom they can manage with black and white declarations of either/or dogma and confessional statements of certainty.

God has been limited by human imagination from the time when codified doctrine was formulated, cast in verbal stone, and then endowed with assumptions of "Truth." The Westminster Confession of Faith states, "There is but one only living and true God, who is infinite in being and *perfection,* a most *pure* spirit, invisible, without body, parts, or passions, immutable, immense, eternal, incomprehensible, almighty; most wise, most holy, most free, most absolute..." (italics added).

That God was "incomprehensible" and "most free" did not stop the preachers and laymen who gathered at Westminster Abbey in July of 1643 (Rogers, 153) from describing, in agonizing detail, a God who was supposedly indescribable. These descriptors, while certainly not lacking in superlatives, are striking because there is no balance in this God. Their God has no shadow, no anger except for righteous judgment, no passion, no lack of wisdom, and no limitations. Yet they have created a God who is fraught with limitations. The God they describe has been made into a pure, perfect one-sided shadow of the former indescribable God of magnificent Old Testament proportions.

These men labored for more than four years creating a doctrine encompassing thirty-five chapters. The shadow is never more evident than in their attempt to place a verbal corral around a God who cannot be circumscribed in any way. This inflated attempt by humans, an attempt to find appropriate adjectives and adverbs—

particularly ones that epitomize perfection in its purest form—continues as Jesus is described.

The most recent contemporary Affirmation of Faith in the Presbyterian Church, USA uses similar kinds of superlatives to describe Jesus. "A Brief Statement of Faith" was written and approved for inclusion in the *Book of Confessions* of the Presbyterian Church, USA by a majority of presbyteries in the decade that ended the twentieth century. These lines leap off the page: "God raised this Jesus from the dead, vindicating his sinless life, breaking the power of sin and evil, delivering us from death to life eternal."

These words would seem to imply that sin and evil simply disappeared from the world, either by osmosis through the sinless life of Jesus, or when Jesus was raised from the dead. Of course, these words are euphemistic in their content and intent, since sin and evil are as much a part of the modern world as they were in the ancient time of Jesus. Relying upon the canonical pronouncements of the New Testament (II Timothy 1:10), the authors of this statement of faith revert to old forms of proof-texts and fail to articulate a more contemporary assertion of the mysterious word of God, incarnated in the human Jesus. While Christians believe Jesus left that legacy of resurrection and life beyond the one lived in the human realm, no human is delivered from death itself. Death is the appropriate and natural ending to our human condition, and only shadow understandings of self would imply that death is not necessary.

More difficult are this confession's words about Jesus' "sinless life." Jesus was human. Jesus had a shadow. Jesus' shadow is evident in two different gospel accounts of his encounter with the woman of Tyre and Sidon. The canon implies that he had gone there to rest, weary of the crowds who followed him everywhere. This Gentile, a Greek-Syrophoenician woman, has an audacity of spirit that persisted, despite the apparent fatigue Jesus exhibited when they met.

She questions his faith and his ethnocentric values, when he answers her request to heal her daughter with these words (from the gospel of Matthew 15:24), "I was sent only to the lost sheep of the house of Israel."

Still, the woman persists. Coming to him and kneeling down in front of Jesus, she begs, "Lord, help me."

And then perhaps the fatigue Jesus was feeling colors his answer. He responds, "It is not fair to take the children's food and throw it to the dogs" (Matthew 15:26).

Here the pivotal word is "dogs." The Canaanites and all other Gentiles were labeled "dogs" by the Jews because they were believed to be unclean. Their life patterns and practices did not conform to the purification laws set forth by the Jews for the Jews. What cannot be subtracted from this text is that Jesus was a Jew. His understanding of himself was Jewish and, at the deepest levels of his psyche, he held many of the same notions as his Jewish peers. That belief system included an understanding of the Jews as God's chosen people. Thus, Jesus here indicates his belief that he has been sent only to the chosen ones of Israel, not to the Gentiles.

With one statement, in response to these words by Jesus, this Gentile woman confronts his prejudice *and his shadow*. Pointing out the parochial limitations of his assumptions, she deftly parries his shadowy thrust with one sentence. She answers, "Yes, Lord, yet even the dogs eat the crumbs that fall from their masters' table" (Matthew 15:27; see also Mark 7:28).

Then, unlike most humans, he instantly recognized his shadow for what it was, and turned away from acting upon it. Initially, Jesus had offered a shadow retort. When this foreign woman confronted his inborn presumption of superiority as a Jew, he immediately responded with compassionate understanding. Her mentally ill daughter was healed because of the mother's faith energy.

Jesus was called to account for his preconceived notions of Hebrew superiority when this woman confronted him about his Jewish prejudice. This bold woman stands with obstinate courage and pushes Jesus to a new awareness of his old assumptions. Because of her tenacity, her little daughter was healed. This foreign woman confronted a man who is truly human with a shadow that showed in his reference to "dogs."

To say that Jesus exhibited a human tendency to prejudice may be worse than declaring he was capable of anger. I once had a New Testament professor who argued that Jesus was not angry when he drove the moneychangers from the temple. At the time I argued in opposition to his stance, and he was not pleased. Apparently my professor subscribed to the images of "gentle Jesus, meek and mild," but when such imagery became the overriding image cast upon Jesus it castrated the strength he embodied and modeled for humanity. This account of Jesus' action against those merchants, who had set up shop in the outer courts of the temple, can be found in all four gospels. Known as "The Cleansing of the Temple" text, the Johannine author (John 2:13-22) adds a detail not found in the three synoptic texts. He wrote that Jesus made a "whip of cords" and used it to drive out those who had defiled the temple with their commerce.

When a whip is used, there is little doubt about the one who wields the weapon. Here Jesus proves he is someone to be reckoned with, who knows who he is and what he is doing. Jesus exhibits a fierce spirit and a temper when he encounters those who defile sacred space. That John is the only gospel with this reference to the whip is troublesome, however, because a secondary legend may have overtaken the historical narrative by this point, since this gospel was written so much later than the synoptic gospels.

Despite this disclaimer, the man described in this text is not "gentle Jesus, meek and mild." Even without a whip in his hand, Jesus did not compromise or negotiate. His actions would not provoke images of a diplomat. In this text, Jesus shows that anger can be a legitimate emotion, and that shadow used consciously may be an appropriate response to the unacceptable. Jesus proves he is, indeed, "fully human," with all the multiple traits of that humanity, for he is angry, and his shadow shows.

In some ways it is astounding that this particular story survived the editorial pen of later scribes and canonical authorities. This is the passage where Jesus, without equivocation, challenges the orthodox leadership of the day. In this text it is clear—Jesus has assumed an authority that threatens those who define the faith. One canonical scholar believes this is the decisive act that calls forth the executioners' reaction (Sanders, 301). The physical act of driving these commercial agents from the temple sets the stage for a plot that ends in arrest for sedition and ultimate death by crucifixion, Roman style.

This was the courageous action of a prophetic presence. With the bold and decisive undoing of a thriving commercial marketplace inside the sacred space of the temple, Jesus thrusts the status quo into chaos and demonstrates his revolutionary character. This action was a risky interruption of their assumptions. It disrupted the prevailing acceptance of the profane imposed upon the sacred. Jesus, like the prophets of an earlier day, confronted the orthodox leaders of that time with a terrible reality, one of desecration of their own place of worship. Beyond that, his teachings and his revolutionary presence had pushed the orthodox leaders to the wall. His overt action of cleansing the temple is symbolic of a far more covert reality. The old assumptions of the orthodox leaders have been torn asunder by a homeless rabbi with dirty feet.

That sundering was the equivalent of heresy, in that it was perceived as far more dangerous than treason against one's country. Edward Edinger wrote, "Heresy for the true believer is the ultimate threat. It threatens the supreme psychic value and is therefore more dangerous than death which threatens only physical existence" (86).

It is the essential difference between the questions asked by those who examine Jesus. The high priest, Caiaphas, seeks to limit the power of Jesus' divinity when he asks, "Are you the son of God?" It is clear that Pilate, the Roman procurator, is far more concerned about Jesus' earthly power because he specifically asks, "Are you the King of the Jews?" Jesus is only a threat to Pilate if he decides to incite a political revolution. Pilate is less troubled by a theological upheaval in the Jewish community. Nevertheless, Pilate's subtle respect for Jesus is apparent in the text. Pilate is wise enough to know, this is a man to be reckoned with. Pilate, at least, may have recognized the power of Jesus' shadow, both its dark and its light side.

When Jesus launched himself into the middle of the temple marketplace, he did not do so from some elevated stance of "righteous indignation," although his anger might have had some righteousness at its core. Driving out the animals offered for sale (to be used for sacrifices), he overturned the tables of the money changers. Those who sold shekels to be used for the temple tax had their business abruptly halted. Flinging the coins that replaced the Roman denarii aside, he swept all and sundry from the sacred space of the temple.

To argue that Jesus was not angry, or that his actions were meant to foreshadow the destruction of the temple at Jerusalem, is to argue from a place of historical and revisionistic retrospect. Neither of these arguments gives full credence to the humanity of Jesus, but rather strips him of that humanity, while at the same time robbing him of the diverse aspects of his personality and character. The magnitude of his being is diminished each time Jesus is cast into a one-sided persona of purity.

To project pure goodness, without an opposite dark side, upon either God or Jesus is a distinguishing pattern of Christian tradition. In Judaic belief, good and evil are accepted as "both/and" aspects of the world, and of divinity; to perceive God in an either/or way is not typical of Jewish thought. Only the writers of the New Testament text seem to ascribe this peculiar one-sided personality to both Jesus and God.

If you take the contrast between the strident God-imagery of the Old Testament, and the pure, perfect imagery of the New Testament, there are two opposites. The warrior God of the Hebrews is a reflection of the negative aspects of the unconscious human shadow. This God exhibits anger, revenge, jealousy, resentment, and divine petulance, thus seeming to possess a personality more like other gods familiar to the civilizations of the Near East. This God is a punishing god who drives the first humans from Eden's paradise when they are disobedient. There is no question that this God is a warrior god who reflects the shadow side of the tribes of Israel. The Old Testament God then becomes the archetypal God who encompasses the negative aspects of the human shadow.

However, this God is not presented as one-dimensional, since this is the God who also comforts in times of sorrow. The psalmists turn to this compassionate God when they are in distress and grief. These Hebrew writers describe this God as one under whose sheltering wings they find security, whose presence has the strength and substance of a rock, who satisfies them when they are thirsty or hungry, who heals them when they are sick, whose "steadfast love endures forever." This may be the God who goes into war with them, but this God is not limited to one archetypal image. The God described in the Old Testament is both warrior and one who leads them into still places and green meadows to find peace.

When the writers of the New Testament created their theological imagery for the man, Jesus, they reflected the societal influence of their time in history and cast him into the ideal perfection of Hellenistic philosophy. They wrapped a stunning narrative around a vagabond traveler, whose day-to-day wanderings may have been an embarrassment to his own family. Throughout his lifetime, those he encountered shook their heads and wondered how this ragged itinerant preacher could have such influence on the common people. Those who later wrote about him rarely allowed the reader to catch a glimpse of Jesus' dark side. Thus, these apologetic writers carved out a new god, who is a reflection of all the positive aspects of the human shadow, but who does not often reveal his dark side.

Paul's writings are one of the reasons the Christian tradition has insisted upon the image of Jesus as a perfect human being. As noted earlier, Paul's writings were completed earlier than the four gospels, despite their location in the canon where one might assume they had been written later. His elevation of Jesus to a place of perfection is part and parcel of his obsession with perfection in those to whom he preaches this new gospel. It was part of his Pharisaic personality, this striving toward perfection.

The words be perfect, perfection, perfect, perfect harmony, make perfect, and more perfect appear often in the writings of

Paul. The only other writer who uses these same kinds of references to perfection is the author of the book of Hebrews, who is believed to be one of Paul's disciples. The writer of Hebrews used words referring to perfection more than any other New Testament author. Yet both may have been reflecting the influence of the Greco-Roman world upon their values. The basic concepts of Hellenistic philosophy are strewn throughout the writings of the apostle Paul and cannot be discounted. The notion of the mind or the intellect as greater than, and ascendant over, the physical body is typical of this philosophy. By perceiving the intellect as capable of achieving perfection, the body is denigrated into a place of defiled impurity. Many biblical scholars also believe that similar Gnostic influences colored Paul's beliefs, and thus his writing. The canonical writers who espouse this kind of perfection had replaced the heart with the head, when the original Hebrew faith understood the heart to be the source and core of the intellect. By trying to differentiate themselves from the earlier orthodox understandings of faith, perhaps they tried too hard to be different. The author of Revelation was the exception, since this author chooses apocalyptic pronouncements of a vengeful God to emphasize the central theme of this New Testament book.

Such perfectionist projections onto those who are the earliest converts to a new faith have left their mark in the inherited assumptions held deeply within the lowest levels of the Western psyche, the collective unconscious. Whether one has been inculcated with the doctrine of the Christian tradition from inside the institutional church, or whether "being good" has been thrust upon one through other socialization processes, the end result is the same. The common notion of being good precludes an acceptance of one's negative personality traits. Those particular or even peculiar aspects of the personality are pushed down and lodged in the shadow, where they are repressed and denied with a vengeance, for after all, denial of one's shadow is part of "being good." So it is that historically the Christian tradition has fostered an environment which not only denies the shadow in both God and humans, its socialization processes require that the shadow be denied.

An unconscious rebellion against this socialization pattern has given us the idols that are particular to the American culture. Here we encounter, as in no other place, the shadow side of God. As the American culture moves through this time in history, we are bombarded with daily reminders of God. "God" and "Jesus" and "Christian" and "faith-based" and "family values" and "born again" have become formulaic key phrases to open political doors, to persuade middle America that leaders are trustworthy, and to convince voters that certain political candidates are superior to their opponents. If these same opponents are reticent about readily announcing their born-again status, they are often branded with the "liberal" brand, the new obscene label for one who must surely be an atheist. Certainly it is the newest branding for those who are perceived as anomic for refusing to loudly proclaim their Christianity, along with all the other political lemmings. This contemporary American phenomenon is not an indicator that religion is more important to us than to the citizens of other nations. Instead, it shows we are egocentric enough to think we can use God as a manipulative tool for unholy political purposes.

This practice fails to acknowledge the profound divine energy of the God Annie Dillard holds in awe. Despite a tendency to inject "perfection" (which in the Greek could have been translated, instead, as "wholeness") into his works, the writer of Hebrews also declares, "You have not come to something that can be touched, a blazing fire, and darkness, and gloom, and a tempest, and the sound of a trumpet, and a voice whose words made the hearers beg that not another word be spoken to them" (Hebrew 12:18-19). Here this canonical writer is not describing Christ, but the God, Yahweh, whom this writer holds in absolute awe. The author of Hebrews concludes chapter twelve with this sentence: "Therefore, since we are receiving a kingdom that cannot be shaken, let us give thanks, by which we offer to God an acceptable worship with *reverence and awe, for indeed, our God is a consuming fire"* (Hebrews 12:28-29, italics added).

This writer is describing a God who cannot be bridled for personal, political or any other human purpose. The author of Hebrews is describing the wild, untamed side of God. It is that supraliminal side of the Supreme Being that Moses must have encountered. It is that aspect of universal intelligence that inhabits a region "above the threshold of consciousness." The only appropriate human response to such a God would be unremitting, overwhelming awe, but finding an example of such an interaction in the human realm is not easy.

A feature documentary, *Living with Wolves*, on the Discovery Channel recounts the story of a family of wolves. A human husband and wife team, who had chosen to live among these animals, detail the complexity of the instinctive canine family structure and the ways its enduring purposes cast each wolf into a particular role. The two of them are equal partners in caring for wolf pups they later release into the compound where the established family of wolves has been living. The daily activities of these wild creatures are carefully recorded by this couple, whose singular understanding that the wolves are wild things infuses their work with brilliant meaning. They never forget the wild side of the wolves, and strive to always enhance it. They make no effort to domesticate the pups they raise on a bottle. They are especially careful not to project their need for something warm and cuddly onto the wolf pups. Their clear intentionality undergirds this beautiful documentary; they do not foist domestication in any form upon these wolves. It is as if the adult wolves understand that. Deeply imbedded within the interactions between wolf and human is an exquisite unspoken agreement. Nonverbal communication is more than sufficient.

When the humans go into the compound to sit in motionless silence among them, the wolves accept them with a kind of untamed grace. Instinctively they seem to know their wildness (and their existence) is not threatened and, in return, they come willingly to lick the faces and hands of the humans among them. They look into the eyes of the humans with primitive animal wisdom.

When the time comes for the wolves to be relocated to another wilderness area, the couple travels through the night to deliver them to their new home on the Nez Perce tribal reservation in Idaho. They release the wolves and sit down upon the ground in this new habitat. The time has come for farewells. Beginning with the Alpha male, and proceeding through the entire clan, ending with the Omega wolf, each wolf comes to the husband and then to his wife to bid them good-bye. The Alpha male walks up to the husband and thrusts out his paw, laying it into the man's open palm, offering him this symbol of friendship and love. The wolf bobs his head up and down; then he licks the man's face. All the wolves greeted this husband and wife with licks upon the face, or out-thrust paw into the hand, or by rubbing their face against the face of the human (Dutcher Film).

In that moment, the wolves, always wild, make a choice. They choose to sublimate their wildness even as they choose to safely connect with, and not harm, the human. The wolves controlled this interaction between species. This husband and wife team sat in positions of submission, with heads lowered, in order to be received by these wild creatures and touched by them. To witness these animals bid their human friends good-bye was to witness both the magnificent wildness of the wolf and the profound mourning and loss in the humans. When the wolves had each, in turn, come forward to offer their good-byes, they turned away, and were led off into the unknown places of their new home by the Alpha male. The wolves never looked back.

Two humans lived in close proximity with wild animals that have been feared for centuries. Hunted almost to extinction, the wolf had been reviled as a vicious predator in literature down through history, but this documentary showed the true nature of this wild canine. The careful and respectful manner in which these two humans treated the wolves was exemplary. Their profound awareness of the wolves' untamed wildness colored every interaction between animal and human.

In my introduction I mentioned a dream in which a lavender leopard, which I saw as symbolic of the Holy Spirit, showed me that improbable change is not impossible. If she could change her spots, what changes are possible for each of us? Two other animals skulked about in this same dream. The setting was a church where I was the pastor. Wherever I went inside this church, the lavender leopard would come slipping into the same room. She would curl up in a corner and simply watch me. The other animals (who seemed to represent the other entities in the Trinity) never came into full view. They were quite adept at hiding, and the adults in the church were unaware of their presence. Completely unaware. Only the children knew these wild animals. Only the children could see them. The children were the only ones who were aware of the wild side of God, and could embrace it fully.

If we could understand, to some small degree, the dimensions of the wild side of God, we would be struck with an awe of immeasurable proportions. It would not be one we could easily cast into noun or verb or metaphor. The *mysterium tremendum* of God's being lies far outside the universe of quantifiable scientific measurement or formula, for mystery cannot be measured or described. Linguist George Steiner would remind us that we have "used up all possible symbols without really penetrating their meaning." We live in a vast sea of words, assaulted during every waking moment with commercial words that intend to draw us toward a particular person, product, or event. Steiner concludes, "The fact is that words say nothing.... There are no words for the deepest experience" (Steiner, 185).

Unfortunately, we have spent centuries trying to wrap words around an indescribable force in the universe that we have named "God." We have spent almost the same amount of time trying to domesticate a God with scant appreciation for this same God's untamed nature. The Valley Girl slang articulation of the word "awe" falls far short of the mark in encounters with the wild side of God. When teens use the word "awesome" to describe everything from a trendy color in lipstick to a "hot" boyfriend, this word is diminished into the vocabulary of the secular and mundane. A God who is a "consuming fire" should provoke human awe, but therein is the problem. When we use terms like "shock and awe" to describe our attack on another nation, we fail to recognize the ways such terms alienate. In a nation driven by the ego, inflated egos are accepted daily as the authority on everything from leadership in the government to scientific accomplishment. The opposite ability to surrender to a god of any kind is viewed as almost impossible. Certainly such a surrendering does not come easily in a nation that extroverts every whim, feeling and physical need. We have no inclination to be still or silent with the God-spirit within, when we fill our environment with the noise of television, radio and cell phone. Our souls are accosted by constant sound in this culture. In an egocentric nation, where extroversion is rewarded and introversion is regarded as anomic, to find a place of soul-stillness and spirit-quietude is almost impossible.

We Americans prize our independence. We like control. We like to be in charge, of our lives, of our values, of our destinies. We consider ourselves a can-do nation filled with bright, capable individuals who are quite good at a vast and diverse variety of occupations, professions, and trades. American Christianity is honed in the same marketplace. For decades business models have been thrust upon everything in the church—from the ways worship is conducted, to the method employed for stewardship campaigns. Outside consultants bring in business models and church leaders believe they are worth every penny of their often steep consulting fees. In a morass of marketing ploys, where we are bombarded daily with literally thousands of commercials and advertisements, why not use successful models from the business arena if they work? What's wrong with using what works? If the church is a part of the culture, it must be prepared to respond to that culture. Right? The secular notions of process, structure, organization, and policies all have a daily impact upon the church as a social institution. The people who are "the church" within the church bring their contemporary expectations along with them. Sometimes it is impossible to honor those expectations.

I've never forgotten a conversation with the mother of a student who came to the church and stepped into my office to voice her anxiety that her daughter might not be happy taking classes that I would teach. When the dust settled, the mother's angst wound itself around the daughter's personality trait (or a learned attitude) of assuming entitlement without work. The child also assumed she could say anything she chose, no matter how disrespectful or vulgar, to an adult. She had been so coddled that any adult who would deny her demands provoked rage in reaction. Her mother feared the worst; it was a self-fulfilling result of her previous interactions with her own daughter.

This teenage girl reflected the society in which she lived. She wanted what she wanted when she wanted it, period. She was unused to having anyone expect that she be responsible for anything, but she wanted to claim her autonomy with every sentence. She was a living, breathing example of a narcissistic personality, brought to birth in a narcissistic age, and *it wasn't her fault*. This adolescent child mirrored a whole culture in love with itself. She was growing up in a nation that had gone from the societal rigidity of the forties and fifties, through the changeling looseness of the sixties and seventies, back-pedaling its way through the regression of the eighties and nineties, to find itself swimming in an illusionary lake of nostalgia and pseudo-religiosity in this first decade of the twenty-first century. The cultural climate of the United States in the present moment is so fraught with extreme opposites, most of us don't know where to turn or what to do after we've turned. No wonder our children are confused and obstreperous and troubled.

The gods of extreme technology have allowed us to believe we are super beings. The gods of self-absorption, self-centeredness, self-focus and self-comfort-above-all-else are the new idols we have substituted for a God who is much larger than our imaginations or verbal descriptors. A God who is "a consuming fire" is a being who might provoke awe, or wonder, or questions beyond all answers—if we were courageous enough to let go of our trite idols for one nanosecond. But in America our God better make us feel good, fast, if we are going to accept her, him, it or them. Our church better provide for the multiplicity of needs we bring through its doors, or we go church-shopping in a competitive ecclesiastical marketplace. We want a god who is an amalgam of Dr. Phil, Oprah Winfrey, Deepak Chopra, and Suze Orman. We want a god of financial security and prosperity, a god for an ideal family, an American god for any war we want to wage, a god who affirms our life journey, and a god who has the same gender and skin color as ours. All these gods are part of a panoply of gods we seek, because they reflect our individualistic need to have our specific personhood and our arrogance as a nation affirmed by the divine.

By falling in love with a small god, who serves whatever purposes our egos demand, we have fallen in love with the shadow side of god. This god is the small, limited reflection of our own ethnocentric egos which are driven by the particularity of our own collective shadow neediness. In a world filled with pain and anguish, we are seeking cheap grace without either of the two. Our ability to connect with a God who is "a consuming fire" is further stultified by our own tendency to project national arrogance into a complex global arena.

The fact that this American God has been invoked in the war on terrorism is not new. Whenever this nation has gone to war, people have prayed for God to bless our soldiers. Even during the time of the Civil War, there was an assumption that God was on one side or the other. When asked if God was on the side of the North, Abraham Lincoln answered, "The real question is not whether God is on our side, but whether we are on God's side."

Such clarity is useful for this day and age, when we have reached this stage in the development of global technology. A computer in Pakistan can change the total on an American consumer's credit-card account with the stroke of one key. A hacker in Hong Kong can watch as this confidential transaction is completed. A twelve-year-old Australian can look, through cyberspace, over the hacker's shoulder, feeling elated that he has hacked into the hacker's computer at the same time the hacker has invaded the privacy of the Bank of America system. We live in a peculiar environment of global communications, yet provincial attitudes about our American gods allow us to cling to attitudes of national superiority. We expect God to be on our side, but we may balk if asked if we are on God's side.

The shadow gods we worship in this country are not synonymous with those who might be worshiped in Europe or Asia, or even Australia. We have our own peculiar gods who reflect nothing so much as they reflect our collective ego's determination to have comfortable gods who will meet the specificity of our needs. In this contemporary push to have our gods meet our modern needs to the fullest extent, we have provoked an undertow of unholy morphic energy. The Holy Spirit might be what we think we invoke, but our shadows have called in an unholy spirit. As the denial of our shadow has been given energy by the cultural dynamics in this nation, we have increased the energy of our shadow projection exponentially. The more we deny the shadow the greater its strength becomes.

This is the same projection we cast upon the gods we invoke. In response, like the prisoners described by Plato, the shadow sides of these same gods are the only images we can perceive. When we invoke a god to make us successful in killing or in war we are invoking the shadow energy of god, and thus calling forth unholy spirit. When we invoke a god whom we have molded from human expectations or frustrations or resentments or prejudices or values or morality, we have not invoked the God who is a consuming fire. Instead we have invoked a pale substitute, limited by the boundaries of human imagination, and have, instead, unleashed an immense morphic field of unholy energy, filled with unholy spirit.

There must be some pathway to new patterns of living, where we have an authentic understanding of the ways we can enhance Holy Spirit energy in the morphic sea that surrounds us. There must be a more balanced way to perceive God. War is not the only way to settle differences. It is one of the most primitive means for doing so, no matter how sophisticated the weaponry. We must find some other way to settle conflicts. When we understand fully the creative energy of the very shadow we have spent years and years denying, we will understand a little more about the wild side of God and our own connectedness to it.

Chapter 10

Transforming the Judas Shadow in Self

The extreme paradigmatic changes that came in the last fifty years of the twentieth century and during the leading edge of the twenty-first century are more rapid social change than the human psyche believes it can tolerate. These metamorphoses in ruling paradigms have been like major tectonic shifts within the collective unconscious. Our natural reaction to these rapid changes is to run screaming into the perceived security of what we do know: the roles, patterns, and norms of an ancient past. First the denial, then the retreat into the familiar are predictable reactions to rapid change. What we do not understand is automatically resisted by the human psyche. The age of technology has provoked such reactions because it has thrust more rapid changes into the daily lives of the people on this planet than most other eras in the history of humankind. Think of bar codes...remember the time before them...and consider all the other changes that have been synonymous with them.

If we are to heal the global shadow dynamics described in the earlier chapters of this book, we must begin to reflect upon our individual participation in them. This means we must look inward and make peace with our own shadow and mind-habit reality in order to cleanse the morphic field in which we swim daily. To understand this psychic reality requires some understanding of the actual biochemical reality of our individual human physicality. We cannot change the deepest reaches of the unconscious without knowing that these same levels of the psyche are carriers of critical information locked inside ourselves.

Japanese scientist, Dr. Masaru Emoto, began to experiment with the very core levels of the human physical body in 1993. Dr. Emoto began with his understanding that humans are comprised mostly of water, in that at birth we are 90% water, and by the time we reach adulthood we are 70% water. Water is the physical property that every human shares in common. As Dr. Emoto explored the ways water circulates within humans and as a dominant component of the global geography, he discovered that water had the ability to copy information. But, not only can water copy information, it also memorizes information.

Through extensive and carefully conducted experiments with water from different sources, Dr. Emoto discovered that water responds to positive and negative stimuli. Using a high speed microscopic camera, Dr. Emoto found that classical music or words of praise or gratitude changed the molecular structure of water into a beautiful crystalline form like an exquisite snowflake. Water exposed to opposite stimuli or words of derision or anger produced malformed, fragmented shapes.

The process used to test the water's reaction to stimuli was fascinating because the negative words were not spoken aloud! Instead, negative words were written on pieces of paper and wrapped around bottles of water, facing the water. Dr. Emoto wrote, "It didn't seem logical for water to 'read' the writing, understand the meaning and change its form accordingly" (xxiv), but that is exactly what happened. He continued his experiments using various verbal phrases, some spoken aloud, some not, some positive, some negative. What he extrapolated from these experiments is summed up in this sentence: "The vibration of good words has a positive effect on our world, whereas the vibration of negative words has the power to destroy" (xxv).

That old adage about "sticks and stones" will no longer hold, because we understand only too well that negative words can harm or destroy and positive words can enhance or affirm. Words allow us to express the deepest levels of our own beings. Words connect us to soul. Their impact upon the molecular soul of water is obvious in the extraordinary photographs Dr. Emoto has taken. When we consider the countless words that bombard the human cell-spirit during a given day, we can more easily understand the levels of harm these words are causing. Consider the large segments of time that negative words, in news reports about ongoing wars around the world, or reports detailing a sensational murder, are cast upon the receptive waters of our physical bodies. Consider the impact those words are having upon water, the element that comprises the largest percentage of our individual bodies and the global mass. If such words can radically change the molecular structure, and thus the spirit of water, what are they doing to us at a soul level?

An experiment performed at Washington State University gives us another glimpse into the internal chaos created by external stimuli. A team led by Michael Skinner found that rats exposed to fungicides or pesticides had reduced sperm counts in more than one generation of offspring. This occurred even though subsequent generations of these rats were not exposed to the toxic chemicals. These scientists noted they were surprised to discover reduced sperm counts in three more successive generations, even though they found no obvious mutations in the DNA of these same animals (Connor, 6/3/05). What they did discover was that the physical body can hold inherited toxicity.

These experiments come forty years after American scientist Cleve Backster used a lie detector to discover that plants exhibited high levels of emotional reactions to external stimuli similar to the emotional responses in humans. These same experiments are also part of a worldwide scientific effort to understand the deepest levels of plant and bacteria life on this planet (www.mindpowernews.com). They show that plants have the ability to "think" in ways humans are still unwilling to grasp or accept.

If these scientific results are extrapolated to the human soul, that deepest part of the self in each one of us, then we must hold an awareness that both toxicity and blessings can be carried at a molecular level of the human body, and thus imprinted within the soul. The mistaken New Testament notion that we are embodied souls would lead us to believe we have some sort of a free-floating soul that is not bound or reactive to the physical body. We may even think we believe the body is the temple for the soul, but we have no clarity about what that means. That perception is one we carry from the Hellenistic and Cartesian philosophies, thrust into the earliest teachings of the Christian church. It imposed itself upon the biblical text and continues as the predominant habit of the mind in the Western world. When we subscribe to the notion of a "flesh and spirit divided," we are simply extending the imprint passed down to us through the genetic encoding we received from our birth parents, who were themselves the byproducts of similar genetic encoding.

If we could fully accept the findings of Masaru Emoto, Michael Skinner and numerous other scientists, or the philosophy of Aristotle, we would understand that we are ensouled bodies, rather than embodied souls. As I explored this same concept in my book, *The Magdalene Legacy*, I came to the conclusion that ensouled bodies cannot ignore the human spirit, or set it aside to be considered only one day a week. Ensouled bodies understand that every aspect of the human journey is part of a sacred process (170-172). Our souls lead the body; they are the womb embracing our DNA. Definitive research over the last thirty years has shown that the mind is critical to healing the body. The soul/spirit is even more critical to this vital process.

Pierre Teilhard de Chardin once wrote, "We are not human beings having a spiritual experience. We are spiritual beings having a human experience." We cannot ignore the human spirit and heal ourselves any more than we can ignore the global spirit and heal the world. With these understandings in place we can begin to address our own individual soul wounding.

Think of retired superstar Michael Jordan's tremendous ability to dribble a basketball down a court with remarkable speed and grace. For him to almost fly up to the net to drop the ball through the hoop with astounding accuracy was the result of hours and hours spent replicating the same pattern daily. By the time Michael Jordan finally retired from basketball, he could accomplish this repeated pattern of speed and accuracy using nothing more than his brain stem. This freed the rest of his brain to process other information, such as offensive or defensive strategy. We ordinary mortals, who have not played basketball daily, would be required to engage the majority of the brain cortex to do anything close to the same thing. If we had done what Jordan had done, hour after hour, day after day, our response would be automatic, too. We, too, would be imprinted with the ability to almost fly.

Turning inward to the shadow wounding we carry in the core of our souls, we can consider similar ways we imprint the neural pathways inside ourselves. For example, consider the ways addiction has a profound impact upon our physical body and the soul. Any addiction develops because we either consciously or unconsciously recognize, and come to desire, the rush we get from it. The addiction emerges through repetition. If someone is addicted to anger and uses rage to control their environment, this addiction allows that person to create a powerful biochemical pathway resulting in the rush or high. A cascade of internal biochemicals is provoked by the "rageaholic" melodrama whose endorphic end result is the desired high. Since the desired high is often denied by the person who is the rageaholic, the addiction gains greater power in the body because it is fed by shadow denial. Over time the addictive process becomes as automatic as Jordan's abilities on a basketball court, and the neural pathway is equally as strong. By sheer repetition the neural pathway is stamped, again and again, with the same message.

This process occurs with all addictions, whether we are addicted to drugs, sex, sugar, alcohol, religion or any of the other numerous chemicals or activities we use to satisfy ourselves. The neural pathway is imprinted in a more pronounced way each time we provoke the biochemical cascade. Neurotransmitters translate an electrical signal to a chemical one. Made from amino acids and therefore produced simply and quickly, neurotransmitters are biosynthetic pathways that serve as messengers. The various chemicals that people ingest mimic neurotransmitters, or can block neurotransmitters, or can cause the inappropriate release of neurotransmitters. Consider the generational dynamics proven by Michael Skinner. Such research information is vitally important for children of alcoholics or drug addicts, since toxicity can be inherited at a molecular level.

Also consider—the opposite must be equally true. We carry love and compassion and gentleness and the desire for authentic peace at the molecular level as well. Sadly enough, we often remember negative stimuli with more accuracy than we seem to recollect positive stimuli. This habit of the mind may be indicative of the power of negative thoughts, words or actions, or it may be one more indicator of generational scarring. The neural pathways informed by our genetic encoding have been imprinted with patterns we will easily emulate, simply because they are automatic responses.

To change these unhealthy neural patterns requires an intentional decision to change the thought process. Once the decision is made we must also repeat the thought process. If we are to reject negative patterns, we must do so with deliberate intentionality—repeated, again and again. I can remember when my mother would use a particular verbal lament that I found spine-chilling. She would say, quite often, when something was worrisome, "This is just killing me; it's just killing me!" This would happen when one of her offspring managed to throw off the psychic bridle she had tried to fasten firmly in place. Her finely honed skills as a worrier inculcated the same edgy temperament in most of her children. Her continuing insistence that any deviation from her rigid expectations had the power to kill her left the rest of the household in a constant state of suspended animation, as if waiting to exhale. Her worrying and fretting did not kill her for a long time, but during her adult lifetime she was gripped by sundry illnesses of a vague and disquieting nature, none of which were helped by the consistent use of this melodramatic pronouncement. Yet my mother was awash in her emotional addictions.

My mother, like so many other Americans, went to church regularly and was vocal about her Christianity. Perhaps she believed that God needed to be kept for Sundays, since the rest of the week was filled with the incessant labor of running a large farm. Yet, we compartmentalize God into a small niche, like we compartmentalize the feelings in our bodies. We believe they are disconnected from our spirits, when both the body and the spirit are striving to teach us valuable lessons. We hear the voice of our shadow-habits with great clarity. Their constant nagging becomes the message we live and verbalize.

If my mother had halted this mind-habit of emotional outpouring by consciously stopping herself, even mid-sentence, she could have inserted a substitute for it. She could have said, "I relinquish my concern about (fill in the blank) to God's protective care." If my mother had been able to live into her spirit, by being aware of her soul's needs, she could have been more consciously aware of the voice of God's Spirit. She was not only unable to trust her spirit, she could not trust God's either. Our inability to hear the voice of God's Spirit, or to trust it, prevents us from confronting our addictions.

We only become aware of our addictions when we pay attention to our emotional attachment to them. We only change them when we are prepared to detach from this emotionality. In the film *What the Bleep Do We Know?* Joe Dispenza advised, "Emotions are not bad—they color the richness of our experience—it's our addiction that's the problem." In this same film, J. Z. Knight indicated, "We must pursue knowledge without interference from our addictions." Our American culture induces a love affair with emotional addictions through its emerging "norms" of reality television, other media-driven societal impositions or assumptions, and its national history. What is vital for us to understand is encapsulated in this statement, made by J. Z. Knight in the same film: "All emotion is, is holographically imprinted chemicals." These holographic imprints are the neural patterns we must learn to change.

This is not a simple process of "just saying no" since these neural patterns are so locked into place, we mistake them for something we cannot control. We need to stop and examine ourselves, and avail ourselves of information, such as Dr. Emoto's, that will help us evolve and grow. When we do so, we will discover that our addictive actions and habits of the mind, although they are perceived as automatic responses, do not need to become a life sentence with no reprieve. We are making a choice. By making that choice we are creating more addictions and more habits of the mind. The psychic shadow is an active impetus for the choices we make, and because we are as addicted to shadow actions as to chemicals, we participate in the choices the shadow offers in every nanosecond.

By staying addicted to the shadow, we allow the neural network to create a template of biochemical responses that become more and more a part of self, community, nation and world. The most complicated part of this is that the shadow response is deeply encoded. Its imprint covers more than one generation of habits of the mind, and we must examine the assumptions that form those mind-habits in order to change or discontinue them. Furthermore, we carry this encoding locked inside the collective unconscious even from past lifetimes, since the soul is an active participant. Once wounded, the soul strives in each lifetime to learn the life-changing lessons that will free it from the scars left from such wounding.

Just as daily practice on the court created Jordan's automatic response, we have had eons of daily practice in carrying the neural imprinting of previous generations and lifetimes. The influence from ancestral habits of the mind carried into the cellular memory through past-life memory provides a fertile ground for becoming adept at shadow addictions of all kinds. These autonomic responses go unnoticed because they are automatic. To stop an addiction, we must get to know what we are doing automatically.

To use a more contemporary example than my mother's habit of the mind, consider the reactions we have in traffic. Any one of us will have encounters when we are driving that might provoke "road rage" if we choose to react in that way. On any given day someone driving a vehicle larger than ours may cut us off in traffic or ride our bumper at seventy miles an hour on the freeway. We choose the reactions we will have to these incidents. If we choose the biochemical cascade of rage too many times, we will discover that we have become road rage-aholics and our responses have become automatic.

If we stop ourselves mid-neural pathway, or mid-emotion, then we can radically change these automatic reactions. This is the reason alcoholic counselors strive to enable alcoholics to name their addiction and recognize its reality. Until the automatic reaction is recognized and stopped, the neural pathway remains intact and when the internal impulse is fired, the pathway already is in place for the automatic response. When we stop ourselves mid-emotion, we can begin a mind-body-spirit process that frees the soul from its imprinted wounding. This process looks with honesty, which may sometimes be painful, into the shadow habits of the mind and begins to untie the neural connection.

The biochemical activity along the neural pathways produces the vibrational energy of each individual human body. That vibrational energy is picked up by all those we encounter in home, school, church or workplace. It is also carried by the earth's very receptive water and moves in waves from place to place. By interrupting our habits of the mind and urges to addictive behavior repeatedly day-after-day, new neural pathways are formed. Then the old neural pathways atrophy so that we no longer remain victims of our own emotional melodramas or addictions. By changing our minds, we change our lives. When we change our thoughts, we change the neural pathways and thus our biochemistry.

This healing occurs from the inside out, and has the potential for healing backward in time, as well as forward. We will automatically leap to a habit-of-the-mind conclusion that the previous statement makes no sense. Surely no rational person would declare that we can heal the negative neural pathways of previous generations in this process! By healing the neural pathway, we heal the body at a molecular level. When we heal the body in this way, we are healing the soul. When we heal our souls, we heal the spirit. The changes at the levels of the DNA heal past wounds inflicted upon the soul. Just as these changes heal the autonomic tendency to genetically encode future generations with these same old wounds, the reverse is also true.

What does this healing look like at a shadow level? The shadow is finally acknowledged, making room for our creative ability to recognize its characteristics, to notice them without judgment, and to learn where the negatives need to be healed and the positives need to be enhanced. Our wild shadow side is released from its psychic prison.

I love the beautiful way John Muir wrote of the wild side of God when he said, "In God's wildness lies the hope of the world." When we encounter the wild side of the shadow with an attitude of open acceptance, we can more easily understand why we have rejected it. We have only rejected it out of fear. The fear of the wild side of God reflects our fear of the wild side of our spirit/shadow/soul. This fear paralyzes our ability to express our inborn native intelligence in a way that others will easily receive. A vicious fear cycle ensues. Afraid of the wild side of God, we are afraid of our inborn wild spirit. This fear causes us to stop the truest part of our "self" from authentic expression. At some level, we seem to have an awareness that if we express this authentic aspect of ourselves, this essence of who we really are, we will be perceived as "out of control" and subsequently ostracized for it. Afraid of being out of control, or being seen that way, we allow fear to drive our lives in an ever-continuing spiral.

I remember a time when, as an elder in a large church in the Midwest, I agreed to teach a class on spirituality. The man who had taught this class in the past had opted not to teach for that semester, but he was there every Sunday and his shadow would not allow him to move beyond his old understandings of God or religion. Every Sunday, without fail, he would demand that we define "spirituality" before we could actually have a conversation about it. A dean at a nearby university, he could not allow himself to delve into the depths of his own soul's substance. By his relentless insistence upon a definition, he revealed how much he needed the comfort levels of defined religious imagery. He would never have been able to articulate his profound fear of the wild side of God or of his own equally wild internal shadow. Nevertheless, his shadow drowned out any substantive conversation that might have explored spirituality in new ways. Both his academic training and his natural inclination to the linear and precise kept that from happening. His negative spirit energy emerged in such powerful ways, Divine Energy was sent out to wander in the wilderness. We were never able to move past these attempts at definition.

If we express our wild, energetic spirit, we cannot be "controlled" by a parent, a school or church, a corporation, or the government. The basic assumptions of our socialization process from birth to death inculcate a cellular-level fear of being out of control. From this fear, our denial of shadow emerges, for the fear is embedded in our cells. We have been socialized to become our own Judases and to betray the very core levels of our selves. Our parents were not to blame, because they held no more awareness of this phenomenon than do we. Our teachers were not to blame; they held genetic encoding provoked by generations of cultural norms and habits of the mind passed down through their families and past lives. Not even the government, or the church, or any established social institution is to blame. Every one of these social institutions was, and is, comprised of individual human beings who carry complex genetic encoding that reflects our cultural assumptions, beliefs, and values, all of which are part of our habits of the mind.

While blaming a particular person, event, or institution is not helpful, all individuals must be responsible for their specific soul's journey. The innate, inborn intelligence of the human spirit/shadow/soul does not need the entrapments of modern civilization or our stunted culture to express itself. This wild side of ourselves is that mystery lodged within us. It has the ability to bring to birth such splendid accomplishments as the great music of those like Bach, Beethoven, or Mozart. From this same core level of human psyche/body came the astounding scientific discoveries of Marie Curie, Candace Pert, Albert Einstein, Jonas Salk and Masaru Emoto. Many scientists will tell you that the ultimate understanding of their discoveries did not come from rational, linear, empirical thought processes, but from a deeply felt intuitive urge.

We must break away from the generational assumptions that

stultify our souls at a purely individual level, and contribute to the contamination of the collective soul of the world. We must break away from the hypnotic entrapments of our daily culture, because they serve to continue the creation of unholy morphic energy. These illusionary norms do not provoke self-reflection. Instead, they smother authentic creativity and subtly persuade millions of people to live mediocre lives, without hope, without joy. Breaking this cycle is possible through daily self-reflection that brings us face-to-face with both the creative potentiality of our shadows and their equally potent negative habits of the mind.

Only through a conscious awareness of the ways our old assumptions are unhelpful, and actually harmful, can we change our habits of the mind. Our habits of the mind only change when our thought processes form new neural pathways. Never has the concept of "Every Thought is a Prayer" been more critical to the healing of humanity. When we understand that every thought is, indeed, a prayer in some form, then we know: whether we choose to bless self and other, or curse self and other, our choice is critical to such healing.

We resist this understanding of the prayer-power of our thoughts as much as we resist the shadow. We don't want to consider that all the less-than-noble thoughts that rise to the surface during every waking moment are forms of prayer. We don't want to claim the magnitude of our chaotic thought processes or our own internal confusion. Perhaps this is the reason we also resist empirical data that clearly shows how our thoughts create our individual reality, moment by moment. Yet, as more and more definitive research shows, our thoughts are active participants in forming our vibrational energy. Every single thought has the capacity to harm or to heal.

Our vibrational energy has an immeasurable influence upon our environment, and affects the vibrational energy of both living things and what we have heretofore regarded as inanimate objects. The sum total of this effect becomes our morphic field. Every one of us participates in forming this morphic field and in determining whether it will be healthy or not. Each of us participates in the collective that ultimately makes the choice between holy morphic resonance and unholy morphic cacophony. If every leader of every nation on the planet understood this, they would step back from choosing war to settle conflicts. Going to war would be their last choice.

As individuals we can begin the process of altering the neural patterns that link us to addictive behavior, obsessive thinking, and shadow projection by intentionally finding moments of stillness during the day. In a culture where speed, noise and external influences make such quietude seem impossible, our first challenge is to create these moments in opposition to cultural imperatives. Not only is stillness necessary, but silence is also an important component of self-reflection. If we are never still and silent with our own spirits, these same spirits have no opportunity to speak to us.

This one-on-one dialogue is an example of the difference between religion and spirituality. Corporate worship is, too often, the practice of religion. Intentional one-on-one silence and listening to Divine Spirit is the way we live spiritually. In a corporate worship service, with the vibrational energy of other people swirling around us, it is very difficult to sink into this kind of surrendering of the ego. Step into any church on any Sunday morning and notice whether the people there have an awareness of their environment. Notice their reaction to space that has been dedicated as sacred, as holy space. Notice whether they are talking with great animation, or sitting with eyes closed in prayerful attention toward God. Visit more than one church to see if you can discern similarities. The one place where you might find this silence is in the context of a Quaker meeting.

The voice of the spirit has so many obstacles to overcome, it may more often sit silently among us in corporate worship. My experience of corporate worship is that few churches offer appropriate moments of silence during the context of worship. If silence is observed, most people cannot sustain the energy of stillness and silence much beyond thirty seconds. Then an uneasiness emerges and the people will begin to shift about and squirm in their seats. Only a rare worship service is conducive to silent approaches to

God.

Once we learn how to create individual quietude for ourselves, we can slip into the internal rooms of the soul and become acquainted, maybe for the first time. The dialogue with the soul can include such questions as: What is meaningful for my soul? What do you, my soul, need in order to feel nurtured? How can I live a more meaningful life? What is my life's purpose? What happens after I die? Down through history those who asked these questions most vehemently were often regarded as demented, or at the very least unstable. Sometimes this dialogue with the soul may provoke similar reactions within us, but the dialogue is vital for our soul's growth.

Appropriate conversation with our own souls leads us naturally into dialogue with Divine Spirit. The more we engage in these still, silent conversations with our own souls, the more we are able to hear the voice of Divine Spirit. Stillness and silence create an opening for the voice of the Spirit to enter and speak to our hearts. This is not a corporate endeavor to be undertaken in the context of worship, where other soul energies potentially (but unconsciously) present obstacles to it. This is a one-on-one dialogue between the mind and the human spirit, which enables an encounter with Divine Spirit.

We Americans have not been socialized to stillness or silence. Our discomfort with it is an indicator of our cultural assumption that filling all waking space with sound is not only acceptable, it is desirable. Drowning in a sea of stimuli, we do not know how to quiet our own noisiness in order to find God. To seek out and hear the voice of the spirit, we must learn how to be disciplined enough to sink into solitary silences and trust them. Our innate distrust of such silence is anchored in our own fears. What if I go so deeply into the realm of this wild spirit I can't find my way back? What if I flounder there and slip over the edge into madness? These fears are rarely given voice because we deny them. We can own a fear of terrorist attack more willingly than we can claim our fear of silent attention toward God.

Back in 1996 I attended a conference in Philadelphia where

Caroline Myss taught her innovative concepts on the "anatomy of the spirit." At the end of her day of teaching, she asked those who were Christians to raise their hands. A majority of the large audience did so. Then she cast this challenge out upon the waters of our spirit/bodies. She said, "If you claim to be a Christian, then you should be able to pray, 'Into your hands I commit my spirit,' each day. You should be prepared to follow the voice of God's Spirit in your daily living, and you should be prepared to commit your spirit daily into God's hands."

I left that conference determined to heed her advice. After all, I was a preacher in the Presbyterian Church, USA, which surely meant I should be able to pray this very prayer. That night I prayed it for the first time, and in the days to come I prayed it again and again. Soon I noticed a subtle change in my thought patterns. Over time this change became less and less subtle, and more and more pronounced. One very real change was the diminution of my internal fear factor. I was no longer living with a daily undertow of fear. By the very repetition of this prayer I found I stopped feeling any concern about my next position as an interim pastor. I very quickly learned that as soon as I asked for a new position, it was being sent by Divine Spirit. More than once the position I thought was the best one for me turned out not to be the one God had chosen, and I was sent into another place.

In talking with other ministers who specialized in interim work, they detailed their experience of having three to six months or more between positions. Yet I went from position to position with not even one day between contracts. I never had even one day of lag time when leaving one parish and entering another one. This pattern emerged immediately after I began to pray, "Into your hands, O Living God, I commit my spirit, today and every day." Later I also added, "Show me where to go and I will go where you send me." In the past I had thought I was going where I was being sent before I began to pray the intentional second sentence of this prayer. But I suspect I had foisted my own ego upon the choices in the past. By opening myself to much more risky unknowns, a whole new world of experiences with different congregations in diverse locations was opened for me.

I include this example here because Caroline Myss' challenge literally changed my life. My own experience of the lowering of my own fear leads me to believe it can help countless others for whom fear has become the driving impetus for daily living. I learned to trust the Holy Spirit for guidance in new ways. I learned that I did not need to control nearly as much of my life strand as I had thought important before. If a substantial number of the people on this planet prayed this prayer to their gods, whatever form or name those gods might have, the morphic energy of the entire planet would be changed in a positive way. Individual healing would emerge and from it, collective healing would become a reality.

Some years ago I was fortunate enough to meet a woman who is a cantor. Linda Baer has an extraordinary ability to interpret the biblical text in innovative ways that speak to the heart of contemporary cultural angst. I can think of no better way to end this chapter on the healing of individual shadow than with the words from her exegetical work on Abraham and Isaac.

Hineini

Words and Music by Linda Baer ©1998

1. Abraham heard a distant voice
From far, far away,
Far, far away,
High above.

And the distant voice said to Abraham.
"Give me a gift,
Give me Isaac's life,
And I'll give you love."

And the Voice called out, "Abraham!"
And Abraham answered,

"HERE I AM, HINEINI,
WHAT DO YOU ASK OF ME?
HERE I AM, HINEINI."

2. Abraham and Isaac
Went walking up the mountain,
Walking up the mountain
To see God.

And Isaac said to Abraham
"Here is the firestone,
Here is the wood,
Where is the ram?"

And Isaac cried, "Father, father"
And Abraham answered,

"HERE I AM, HINEINI,
GOD WILL ANSWER ME
HERE I AM, HINEINI."

And Isaac laid his body down,
For the God of his father
His anger bound in sorrow,
And his love stained with fear,

"Why is my love not enough?"
Isaac cried
As the hand of Abraham
Gently raised the knife.

And suddenly Abraham heard a voice
Rise up on wings, shining deep inside,
Calling, "Abraham, Abraham"
"Choose Life!"

And Abraham answered,
"HERE I AM, HINEINI,
GOD IS WITHIN ME,
HERE I AM, HINEINI."

3. By the waters of Beer Sheva
  Abraham was weeping,
  Abraham was weeping
    All alone . . .

And high up on the mountain
  Isaac in his silence,
  Made the first shofar
    From the ram.
  And the shofar blew,
Crying "God, where are you?"
And the Still Small Voice answered

"HERE I AM, HINEINI,
LOOK INSIDE AND SEE,
HERE I AM, HINEINI."

Chapter 11

Transforming the Judas Shadow in Culture and Church

The ability to integrate or transform the shadow in the collective must begin with an individual and personal realization of our own soul's journey. That realization comes through self-reflective encounters with internal Holy Spirit—found in the amazing creative energy of the shadow's bright side, and the contrast cast by the shadow's negative echoing unholy spirit. When we look into the face of, and acknowledge, the shadow's urging toward balance, we do the hard work of self-reflection. Without self-reflection and the healing that emerges from it, the collective remains contaminated—and spiritually constipated.

The American culture is suffering from so many wounding aspects of our historical past and our contaminated present. Perhaps the recent trend in corporate packaging of spirituality along with "Christian" products is a strange, abortive attempt to heal what is wrong. Yet corporations that try to package Jesus along with hamburgers or chicken seem more intent on following the recent American trends in sideways religion. By marketing a drive-through God packaged for those in a hurry (but not wanting to be "left behind"), these corporations drive their market by using God or Jesus or Christianity as a marketing tool. This practice is no more admirable than the notion that God can be employed for political or military purposes. The Judas energy cannot be healed by employing the shadow for that purpose.

Two generations ago the Lebanese poet Kahlil Gibran wrote of a nation that reaches levels of pseudo-sophistication in which "it does not weave what it wears, nor plant what it eats, nor press the wine that it drinks." Gibran saw this as a woeful condition as the same nation "departs from religion to belief, from country lane to city alley, from wisdom to logic." Gibran's poetry and prose reveal the deep reflective thought patterns of a truly wise man. He despaired of a nation "that does not raise its voice save in a funeral, that shows esteem only at the grave, that waits to rebel until its neck is under the edge of the sword" (25-26).

Healing the Judas Shadow means we look at ourselves in a therapeutic way. We must stop passively accepting the pronouncements that harm our people and all other peoples in the world. We must halt actions that harm the earth and the air on this planet. We must be engaged in soul-healing and spirit-building.

This society cannot be healed without recognizing its wounded soul. If we consider the earliest history of our nation and the peoples who dwelled here when we found it, we know that our treatment of them was the beginning link in a long history of unapologetic violence. By assuming that what we found was something we could possess, we took over so-called ownership of this land by driving its previous inhabitants into small corrals where they were expected to live happily ever after. How those old wounds need to be cleansed and healed.

Native Americans of diverse tribes and beliefs held one dominant value in common: they cherished the earth and knew it nurtured them. Our disconnect from this one aspect of spiritual nurturance could be healed if we were intentional about creating healing ritual for that purpose. We need to repent and be forgiven for what we have done to these people and to their land. There are those familiar with the history of those times who would say these same Native Americans fought us tooth and claw. Would we not do the same if invading forces walked onto our shores and declared that they were taking over the land and everything on it? If we also look at our history from the perspective of those who were here when we arrived, we would understand our need for some form of ritual repentance. That ritual would, of necessity, be part of cooperative ritual undertaken together with Native Americans.

I live in a beautiful part of the world known as the Shenandoah Valley of Virginia. Before this place was taken away from the Native Americans who lived here before us, they had given it this name. A form of this name was Senedo. One translation of this word is "Daughter of the Stars." The connotation of a place as the daughter of the stars links us to a mystical knowing of the land as intimately and inextricably bound to the universe and to something beyond itself. We came and "possessed" the land, but failed to honor its sacred meanings. This underlying "daughter" meaning is far greater than seeing the land as real estate to be bought and sold, a notion with pure profit, power or control at its center. The uncoupling from its daughterhood, its very real association with mystery, is just one part of the cultural damage we have inflicted upon this land and its early inhabitants.

Our vast mistreatment of Native Americans continues right up to the present moment as slick lobbyists take millions of dollars from tribes whom they treat with ultimate disrespect. We would heal the soul of this nation if we came together to use cross-cultural ceremony to ask forgiveness for the harm we have inflicted. We have a responsibility to become keepers of the land and of each other's wisdom. That can only happen when we are intentional about seeking out the wisdom offered by these ones who were here before we were. Our American culture can only be enhanced when we educate ourselves about others' religions, traditions and ethnic particularities. We cannot hope to participate in healing the soul of the world without first understanding others, especially those we do not know in our own country.

The soul of the world cannot be healed unless we are willing to strive toward national healing. Huge fragments of our national and historical soul wounding are strewn about in the energy left over from the clashes of the Civil War and the slavery at issue in that war. African-Americans have made many advances since Martin Luther King Jr. was assassinated, but the shadow energy that drove his assassination is still lurking in a more subtle form in the present day. If you add only one other cultural piece of wounding to racism and consider the immense losses of the Vietnam War, it is small wonder that those who chose to seize tyrannical power in the present moment are successfully thwarting the accountability built into our U. S. Constitution.

The collective soul of this nation carries unresolved grief from the Vietnam War. That unresolved grief has been compounded by the war in Iraq. The war in Iraq has added insult to an injury that had never healed from the inside out. Any physician or nurse knows any deep wound must heal from deep inside the body before it heals on the outside for complete healing to occur. The deep wounds of the Vietnam Era have been left untended and unmourned. Our failure to properly tend the deep levels of collective soul injuries means that these soul infections have been allowed to fester for decade after decade. We pretend there is no infection, but the cultural soul is carrying around this unrecognized and unhealed injury, made more painful because it has been replicated by the war in Iraq. That replication provokes and promotes cultural depression.

Formal declarations of war allow humans to engage in blood rituals that have been accepted by nations for all the yesterdays we have known and not known. Wars still contaminate the world we inhabit, but they serve no good purpose. Most of the years our nation celebrates as its singular history have been marred by the blood ritual of war. We have funded a war department that did not change when we renamed it the Department of Defense. Whatever euphemism is encapsulated in the labeling we use, its purpose is the same: to wage war. I suspect that John F. Kennedy had a vision for world peace when he created the Peace Corps. I also suspect those individuals who have served in the Peace Corps entered that work with the same or a similar vision. Visions of peace are sublimated when war is waged.

Our inability to imagine a peaceful world is reflected in the absence of a governmental Department of Peace. Yet, peace is a vital aspect of healing a world filled with conflict and hunger. Almost twenty years ago a Canadian scientist, Gary Whiteford, came before a United Nations conference to report on his research. He had studied the number of earthquakes that measured more than 5.8 on the Richter scale during the last century, and their correlation to underground nuclear testing. Before the United States and other nations had begun these underground tests, there was an average of sixty-eight earthquakes per year. After the underground testing began, the earthquakes increased to one-hundred, twenty-seven per year. Forty-eight hours after Pakistan set off five underground nuclear bombs, a severe earthquake killed four-thousand people in Afghanistan (Courteney, 128-129). The correlation is obvious.

We need visionaries in the world, and in this nation, if we are to survive in the culture we have created for ourselves. Unfortunately most visionaries are cast out of the realms of human power and their wisdom is not only disregarded, they are treated without respect and castigated for their failure to fit in.

I was working in the oil industry when Jimmy Carter was elected president. During that period of time, it was increasingly evident that fossil fuels were a limited global natural resource. The North Dakota company I was working for was reduced to importing oil products from Canada. President Carter did everything in his power to convince the American people of the gravity of this situation. For the first time solar power was explored as a viable option for powering everything from corporate office buildings to private residences. When Carter was defeated for a second term, I watched as every one of his initiatives was stripped down to the bone and/or discarded like so much rubbish. Despite this national lack of respect for Carter during his presidency, he has emerged as a global visionary who was awarded the Nobel Prize for Peace in 2002. Carter was only the third president in the history of our nation to be recognized in this way.

By the time Reagan was elected, the nation was busily covering its Watergate mistakes. Deficits were the order of the day and conversations about fossil fuels were halted in favor of corporate profit. Sport utility vehicles were dreamed into being by the automobile industry as if there was an endless supply of oil on this planet. Lax fuel standards were created to accommodate these monster machines, and Americans embraced them with glee.

Solar power disappeared from our national dialogue, just as tax credits for it disappeared from the IRS code. Now we are told we are addicted to fossil fuels, as if this is news and we had not been addicted for decades.

During this same time period another international visionary was thrust into the global consciousness. Mikhail Gorbachev, president of the Soviet Union, arrived at the October 1986 summit meeting in Reykjavik, Iceland having prepared well for talks on nuclear weapons. He went to the table for this famous conversation with President Reagan with a fully articulated plan to reduce intermediate-range nuclear weapons in Europe. Reagan went to the table empty-handed. The conversation had to be recessed for some hours after Gorbachev presented his proposal to Reagan. Reagan had no counter-proposal to offer; he had to scurry out and meet with his staff in order to catch up. Despite Reagan's ill-equipped entrance into these talks, they led to the signing of the Intermediate Range Nuclear Forces Treaty (INF) in 1987. That same year, Gorbachev was named Man of the Year by *Time* magazine. Later he was named Man of the Decade by the same publication for his work toward peace and democratic forms of government. The American nation has been fed the revisionistic history that the cold war ended because of Reagan, but Gorbachev was awarded the Nobel Prize for Peace in 1990.

If you consider all the living people around the world who have received the Nobel Prize for Peace, it is unfathomable that these same individuals are not active participants in advance considerations before military actions. We always turn to the warriors because that is our overriding impetus when we want to go to war. What would happen if we were willing, instead, to delay any military action until we had spent at least ten days (or thirty days) in conversations, and prayer, and silent meditation with world peacemakers? How would war look then? Would it be so seductive? How could Nobel-Peace-Prize winners change the assumptions that precede war? How could their perspective aid in decisions related to such blood sacrifice?

In 2006, the Nobel Peace Prize was awarded to a Bangladeshi

economist and banker, Muhammad Yurus. More than thirty years earlier, Yurus had founded the Grammen Bank to fund small loans to poor peoples in villages. Initially he made a list of forty-two people to whom he would lend money, none of whom owed more than $ 27.00, but many of whom were suffering from conditions set by loan sharks. These loan sharks were flourishing, and some of their borrowers were even cast into slavery because of their inability to pay off small loans.

Muhammad Yurus responded to a question about his singular achievement by answering, "I did something that challenged the banking world. Conventional banks look for the rich; we look for the absolutely poor." Yurus is the kind of visionary who may not even see himself in that way, but the opportunities he has offered to the poor, especially poor women in Third World nations, have been ones that changed their lives and those of their families.

In the same ways, Bill and Melinda Gates have formed a foundation with the underlying belief that "every life has equal value." With that as their primary standard, Bill and Melinda Gates "work to reduce inequities and improve lives around the world." In developing countries this foundation "focuses on improving health, reducing extreme poverty, and increasing access to technology in public libraries." Here in this country the foundation works to "ensure that all people have access to a great education and to technology in public libraries. In its local region, it focuses on improving the lives of low-income families."

Their Web site, www.gatesfoundation.org, includes a list of fifteen guiding principles. These principles reveal a consciousness that far exceeds that of many leaders in the American government. Among them: "Our focus is clear—and limited—and prioritizes some of the most neglected issues...; we must be humble and mindful in our actions and words. We seek and heed the counsel of outside voices. We treat our grantees as valued partners, and we treat the ultimate beneficiaries of our work with respect.... We demand ethical behavior of ourselves. We treat each other as valued colleagues.... We leave room for growth and change."

This last principle is vital to a living organization, because adapting to global change is critical to life itself. Every living species must change as its environment changes. Adaptation is the means to survival. Yet changes that are necessary at a national level are often ones that are resisted the most. Our old habits of the mind stultify adaptive thinking and keep us from making the kinds of structural changes that could improve our governmental and/or electoral processes. The American political environment is highly resistant to positive changes, even as it is a strong indicator of our Judas legacy.

Of all the changes that need to be made, abolition of the Electoral College mandated by the Constitution is one. Mass communication was far from the imaginations of those who wrote the Constitution. The Electoral College was a stipulation that made perfect sense in that day and time. Now it represents an anachronistic instrument that carries forward a dysfunctional tradition. For more than forty years this nation has had access to mass communication fully capable of allowing the majority vote of the people to choose the president and vice-president of this nation. If one sets aside the lingering problems with paperless voting machines or flawed processes in many states, the technology still exists whereby citizens can choose the leaders of this nation by a majority vote. There is no reason for continuing the Electoral College.

Election campaigns have become one of the huge financial enterprises in this nation. Millions of dollars are spent at the federal, state, and even local levels during election campaigns. Political consultants may not be a dime a dozen, but their share of this take is substantial. Thus, lobbying against anything that would change the status quo is a predictable aspect of the resistance to this change. If the campaign process, from primaries to election day, had a time limit of ninety days, consider how much money could be saved.

On February 24, 2007, John Hendren of ABC News reported that the 2008 campaign for the Office of the President would cost between "2 billion and 3 billion dollars."

If the twenty-second amendment to the Constitution were abolished and individuals elected to the Office of the President served only one term, many of the dynamics that plague our government and society would change. By repealing the twenty-second amendment, we could replace it with an amendment that stipulated one six-year term for the Office of the President. This one six-year term would match the terms U.S. senators serve. By adding a provision that would prohibit re-election to the Office of the President, any person elected to this office would be forced to focus upon the work of the executive branch of our government. Incessant fund-raising for election campaigns could be set aside for far more important work. Indulging in across-the-aisle catfights might be less seductive. Ideological focus groups would hold less power, since the Office of the President would not be a re-elective office.

Since war, and the waging of it, forms a large part of our collective history, we should have more clarity about it. If a president chooses to go to war, he or she should have some exit strategy that is clearly articulated to select Senate and House committees, even if it is not revealed in its entirety to the people. A failure to create such an exit strategy prolongs war as disorganized leaders scramble to cobble one together. As we arm our nation in unimaginable ways, we consistently and constantly set up others as alien and continue an ancient practice of dualism. By seeing ourselves and those others as separate and distinct from each other, we continue the old warring ways of our ancestors.

A quantum leap in both consciousness and theology would allow the church and the state to move beyond these old ways into an understanding of the interdependency of our planet. Only when we recognize that all those others are vulnerable, flawed, searching, struggling human beings, many with wounded souls and impoverished spirits, just like ourselves, can we begin to live into the healing that is vital for the world's soul. Such recognition can only come when the church and the nation step back from the egocentric and ethnocentric rigidity of American superiority. Power and control are driven by this stance, but soul-healing cannot emerge from it, no matter how many times scripture verses are printed on a hamburger wrapper.

Our odd mixture of religious, militaristic arrogance has gotten us to an outer edge of hyperbole that must be changed if we are to heal the soul of this nation, or participate in the healing of the world's soul. At a deep, primordial level of the human psyche we call out war in an unconscious effort to heal our own souls. Without appropriate self-reflection we will continue to create blood ritual to satisfy this psychic need, since we fail to understand or acknowledge it.

As the United States military wearily stumbled forward on the third anniversary of the second war on Iraq, states and counties began to have the courage that was lacking among national leaders. Residents in counties across the state of Wisconsin passed resolutions calling for U.S. troops to pull out of Iraq. At the same time, "seven states (Alaska, Arizona, Colorado, Hawaii, Maine, Montana and Vermont) voted either to criticize or ignore the Patriot Act" (Kingsbury, 26).

Then seven retired military generals, all with battlefield experience and more than thirty years of service each, stepped out of "the fog of war" and declared the Secretary of Defense incompetent, asking for his termination. Writing on "Why Iraq Was a Mistake," Lieutenant General Greg Newbold (Ret.) said, "I am driven to action now by the missteps and misjudgments of the White House and the Pentagon, and by my many painful visits to our military hospitals" (42).

As literally thousands of injured veterans of the Iraq war lie in hospital beds and hobble about with crutches, on prosthetic legs that replaced the ones blown off in that bloody altercation, we must find ways to respond to their wounding, both physical and psychic. We cannot ignore the deeply held pain these soldiers carry back from the battlefield. By doing so we again pretend that the cost of war is an acceptable one, when it is far from it.

Newbold continued with an eloquent plea: "The cost of flawed leadership continues to be paid in blood. The willingness of our forces to shoulder such a load should make it a sacred obligation for civilian and military leaders to get our defense policy right. They must be absolutely sure that the commitment is for a cause as honorable as the sacrifice" (42-43).

If the collective is ever to be healed, we need to hear this retired warrior's advice. Blood sacrifice is far too often disconnected from sacred purpose. Blood sacrifice is thoroughly and completely anachronistic, whether used as a means of settling disputes or of worshiping a god. Blood sacrifice is not necessary for transcendence and does not create it. The church where symbolic blood ritual was once assured has become like so many other competitive enterprises in America. By marketing itself to appeal to the masses of the commercial arena, it has become one more form of entertainment, invoking the name of God as if this God is synonymous with Mickey Mouse. In the doing of it, we lose our connectedness to God and to each other. We must find ways to reground ourselves in the sacred.

There is a deep longing for hallowed ground lying within some nether region of our souls. This is the longing that provokes many people who walk through the doors of any church on Sunday morning, any synagogue the day before. It is a longing for spiritual nurturance, for soul food. In such a hallowed place burning bushes would spring into spontaneous flames and sacred groves of trees would march along the horizon.

Kahlil Gibran once wrote, "You work that you may keep pace with the earth and the soul of the earth." This man understood that we must respect not only the souls of other humans, but the soul of the earth. He knew that our healing came through understandings of ourselves in relationship with others and with the earth. Our souls are nourished through such deepening understandings. We are all part of the vast whole that is this planet. The only way we can heal both ourselves and the planet is to embrace others who seem to be different from ourselves. Those differences, whether of language, tradition, government structure, or values and beliefs, can be celebrated when we understand that we are all part of one great amalgam of humanity in a shrinking global environment. That rapidly changing environment is part of the changes we ourselves have thrust upon our world.

Noah ben Shea has written, "Look carefully and you will see

we are all orchards hiding in seeds. You will see inside each of us is the Pharaoh. And inside every Pharaoh is a slave. And inside every slave is a Moses." It is this understanding of the soul within a seed that we must bring to our own healing and to the healing of this nation.

There are times when the unfamiliar presents a visual image that is so unforgettable, we know we were meant to embrace it and ponder it for many succeeding moments thereafter. Lingering in my mind is an unforgettable image of the saffron-yellow robes worn by a large group of Buddhist monks who came to a Christmas Eve worship service at a church where I was serving as an interim pastor. I had been with this congregation for two years. This was my last Christmas Eve in this church located just outside the beltway in Washington, D.C. I believe the presence of these men enhanced my last holy day with that church. Their visible presence in the midst of that congregation became a prism for us to enlarge our awareness of the ways God can be imagined.

Writing in *The New Convergence,* Albert Einstein declared, "Science without religion is lame, religion without science is blind." If religion lacks new imagery it is not only blind, but deaf as well. If religion refuses dialogue with those who hold other views, it chases away new potentiality in favor of old dogmatic tradition. If religion perceives itself superior to all other thought forms, it rides upon the crass horse of its own collective ego, but knows nothing of an authentic God. That horse wears a saddle formed of pure shadow.

The shadow has emerged in this powerful way because both the church and the culture have been partners in collusion. That collusion has fostered the diminution of the God-being to such small, anthropomorphic levels, God is no longer God with a capital G. This god has been limited by human definitions, doctrine, elaborate argument, and tradition.

Theologian Walter Brueggemann warned against both an intellectualization and a psychologization of the image of God when he wrote:

> Twin temptations beset us in our presentation of God. On the one hand, we may be tempted to a scholastic reductionism about God, so that all things are thought to be settled about God and nothing is left open. On the other hand, we may be tempted to render God only in psychological, personalistic terms so that the terrible sovereignty of God is nullified. Neither way will make the God of the Bible available to us. Both are idols lacking in power and vitality (15).

The God who has been adopted as the "traditional" God of Christianity is lacking in such vitality, because that vital life force has been sucked dry through generations of human determination to make this God into a one-sided idol of goodness, purity, and love. The God of psychology, and/or of New Age imagery, is no less sentimental, no less filled with love, no less impotent. Clearly neither the traditional Christian God, nor the New Age-psychopop God, has been allowed the balancing power of the shadow. The absence of shadow strips all these gods of the vitality necessary to feed the spirit of a complex society.

When both Christianity and pop-psychology/New Age leaders fall into the trap of allegiance to a one-sided image of divinity, the shadow emerges to claim a balance. On the one hand, the God of Christianity has been the focus of projections of pure goodness, ones the institutional church could never live up to. On the other hand, psychology either declared that God did not exist, or that God could be found in the office of a therapist, or upon a psychiatrist's couch. This either/or god is still frozen within the perfectionistic, albeit reductionistic image of projected goodness, while the shadow is cast out of this Eden-like place to be unconsciously extroverted in sometimes subtle, sometimes terrible ways. Both frames of belief stimulate a denial of shadow, while substituting an idolatrous image for an authentic image of the divine.

Theologian and Jungian analyst Ann Belford Ulanov wrote this about psychology as a substitute for religion:

> The insistent strength of the psyche points to the spirit, not to be diminished by it, certainly not to be eclipsed by it, but that both may be enhanced in the meeting.... Some who have thought about this want to explain away religion by translating it into psychological terms, entirely reducing the epistemology of spirit to that of the psyche.... One discipline cannot be collapsed into the other without both falling apart. A gap properly exists between them. Their differences inform and stimulate research, knowledge, dialogue, every sort of discovery of what lies below the surface of things (110-111 & 114).

I am arguing for a meeting of social psychology and theology, certainly where matters of the shadow are concerned. Our society is far too complex and our global arena too easily accessible through modern forms of communication for us to regress any further. We can no longer use old forms of projected hatred to scratch the itch provoked by the shadow within each one of our psyches and, by extension, in the collective.

We will never mature as human beings until we have owned the shadow within, made friends with it, and stopped projecting it onto some supposed enemy. If we need a scapegoat, any scapegoat, we have failed to claim ownership of our own shadows. We will never mature, as individuals, or as a nation, until we claim our collective shadow. That is why the shadow and understandings of it matter. To accomplish this we need first to be made aware of the shadow, in all the multiplicity of its personality. We need, as well, to recognize the shadow side of God. The latter of these two tasks is not as difficult as the first, for we have the multidimensional God of the Old Testament to inform us as we search for God's shadow side. Yet, the New Testament also encompasses far more mystery and far more ambiguity than the church seems willing to own. Accepting the biblical text, either the Old or the New Testament, as inerrant or literal is an acceptance of incongruous opposites set over against each other, neither one of which make complete sense in our contemporary, complex world.

To place theology and psychology in the same room with each other, where a deeply meaningful dialogue could occur, is to own the aspects of each discipline that have been interwoven and inextricably intertwined for centuries. Ulanov told us, "Theology and the church hobble themselves when they fail to recognize the broad deep rich life of the unconscious life already there in religious ritual, symbol, doctrine, and sacrament. It is a failure to take seriously the transcendent in its persistent immanence, in and among us" (118).

When Jung's psychological theory is cast in dialogue with theological statements by well-known twentieth-century scholars, it provokes questions that might never be asked otherwise. Those who inhabit the professional corridors of both disciplines might protest Ulanov's statement, but there is an undertow of disrespect between the two. It was palpable in my experience at a seminary that perceived itself as open to dialogue from other disciplines, but faltered when such dialogue was attempted.

What if it were possible to dream an ideal church into being? As a woman and a mother I believe both the church and the government could radically increase the positive morphic energy in our nation with universal day care. If the government chooses to fund faith-based programs, day care for children and elderly adults would be an ideal place to start. The soul of any nation is measured in the ways it cares for those who are too young or too old to care for themselves. When shadow energy gathers around discussions of day care, we know how much our old assumptions and mind habits present an obstacle to finding solutions for contemporary problems.

More than twenty years ago I had been invited to speak to the annual meeting of a women's group in a Midwestern suburban church. I can no longer remember what my topic might have been, but apparently it was provocative enough to call out the shadow. When I had completed my prepared remarks, I was taking questions from the group when a woman, who was probably in her early sixties, asked this: "What program should every church offer its congregation?" I answered that, in addition to at least one weekly worship service, every church should offer day care for children.

With a look of pure shock upon her face, the questioner blurted this emotional reaction: "What are you, some kind of socialist?"

In response I said, "Churches that are locked-down fortresses six days a week don't function as churches and for all practical purposes are dead. If a church is alive, it opens its doors every day of the week for some compassionate purpose."

A lively cross-generational discussion ensued, with women of child-bearing age verbally applauding my statement and women whose children were grown opposing it. It was a classic example of our psychic inability to make a paradigm shift. As I silently withdrew from the conversation and watched the women argue from their particular perspectives, I also saw the emotional energy around this one issue in the lives of women. Older women who had never worked outside the home seemed adamant that young women should stay home and raise their children. Young women who had to work outside the home could not articulate their concerns in ways that could be heard. I watched as an outside observer with no authority in their community of faith, and no credibility to turn the shadow energy. The conversation ended in a stalemate and I crept out the door feeling overwhelmed with the unleashed shadow backlash. I suspect many of those women left feeling the same way.

Churches in the United States believe they must compete in the highly competitive marketplace we have created in our culture. What if no church could declare itself tax-exempt unless more than 50% of its income was used for outside ministry beyond itself? Would mega-churches have become such a phenomenon if, every year, every church had to provide evidence that it was functioning as a church, and not as a social club for those who were most comfortable with each other? What if documents showing this ministry in some detail were required for a church to hold its tax-exempt status?

The natural inclination to use business marketing practices is apparent in mega-churches, which are becoming an insistent model for others. One young pastor of a Texas mega-church declared, "To me, we're marketing hope."

CBS Reporter Byron Pitts said, "And hope sells. Last year, Lakewood brought in $55 million." Pitts continued his report, indicating the style of worship offered in this gigantic church, and the ways in which it, and other evangelical organizations, "have mastered" marketing religion—as they appeal to adolescents with rock bands and "Christian-themed parks."

In a conversation with Notre Dame sociology professor Michael Emerson, Pitts noted Emerson's response about "feel good theology." Michael Emerson declared, "Religion changes to nothing more than 'make me feel good,' and there's no sacrifice."

Therein is the crux of modern American Christianity. On the one hand the government asks young men and women to make the ultimate sacrifice by dying in a war with ambiguous endings. On the other hand, the church that elevates entertainment as ideal worship may ask for only one sacrifice, your money. Soul-level nurturance can be found in neither of these extremes.

Professor Barry Ulanov once wrote, "The astonishing fact is that each of us is himself or herself and nobody else. What our imagination has brought us to, in this meeting of knowing and unknowing, is the eternal moment where our small being confronts Being itself." If the church does not offer us ways to confront "Being itself," it dissolves into an emulation of every other social club.

The church has the opportunity to radically change the culture in positive ways. By offering day care, the church could become the safe haven for children whose mothers must work. When women have no choice but to work outside the home, the church can support healthy families by offering day care. Families where elderly women and men need assistance during the day but live with extended family would also benefit from elder day care. Few of these day care facilities exist in this nation. Elderly folks are more often shuttled off to live in isolation, their accumulation of years a walking death sentence in a nation which elevates youth as an ideal.

By offering opportunities for stillness and quietude, the church could provide places of retreat from the noisy chaos of the American culture. The Roman Catholic Church has understood this for eons. Most Catholics can find a place to light a candle and be still with Divine Spirit any day of the week. Protestants have not been as aware of the need for a place of sanctuary. If every Protestant church in this nation encouraged individuals to slip into their sanctuaries on a regular basis for prayer and stillness, the morphic energy swirling around us would shift dramatically.

Ultimately I have reached a place where I have more questions than answers when I consider how to transform the church. This concretized social institution is firmly established in our nation and the world, and that solidification is a profound habit of the mind. It is equally as solidified in its sense of its own necessity. I know this. Thus I have far more uneasiness whenever I am presented with suppositions about a concrete, dogmatic version of anything. I have more questions than answers, because mystery is not easily defined and I believe God is more mystery than anything else.

In some ways we are attuned to a God whom we claim as "our God," and to a God that not only blesses America, but is our warrior ally. Yet we are forced to turn inward and consider that to be Christian we claim Jesus as our model. To claim Jesus as our model calls us to the hard places of confrontation with our own maturity as a nation, with our own faith in this Jesus, and to encounters with a multitude of unanswered questions.

Shortly after September 11, 2001, E. J. Dionne Jr. wrote in the *Washington Post*, "Faith is suspect when God is harnessed to immediate human ends and identified entirely with a person, political or national cause. Faith is brought down by a pridefulness that expresses an unwavering conviction that our own desires and interests coincide perfectly with those of the divine. Faith is more credible when it stands as a challenge, when it insists on aspirations beyond those of our own political movements, communities or nations. The prayers of such a faith do not express certainty that God is on our side, only the hope that this might prove to be true."

If anything is most troubling about the church in America in the present moment, it is that strange melding of patriotism with absolute nationalism, commingled and melded with supposed Christianity. The separation of church and state envisioned with such clarity by James Madison and Thomas Jefferson has been contaminated by this patriot-religiosity.

Back in 1986 Andrew Greeley wrote about our need to cast our God, or Jesus, as the one who meets our needs in such times. Here is what Greeley wrote: "The only real Jesus is one who is larger than life, who escapes our categories, who eludes our attempt to reduce him for our cause. Any Jesus who has been made to fit our formula ceases to be appealing, precisely because he is no longer wondrous, mysterious, or surprising. We may reduce him to a right-wing Republican or to a gun-toting revolutionary and thus rationalize and justify our own political ideology. But having done so, we are dismayed to discover that, whoever we have signed on as an ally is not Jesus."

In Chapter Ten I introduced the cantor, Linda Baer, to readers of this book. I have chosen to include here the lyrics from another of Linda Baer's sacred songs, "The Café Forever." Her superb exegetical interpretation of a conversation between the two women who were closest to the biblical patriarch Abraham has a powerful lesson for all of us. In this song, Sarah and Hagar meet each other after they have both died. She imagines them coming to a place of soul-melding understanding of each other and of themselves.

During their lives, Sarah is the elderly wife of an equally elderly Abraham. Her desire for a child (and the Hebrew notion of legacy carried through one's children) leads Sarah to urge Abraham to take her maid, Hagar, to his bed to father a child. Hagar becomes pregnant and gives birth to Ishmael, the accepted patriarch of those who are Muslim. Then Sarah, too, becomes pregnant, with the son who will become a patriarch of Israel. When Sarah's son, Isaac, is born, she rejects Hagar and Ishmael. In an act of selfish insecurity, she demands that Abraham send Hagar out into the wilderness to fend for herself, or to die. Hagar and Ishmael survive through the miraculous intervention of an angel sent from God. This story is filled with complexity and passion, human frailty and exquisite miracles. It teaches humankind much about itself. Every one of us is as prone to lying as an Abraham, as insecure as a Sarah, as caught in some form of slavery as a Hagar. But then, we also have to remember the hidden orchard inside the seed. Here is Linda Baer's exquisite song:

THE CAFÉ FOREVER
Words and music by Linda Baer © 1998

At the "Café Forever" two mothers sat watching
The world spin around, as their children pass by,
Sarah and Hagar, alone at the table,
Looking for mercy in each other's eyes.
"If only we had known what we started..."
"If only we had known what we've done...."

CHORUS:

WHAT CAN WE DO? WHAT CAN WE SAY?
ALL OF OUR CHILDREN ARE LOSING THEIR WAY,
ONE BY ONE TO THE WARS THEY RUN,
AND NOW THEY MUST FINISH WHAT WE HAVE BEGUN,
WHAT CAN WE DO? WHAT CAN WE SAY?
HOW CAN PEACE FIND A WAY?

Said Sarah to Hagar, "When you were with child,
I could feel in my heart the hate in your eyes,
So round in your beauty, so full of God's promise
You filled me with sorrow where my emptiness lies,"
"Hagar, you were the blossom,
And I was a desert of shame...."

Said Hagar to Sarah, "You never knew me,
Long, long ago, I was somebody's child,
Torn from my homeland, and sold like a trinket;
Now my dreams and sorrows overflow like the Nile....

*All that I had to give this world
Was Ishmael, the child of God's grace...."*

CHORUS

*4. Said Sarah to Hagar, "Who could imagine?
To be ninety years old with a child at my breast!
The God of All Things gave me love for the giving,
With a new life within me, I am forever blessed.
Isaac is the child of my laughter...
And the rivers danced as he played...."*

CHORUS

*Said Hagar to Sarah, "How could you do it?
To send us away to the desert to die....
To condemn me is one thing, but to banish my child,
As a mother yourself I can only ask why?"
Said Sarah to Hagar, "I was lost in my anger,
By fears and by demons I was beguiled,
I had visions of angels,
And I dreamed they would save you,
And I prayed for the life of you and your child.
Then I woke to the cold wind a' blowing,
Through the wilderness where you both lay...."*

*5. Early one morning a young man awakened,
And bowed down to Allah and loaded his gun,
Down the same street, a soldier said Kaddish for
The brothers he lost, and the man he's become.
Together their prayers rise to heaven,
And in mercy, the mothers embrace....*

CHORUS

WHAT CAN WE DO? WHAT CAN WE SAY?

Rushing

ALL OF OUR CHILDREN ARE LOSING THEIR WAY,
ONE BY ONE TO THE WARS THEY RUN, AND NOW THEY
MUST FINISH WHAT WE HAVE BEGUN,
WHAT CAN WE DO? WHAT CAN WE SAY?
HOW CAN PEACE FIND A WAY?

At the "Café Forever" two mothers sat watching
The world spin around, as their children pass by....

For centuries our culture, and the church which flourished in it, have been unwilling to go into life's necessary dark places. Only through the violence of crime, and the blood sacrifice of declared war, have we allowed ourselves to delve into these dark places. Both the culture and the church need to be willing to accept the contradictory opposites that are interwoven into life's tapestry. To meet wisdom, appropriate sacrifice, gratitude, praise, death, and life in these dark places, we must be willing and able to hold all of what life brings to us. We can exclude nothing from the mix. We cannot turn away from telling ourselves the truth, even the brutal truth. Mahatma Gandhi would remind us, "We must be the change we wish to see in the world." We must be the ones who grieve for death among us. We must be the gratitude that is expressed. We must be the praise that is sung.

APPENDIX A

A GRAPHIC OF JUNG'S THEORY

THE CONSCIOUS LEVEL OF THE PSYCHE

Cultural Mores - Right & Wrong; Laws & Regulations & Policies
Linear, Scientific, Legalistic Concepts; Precise Cognitive Thinking - The Intellect
Technology & Computers; Church Creeds & Dogma

The Ego forms a barrier between the Conscious and the Personal Unconscious levels.

THE PERSONAL UNCONSCIOUS LEVEL OF THE PSYCHE

The Contents of this level of the Psyche are formed
during the socialization process in one's lifetime.

The Personal Shadow is a Powerful Inhabitant of this level of the Human Psyche.

THE COLLECTIVE UNCONSCIOUS LEVEL OF THE PSYCHE

The contents of this level of the psyche are carried by the soul at birth and links humans to primordial, primitive, instinctual levels of understanding. These contents are represented in fairy tales, myth, symbols, and body symptoms.

The Dark Side of Life Habits, Behavior Patterns, & Old Assumptions.
Revealed through Emotions, Feelings, Pain and Joy

Psychic Archetypes are carried here . . . for example:
The King; The Queen;
The Virgin; The Prostitute; The Child; The Mother;
The Saboteur; The Victim; The Warrior; The Coward

Most Powerful Archetype: Archetypal Shadow
[Examples: Hitler, Stalin or Hussein]

Bibliography

Aarons, Mark, and John Loftus. *Unholy Trinity: The Vatican, The Nazis, and The Swiss Banks.* New York: St. Martin's Griffin Press, 1998.

Adler, Jerry. "O Jackie! How Tacky." *Newsweek,* May 6, 1996.

Aland, Kurt, Editor. *Synopsis of the Four Gospels: Greek-English Edition of the Synopsis Quattuor Evangeliorum with the text of the Revised Standard Version.* Stuttgart: United Bible Societies, 1972.

Albright, W. F., and C. S. Mann. *The Anchor Bible: Matthew.* New York, Doubleday & Co., 1971.

Arkin, William M. "Pentagon Unleashes a Holy Warrior." the *Roanoke Times,* October 26, 2003.

Ashley, David & David Michael Orenstein. *Sociological Theory: Classical Statements.* Newton, MA: Allyn & Bacon, Inc., 1985.

Associated Press. "Bush Defends Domestic Surveillance Program." the *Roanoke Times,* August 19, 2006.

Associated Press. "Politics, Emotions Inseparable." the *Roanoke Times,* January 31, 2006.

Associated Press. "Vatican Pledges to Fight Pedophilia Following LA Clergy Abuse Settlement." *The International Herald Tribune,* July 17, 2007.

Ayto, John, Editor. *Dictionary of Word Origins.* New York: Arcade Publishing; Little, Brown & Co., 1990.

Berry, Jason. *Lead Us Not into Temptation: Catholic Priests and the Sexual Abuse of Children.* New York: Doubleday, 1992.

Bly, Robert. *The Sibling Society.* New York: Addison-Wesley Publishing Company, 1996.

Briffault, Robert. *The Mothers, Vol. III.* New York: Macmillan, 1927.

Brown, Peter. *The Body and Society: Men, Women and Sexual Renunciation in Early Christianity.* New York: Columbia University Press, 1988.

Brown, Raymond E. *The Anchor Bible: The Gospel According to John (I-XII).* New York, Doubleday, 1966.

Brownrigg, Ronald. *Who's Who in the Bible.* New York: Crown Publishing Co., 1980.

Brueggemann, Walter. *Hopeful Imagination: Prophetic Voices in Exile.* Philadelphia: Fortress Press, 1986.

Bugliosi, Vincent. *The Betrayal of America: How the Supreme Court Undermined the Constitution and Chose Our President.* New York: Thunder's Mouth Press/Nation Books, 2001.

Buttrick, George A. *Exposition of Luke 13-18. The Interpreter's Bible. Volume VIII.* Nashville: Abingdon Press, 1980.

Byrd, Robert C. *Losing America: Confronting a Reckless and Arrogant Presidency.* New York: W. W. Norton & Company, 2004.

Campo-Flores, Arian. "Who Has the Right to Die?" *Newsweek*, November 3, 2003.

Carey, Benedict. "Who's Minding the Mind?" the *New York Times*, July 31, 2007.

Carroll, James. "A Moral Challenge for all Catholics." the *Boston Globe*, March 27, 2004.

Carter, Jimmy. *Our Endangered Values: America's Moral Crisis.* New York: Simon & Schuster, 2005.

Cerio, Gregory. "What's in a Marquee Name?" *House & Garden*, July, 2005.

Cooper, Matthew. "A Saddam Souvenir: President Bush Keeps the Former Dictator's Pistol at Arm's Reach." *Time*, June 7, 2004, Internet Archives.

"Cost of Iraq War Could Hit $2 Trillion, Studies Say." the *Roanoke Times*, January 15, 2006.

Courteney, Hazel. *Divine Intervention*. London: Cico, 2005.

Cowlishaw, Guy, and Robin Dunbar. *Primate Conservation Biology*. Chicago: University of Chicago Press, 2000.

Cumont, Franz. *Original Religions in Roman Paganism*. New York: Dover Publications, 1956.

Davey, Monica. "An Antiwar Forum in Iowa Brings Federal Subpoenas." the *New York Times*, February 10, 2004.

Dillard, Annie. *Teaching a Stone to Talk*. New York: Harper & Row, 1982.

Diocese Settles Claims of Sex Abuse for $4.2M." the *Boston Globe*, February 9, 2004; "Diocese Pays Millions to Sexual Abuse Victims." the *Roanoke Times*, February 9, 2004.

Dutcher, Jim and Jamie. Film: *Living with Wolves*. The Dutchers have produced two other documentaries on wolves, the Emmy Award-winning film, Wolf: Return of a Legend, and another one entitled Wolves at our Door.

Dyer, Wayne. *The Power of Intention: Learning to Co-Create Your World Your Way*. Carlsbad, CA: Hay House, Inc., 2004.

Edinger, Edward. *The Christian Archetype: A Jungian Commentary on the Life of Christ*. Toronto: Inner City Books, 1987.

Eggen, Dan, and Jonathan Krim. "Easier Internet Wiretaps Sought: Justice Dept., FBI Want Consumers to Pay the Cost." the *Washington Post*, March 13, 2004.

Emmel, Stephen. The Dialogue of the Savior: *The Nag Hammadi Library in English*. James M. Robinson, General Editor. San Francisco: Harper & Row, 1988.

Emoto, Masaru. *The Hidden Messages in Water*. Translated by David A. Thayne. Hillsboro, Oregon: Beyond Word Publishing, Inc., 2001.

"The EPA Follies: A Wrong-Way Agency," Op Ed. the *L A Times*, January 28, 2006.

"Exxon Posts Quarterly Profit of $10.71 Billion." The Associated Press, the *New York Times*, January 30, 2006.

"The Facts of Clergy Abuse," Op Ed. the *Baltimore Sun*, March 9, 2004.

Fitzmyer, Joseph A. *The Anchor Bible: The Gospel According to Luke (I-IX)*. Garden City, New York: Doubleday & Co., 1981.

Fitzmyer, Joseph A. *The Anchor Bible: The Gospel According to Luke (X-XXIV)*. Garden City, New York: Doubleday & Company, Inc. 1985.

Fonari, Franco. Quoting Roger E. Money-Kyrle. *The Psychoanalysis of War*. Bloomington: Indiana University Press, 1975.

Fortune, Marie M. *Is Nothing Sacred?* San Francisco: Harper San Francisco, 1991.

Fox, Matthew. Lecture entitled *Exploring the Cosmic Christ Archetype, Part 1, Tape 1*. Boulder, CO: Sounds True Recordings, 1992.

Frank, Justin, M.D. *Bush On The Couch*. New York: Harper Collins Publishers, Inc., 2004.

Fromm, Eric. *The Heart of Man: Its Genius for Good and Evil*. New York: Harper and Row, 1964.

Gaster, Theodor H. *Festivals of the Jewish Year: A Modern Interpretation and Guide*. New York: Morrow Quill, 1978.

Gates, Bill & Melinda. "Our Guiding Principles." The Bill and Melinda Gates Foundation. www.gatesfoundation.org.

Geldenhuys, Norval. *The New International Commentary on the New Testament: Commentary on the Gospel of Luke.* Grand Rapids: Wm. B. Eerdmans Publishing Co., 1988.

Gettleman, Jeffrey. "When Family Values Clash With Family Secrets." the *New York Times*, January 4, 2004.

Gibran, Kahlil. *Spiritual Sayings of Kahlil Gibran*, Translated from the Arabic and Edited by Anthony Rizcallah Ferris. Secaucus, NJ: The Citadel Press, 1972.

"Go Ahead, Try to Stop K Street," Op Ed. the *New York Times*, January 8, 2006.

Goodstein, Laurie. "Payout is Bittersweet for Victims of Abuse." the *New York Times*, July 17, 2007.

Graham, Bradley. "Military Scolded on Assaults: Senators Seek More Protection for Female Soldiers." the *Washington Post*, February 26, 2004.

"Ground the D.C. Jet Set," Op Ed. the *Washington Post*, January 16, 2006.

Harris, Lis. *Holy Days: The World of the Hasidic Family.* New York: Macmillan Publishing Co., 1985.

Hatcher, Maynard. "Coins and The Kingdom." *Presbyterian Survey.* Philadelphia: The Presbyterian Church, USA, March 1987.

Hays, H. R. *In the Beginnings.* New York: G. P. Putnam & Sons, 1963.

Bob Herbert. Quoting Al Gore. "Masters of Deception." the *New York Times*, January 16, 2004.

"Homeless in America." Washington Profile: A Project of the World Security Institute. 2004.

Jenkins, Sally. "Life, Liberty and the Pursuit of Nothingness." the *Washington Post*, August 18, 2002.

Johnson, Paul. *A History of The Jews*. New York: Harper & Row, 1987.

Jordan, Michael. *Encyclopedia of Gods*. New York, Facts on File, Inc., 1993.

"Judge in Schiavo Case Survives Bush Bias Claim." the *Roanoke Times*, December 11, 2003.

"A Judicial End Run," Op Ed. the *New York Times*, January 17, 2004.

Kasser, Rodolphe, Marvin Meyer, and Gregor Wurst. (Commentary by Bart D. Ehrman) *The Gospel of Judas*. Washington, D. C.: The National Geographic Society, 2006.

King, Colbert I. "Weapons of Mass Intimidation." the *Washington Post*, January 21, 2004.

Kinsbury, Kathleen. "Fifty Windows on the World." *Time*, April 17, 2006.

Klassen, W. *Judas: Betrayer or Friend of Jesus*. Minneapolis: Fortress Press, 1996.

Koretz, Gene. "Yes, Workers are Grumpier." *Business Week*, November 13, 2000.

Kristof, Nicholas D. Quoting Hans Küng. "Believe It, or Not." the *New York Times*, August 15, 2003.

Krugman, Paul. "The Awful Truth." the *New York Times*, January 13, 2004.

Lauer, Robert H. *Perspectives on Social Change*. Boston: Allyn and Bacon, Inc., 1982.

"Less Help for the Homeless." Op Ed. the *Boston Globe*, February 18, 2004.

Neil A. Lewis. "Bush Seats Judge, Bypassing Senate Democrats." the *New York Times*, January 17, 2004.

Lipton, Bruce. *The Biology of Belief: Unleashing the Power of Consciousness, Matter and Miracles*. Santa Rosa, CA: Mountain of Love/Elite Books. 2005.

Lipton, Michael A., and Natasha Stoynoff. "The Blast Tycoon." *People*, January 26, 2004.

"Louisiana in Limbo," Editorial. the *New York Times*, January 30, 2006.

"The Marriage Experiment," Editorial. the *Washington Post*, January 31, 2004.

Marshall, I. Howard. *The New International Greek Testament Commentary: The Gospel of Luke*. Grand Rapids: Wm. B. Eerdmans Publishing Co., 1978.

MassMutual advertisement in *Time*, September 9, 1996.

Meichtry, Stacy. "Gospel of Judas." *Religious News Service*, www.beliefnet.com.

Merriam-Webster Collegiate Dictionary. Springfield: Merriam-Webster, Inc., 1993.

Metzger, Bruce M. *A Textual Commentary on the Greek New Testament*. Federal Republic of Germany: United Bible Societies, 1975.

Miller, Mark and Debra Rosenberg. "Something About Mary: Gay-marriage Proponents Target the Veep's Daughter." *Newsweek*, February 23, 2004.

Miller, Robert J., Editor. *The Complete Gospels*. San Francisco: Harper San Francisco, 1992.

Murphy, Caryle. "At Millennium, Finding Salvation." the *Washington Post*, November 28, 1999.

Nelson, James B. *embodiment*. Minneapolis: Augsburg Publishing House, 1978.

Newbold, Lieutenant General Greg (Ret.). "Why Iraq Was a Mistake." *Time*, April 17, 2006.

"New Era Begins in Miami." the *Roanoke Times*, January 12, 1996.

Nichols, Sally. Quoting Carl G. Jung. "The Devil in the Tarot." *Meeting the Shadow: The Hidden Power of the Dark Side of Human Nature*, edited by

Connie Zweig & Jeremiah Abrams. New York: G. P. Putnam's Sons, 1991.

Ostling, Richard. "Writers Offer Remedies for Catholic Church." the *Roanoke Times*, July 26, 2003.

Padgett, Tim, "Pilfering Priests." *Time*, February 26, 2007.

Paffenroth, Kim. *Judas: Images of the Lost Disciple*. Louisville: Westminster John Knox Press, 2001.

Pagels, Elaine. *The Origin of Satan*. New York: Random House, 1995.

Peck, M. Scott, M.D. *People of the Lie: The Hope for Healing Human Evil*. New York: Simon and Schuster, 1983.

Pert, Candace. *Molecules of Emotion: The Science behind Mind-Body Medicine*. New York: Touchstone Books, 1997; Your Body is Your Sub-conscious Mind. Audio CD. Boulder, CO: Sounds True, 2004.

Plato. *The Republic*. New York: Charles Scribner's Sons, 1898.

"Privacy in Peril," Editorial. the *New York Times*, February 14, 2004.

Quindlen, Anna. "Desecration? Dedication!" *Newsweek*, February 23, 2004.

— "Not So Safe Back Home." *Newsweek*, April 7, 2003.

Raspberry, William. "Their Cheating Hearts." the *Washington Post*, November 22, 1999.

Reuters. "Sexual Abuse Not Just a Catholic Problem: Vatican Declares." the *New York Times*, July 17, 2007.

"Rise of the Righteous Army." *60 Minutes*. New York: Columbia Broadcasting System, Inc., February 8, 2004.

Ritch, Emma. "Thurmond's Daughter gets Tribute in S.C." the *Boston Globe*, February 29, 2004.

Robinson, James M., General Editor. *The Nag Hammadi Library in English*. San Francisco: Harper & Row, 1988.

Robinson, James M. *The Secrets of Judas: The Story of the Misunderstood Disciple and his Lost Gospel.* San Francisco: HarperSanFrancisco, 2006.

Rogers, Jack. *Presbyterian Creeds: A Guide to The Book of Confessions.* Philadelphia: The Westminster Press, 1985.

Rosenberg, Debra. "Amending Their Ways." *Newsweek,* December 8, 2003.

Rushing, Sandra M. *The Magdalene Legacy: Exploring the Wounded Icon of Sexuality.* London & Westport: Bergin & Garvey Division of Greenwood Publishing Group, Inc., 1994.

Safire, William. "Privacy in Retreat." the *New York Times,* March 10, 2004.

Samuelson, Robert J. "The Cartel We Love to Hate." *Newsweek,* February 23, 2004.

Samuelson, Robert J., Quoting Jonathan Chait. "Bush-Hatred: Fearful Loathing...." the *Washington Post,* December 30, 2003.

Sanders, E. P. *Jesus and Judaism.* Philadelphia: Fortress Press, 1985.

Sanford, John A. *Evil: The Shadow Side of Reality.* New York: The Crossroad Publishing Co., 1988.

Sanford, John A. *Mystical Christianity: A Psychological Commentary on the Gospel of John.* New York: Crossroad, 1993.

Schaberg, Jane. *Introduction: Luke.* Editors: Carol A. Newsom & Sharon H. Ringe. *The Women's Bible Commentary.* Louisville, Westminster/John Knox Press, 1992.

"Schiavo Case Has a 2nd Victim: The Rule of Law," Editorial. the *Roanoke Times,* October 30, 2003.

Schmidt, Eric. "Rapes Reported by Servicewomen in the Persian Gulf and Elsewhere." the *New York Times,* February 26, 2004.

Schmidt, Susan & James V. Grimaldi. "Abramoff Pleads Guilty to 3 Counts: Lobbyist to Testify about Lawmakers in Corruption Probe." the *Washington Post,* January 4, 2006.

"Selling God: A Lucrative Business." CBS Evening News, June 28, 2005.

"Sex Abuse Costs Top $1 Billion for Dioceses." the *Roanoke Times*, June 10, 2005.

Sheldrake, Rupert. *The Presence of the Past: Morphic Resonance & the Habits of Nature*. Rochester, VT: Park Street Press, 1995.

Small, Joseph D., and John P. Burgess. "ReImagining: A Theological Appraisal." *Presbyterian Outlook*, March 7, 1994.

Smith, R. Jeffrey, and Jonathan Weisman. "DeLay Departing on Own Terms." the *Washington Post*, April 5, 2006.

Sniezyk, Monsignor Richard S., quoted in "Perspectives." *Newsweek*, March 8, 2004.

Spong, John Shelby. *Liberating The Gospel: Reading the Bible with Jewish Eyes*. San Francisco: Harper San Francisco, 1996.

—*Resurrection—Myth or Reality: A Bishop's Search for the Origins of Christianity*. San Francisco: Harper San Francisco, 1994.

"Squeezing the Poor for Votes," Editorial. the *New York Times*, February 18, 2004.

Steiner, George. *After Babel*. London: Oxford University Press, 1975.

"Support Lieutenant General William G. Boykin," Petition. Christian Coalition of America: Web site: www.cc.org.

Suskind, Ron. *The Price of Loyalty*. New York: Simon & Schuster, 2004.

Tresniowski, Alex, Johnny Dodd, and Siobhan Morrisey. "Freed from the Past." *People*, January 12, 2004.

Tumulty, Karen. "When Tom Met Jack." *Time*, April 18, 2005. Time Internet Archives, January 15, 2006.

Turner, John D. *The Book of Thomas the Contender. The Nag Hammadi Library in English*, James M. Robinson, General Editor. San Francisco: Harper & Row, 1988.

Ulanov, Ann Belford. *The Wisdom of the Psyche*. Cambridge: Cowley Publications, 1988.

Ulanov, Barry, quoted in his obituary in "Barnard College News." New York: Bernard College, May 1, 2000.

Van Biema, David. "A Kiss for Judas." *Time*, February 27, 2006.

Van Creveld, Martin. *The Transformation of War*. New York: Free Press, 1991.

VanderZanden, James W. *Social Psychology, Third Edition*. New York: Random House, 1984.

Velasquez, Mauricio, "Women in the Workplace, Marketplace and Society as a Whole," DTG Research: Sexual Harassment Prevention Center: http://stopharass.com/article-women-marketplace.htm.

Walker, Barbara G. *The Woman's Encyclopedia of Myths and Secrets*. San Francisco: Harper & Row, 1983.

Weisman, Jonathan. "Hastert Moves to Tighten Rules on Lobbyists." the *Washington Post*, January 9, 2006.

Wiesenfeld, Kurt. "Making the Grade." *Time*, June 17, 1996.

Wilson, C. Vincent. *The Westminster Concise Handbook for the Bible*. Philadelphia: The Westminster Press, 1979.

Zagorin, Adam. "Jack in a Box." *Time*, May 2, 2005. Time Internet Archives, January 15, 2006.

Zakaria, Fareed. Quoting Freidrich Engels & Vladimir Lenin. "All That's Left is Violence." the *Washington Post*, March 8, 2004.

Zweig, Connie, and Jeremiah Abrams. Editors. *Meeting the Shadow: The Hidden Power of the Dark Side of Human Nature*. New York: G. P. Putnam, 1991.

About the Author

After spending several decades in the oil and transportation industries, the author became a second-career interim ministry specialist in the Presbyterian Church, USA (PCUSA). She has worked in eight different regions of the PCUSA, and on the executive staff in two of those regions. She holds a dual degree (Summa Cum Laude, Phi Beta Kappa) in sociology and political science, and has studied the theory of C. G. Jung extensively. Her book *The Magdalene Legacy* was used as a resource for a documentary on the life of Christ. Filmed in Israel by a British film company, this film "The Living Christ" was aired for American audiences on *The Learning Channel*. She is also the author of a book of poetry *Essence of Autumn*, a memoir *Dancing with a Kitchen Chair*, and a liturgical resource book, *Sacred Bread and Holy Wine: Communion and Liturgical Poetry*.